Abraham Lincoln and the Virtues of War

ABRAHAM LINCOLN AND THE VIRTUES OF WAR

❖

How Civil War Families Challenged and Transformed Our National Values

Jean E. Friedman

PRAEGER™

An Imprint of ABC-CLIO, LLC

Santa Barbara, California • Denver, Colorado

Library of Congress Cataloging-in-Publication Data

Friedman, Jean E.
  Abraham Lincoln and the virtues of war : how Civil War families challenged and
transformed our national values / Jean E. Friedman.
    pages cm
  Includes bibliographical references and index.
  ISBN 978–1–4408–3361–8 (cloth : alk. paper) — ISBN 978–1–4408–3362–5 (ebook)
1. United States—History—Civil War, 1861–1865—Influence. 2. United States—
History—Civil War, 1861–1865—Social aspects. 3. National characteristics,
American—History. I. Title.
E468.9.F87 2015
973.7092—dc23   2014046730

ISBN: 978–1–4408–3361–8
EISBN: 978–1–4408–3362–5

19 18 17 16 15   1 2 3 4 5

This book is also available on the World Wide Web as an eBook.
Visit www.abc-clio.com for details.

Praeger
An Imprint of ABC-CLIO, LLC

ABC-CLIO, LLC
130 Cremona Drive, P.O. Box 1911
Santa Barbara, California 93116-1911

This book is printed on acid-free paper ∞

Manufactured in the United States of America

"The Moral Imagination of Confederate Family Politics" in Lesley J. Gordon and John C.
Inscoe, eds., *Inside the Confederate Nation: Essays in Honor of Emory Thomas* is reprinted
with permission of Louisiana State University Press.

For Y.
and for Bernard

Contents

Preface and Acknowledgments

The underlying moral rationale for the Civil War was that it was a necessary means to secure greater goods, such as abolition or, conversely, defense against aggression. However, it is not enough to argue that what sectional leaders proclaimed counted for virtue; what happened in families mattered. Poets may delve into the human heart and learn why we are *underlings*, but historians must discern not only the depth but also the breath of the desire to do good in the context of war. There is no virtue in violence, in killing, in war itself. But in the Civil War, there were practices that reached across racial lines, across regional boundaries, and into the most intimate human relations to reconcile, to forgive the harm, the deaths, the losses of war. These are the practices that can rightly be called virtuous. So a question emerged concerning Civil War families: How did it come to be that Northern and Southern governments could expect such virtue from families asked to support a war against, as Lincoln put it, "friends"?

As I explored the family patterns of Civil War families including the Lincoln family, I began to trace the subtext, the underlying narrative that provoked the war, namely, that families believed their lives were lived on unchanging principles that held them together as a community and as a nation. Nonetheless, as individuals evolved, so did their values and their commitment to patriotism, justice, and honor, to name a few family virtues necessary for war. Family virtue while foundational is not determined. Lincoln did not easily call a reluctant nation to war. He did, however, redefine and redirect the homely virtues in such a way that the nation evolved with him across the bridge of sorrows and into the war for Union.

As historians we belong to a community of scholars. *Abraham Lincoln and the Virtues of War: How Civil War Families Challenged and Transformed Our National Values* has been enriched by the works of feminist, political, and military historians. I am indebted to the works of Catherine Clinton, Doris Kearns Goodwin, Drew Gilpin Faust, Mark E. Neely Jr., James M. McPherson, and Emory Thomas. Generations of historians, myself included, are deeply indebted to David Donald's studies of Lincoln. I could not have begun to think about Civil War familial virtues without William Lee Miller's enlarged understanding of Lincoln's virtues.

Much gratitude is due to the Department of History, University of Georgia, for the summer research grants that made this work possible. As a fellow of the American Antiquarian Society, I investigated a rich trove of materials as well as enjoyed an amiable community of scholars. John B. Hench, vice-president for programs and research at the AAS, proved an invaluable support for direction and aid to research. In retirement my alma mater, Lehigh University, provided a scholarly refuge indeed. Stephen H. Cutcliffe, chair of the History Department, facilitated library privileges while opening opportunities for me to offer seminars on Civil War families. His gracious generosity and unfailing support enabled me to complete the project. John Smith, who succeeded Stephen Cutcliffe as chair of the History Department, continued the kind support of the university. And to my friend and colleague, John Inscoe, belongs the deepest gratitude for giving up his valuable time and effort to read the manuscript of this work. He did so with his characteristic good humor and astute advice. Lesley J. Gordon kindly critiqued a chapter; I am indebted to her. I am thankful, too, to my readers of chapters, Marilyn Brownstein, Tom Postelwaite, and Nancy Felson, whose opinion I value and whose friendship I cherish. Thanks to librarians Frances Pollard of the Virginia Historical Society and MaryKay W. Schnare, who contributed her efforts to the Lincoln research. Jennifer Y. Brown, ever supportive, edited the manuscript in a timely and professional fashion. My editor, Michael Millman, ever cheerful and patient, offered critical help in revising the manuscript. And, lastly, to my husband, Bernard Dauenhauer, who wishes to remain unheralded for his unfailing support, much is owed.

By happy coincidence, I finished the initial draft of this book on July 3, 2013, as the nation celebrated the 150th anniversary of the Battle of Gettysburg.

Introduction

Given the destructiveness of war, the phrase *virtues of war* initially sounds shocking, even nonsensical.[1] Since at least the time of Plato and Aristotle, virtues have been regularly understood to be deliberately cultivated habits of thought or action that are conducive to leading a good life. How can these be virtues of war? And yet, one can well ask: What habits of thought or action, what *virtues*, did the people who lived through the Civil War need to cultivate if they were to lead lives that deserve to be called morally good? This question has to do not only with statesmen or soldiers. The war induced strains and conflicts both among and within any number of families. Both North and South, families underwent substantial challenges to their traditional ways of thinking and acting.

One instructive way to frame these challenges is through Abraham Lincoln's February 22, 1861, Address at Independence Hall in Philadelphia. On this occasion, he emphasized his lifelong dedication to the principles and values expressed in the Declaration of Independence. Honor, patriotism, commitment, and justice are the core civic virtues that he called upon his fellow citizens to exercise in order to preserve the Union. Nonetheless, as crucially important as Lincoln's deep dedication to the founders' values, his call did not immediately give rise to a coherent, positive response from the citizenry. That is, not infrequently Lincoln's virtues of war conflicted with how individuals faced up to the demands that a great struggle involves.[2]

Among those striving to answer a call to war, there is always a worry that the call to virtue in war is unwarranted, perhaps hypocritical. This concern leads to self-criticism and an awareness of one's vulnerability. In this work I claim that the long process of reflection that begins inside the family is indispensable for the stability of a nation's long-term engagement in war. How the United States survived its tensions and divisions, not just between North and South but also among many who faced the moral dilemmas that the war posed, is the subject of this study.[3]

Unquestionably, there are more than four virtues that are relevant to war. But the four I emphasize are particularly pertinent to Civil War families. Each of the families I discuss highlights one of them. Taken together, they bring into clear focus the moral complexity that Civil War families faced. As with any work of this sort, my study invites further investigation into the moral dimension of civilian life during the Civil War.

In Chapter 1 I examine Lincoln's moral language in his Independence Hall speech. There he recalled his lifelong dedication to the principles of the Founding Fathers. His schooling, reading, and maternal teaching instilled in him the necessity of the practice of virtue to ensure a good life for all. The deaths of his family members, mother, sister, and kin left Lincoln with a desire for a greater belonging but also a desire to grasp onto life and take his chances. Economic prosperity in the new nation compelled his ambition to succeed. Nonetheless, he demonstrated in his New Salem wrestling match and the Black Hawk War his devotion to honor and justice. Indeed, his ambition for justice and honor earned him a reputation for *practical wisdom*—how to discern the use of power. As president, his patriotism committed him to the Union, but in order to save it, he delayed the emancipation of slaves until a victory on the battlefield of Antietam. That victory secured public opinion and allowed Lincoln to express his deepest desire for justice and liberty in the Emancipation Proclamation. President Lincoln's moral engagement intensified his determination to carry out the national principles of justice, honor, patriotism, and commitment.

Chapter 2 attempts to answer a basic question; namely, if Southern honor dominated all ethical persuasions then how did some individuals develop the moral imagination to subvert that largely masculine code? The answer lies in the individual's particular relationship to his or her family's moral vision. U.S. Major Alfred Mordecai, who headed the New York Watervliet Arsenal, resigned rather than fight his Southern family. The family, which was Jewish and contained renowned educators who introduced enlightened ethics into Southern women's learning, sharply criticized his course, since they hoped he would join the Confederate cause. Enlightened habits of righteousness spurred Mordecai's decision; he loved righteousness more than his family's honor. Dr. George Bagby of Virginia, a victim of his father's abusiveness, led an ambivalent moral life until he faced his own internal moral division and a love that assured his self-worth. Lincoln's call to honor in upholding the Union had conflicting consequences even among Southern families.

Chapter 3 examines the practices, the learned habits of justice, within a single prominent Northern family. Why each family member maintained a different concept of justice with regard to the Civil War is a study in moral development. Nathan Appleton Sr. a wealthy Boston textile manufacturer raised in a family business, would not support a war that contravened his economic interests, regardless of his involvement in numerous charitable causes. Nathan's daughter, Frances, often visited Lowell, her father's model town for textile workers, and practiced social justice in various ways. Frances Appleton married Henry Wadsworth Longfellow, a friend of Charles Sumner, the conscience of the Republican Party, who had access to Lincoln. Ultimately, but reluctantly, she supported the war. Frances's step-brother, Nathan Appleton Jr. raised as a privileged child, reveled in his wealthy status and elite male associates. He joined the Union army only to discover the narrowness of his self-regard against the larger demands of justice. Each of the Appletons interpreted the war as a measure of *the good life* in dissimilar ways. Slaves were not members of Nathan senior's moral community. Fanny's *practical wisdom* allowed her to arrive at a political notion more applicable to different racial communities rather than her own privileged status. Nathan junior had merely the vaguest notions of *a good life for all* and perceived it only in a peaceful Union camp.

Chapter 4 presents an overview of African American families' dilemma that set family and community loyalty against loyalty to the Union cause. Historian James M. McPherson writes of black volunteers' singular devotion to freedom and constitutional rights in the Civil War. My study argues that African American loyalty remained divided during and after the war. African American patriotism, fired by sacrifices in combat, became increasingly strained by inequities in the military and federal neglect of ex-slave families. These burdens culminated in dissent and even mutiny in the ranks. Despite the suffering and oppression, African Americans held to a core sense of identity and celebrated the passage of the Fourteenth Amendment, which granted them citizenship. Most black people retained their sense of community belonging by remaining in the South. Black patriotism emerged in a few New England cities under the patronage of black Yankee families, such as the William Brown family of

Worcester, and conscientious white families. Thus, African Americans held twin loyalties in the Civil War and postwar period.

Chapter 5 examines three families who demonstrate that a genuine virtue of commitment cannot exist without a sense of vulnerability and self-criticism. In this chapter, I show how two Northern families and one Southern family contend with their personal weaknesses in order to ensure stability in their lives and that of their nation.

Maria Weston Chapman and her family actively supported radical abolition. Chapman, a leader in the movement and a compelling and domineering personality, suffered a breakdown following a speech to the women's Anti-slavery Convention in 1838. Grieved by the deaths of her husband in 1842 and of a close friend in 1846, she encountered a Quaker couple who opened a new spiritual dimension within her. Thereafter, she pursued the cause with renewed energy in Europe, and with the new techniques learned there, she brought greater international influence to bear on the American cause. The North Carolina Edmondston and Devereux families' basic commitment was to the securing of their own interests. Though they expressed support for the Confederacy, they were so fearful of their vulnerable condition that they were very reluctant to put their slaves at the disposal of the Confederate war effort. William Lincoln of the New England Lincolns had no interest in abolition, but he joined the Union army and endured a harrowing escape from Confederate imprisonment. He accomplished his feat only after he came to terms with his failures as a husband and father. Commitment is not a virtue without an understanding of the vulnerability that creates a need for solidarity.

This study attempts to enlarge the notion of virtue, by suggesting that conflict and complication arise at the intersection of familial and national habits of thought and action. Such a notion can only admit that in the time of war, self-reflection and criticism are crucial. Those Civil War families who succeeded in building a new and more just Union allowed themselves to experience not simply the effects of war but the internal displacement or transformation of their learned values. Thus, they had both to challenge and to transcend their earlier conceptions of fundamental national values.

1

❖

Lincoln's Testament
to the Virtues of War

I have never had a feeling politically that did not spring from the sentiments embodied in the Declaration of Independence.

—Abraham Lincoln[1]

Amid the joyous cheers and ominous assassination plots that accompanied Abraham Lincoln's preinaugural journey to the White House, the president-elect maintained an uneasy balance between a hopeful message of conciliation with the secessionist South and a firm commitment to preserve the Union. In Tolono, Illinois, on February 12, 1861, Lincoln quoted a "poet's" words, "Behind the cloud the sun is still shinning."[2] As he traveled East to Buffalo, New York, Lincoln remarked that the crowd's enthusiasm "is evidence of the devotion of the whole people to the Constitution, the Union, and the perpetuity, of the liberties of this country."[3] While Lincoln addressed northern audiences, Jefferson Davis moved toward his own inauguration in Montgomery, Alabama, February 18, 1861, as provisional president of the Confederate States of America. And on February 22, Davis was sworn in as permanent president of the Confederacy. That same say Lincoln spoke at Independence Hall, Philadelphia. In his speech Lincoln invoked his own moral strength and that of the nation. Of all his memorable speeches, none evoked his emotion as plainly as did this one. The speech contained his deep regard for

the Founding Fathers' patriotism and his faith in the just principles of the
Declaration of Independence, freedom and equality. He said:

> I am filled with deep emotion at finding myself standing here in the
> place where were collected together the wisdom, the patriotism, the
> devotion to principle, from which sprang the institution under which
> we live … I have never had a feeling politically that did not spring
> from the sentiments embodied in the Declaration of Independence.
> I have often pondered over the dangers which were incurred by the
> men who assembled here and framed and adopted that Declaration.
> I have pondered over the toils that were endured by the officers and
> soldiers of the army who endured that independence. I have often
> inquired of myself, what great principle or idea it was that kept this
> Confederacy so long together. … It was that which gave promise
> that in due time the weights should be lifted from the shoulders of
> all men, and that *all* should have an equal chance. This is the senti-
> ment embodied in that Declaration of Independence. … If this
> country cannot be saved without giving up that principle … I would
> rather be assassinated on this spot than to surrender it.[4]

With his Independence Hall speech, Lincoln testified to his lifelong political embrace of the national values, liberty and equality.
He affirmed his commitment to them by asserting that he would rather
be assassinated than surrender the principles of the Declaration. Lincoln's
honor, sacred to him, impelled the president-elect to uphold the Founding
Fathers' promise of equality for all. The stirrings of patriotism overwhelmed
Lincoln as he recalled the Founding Fathers dedication to those same principles. In assessing the danger of Civil War, Lincoln vowed that there would be
no war unless "forced upon the Government."[5] In this, his testament to the
Declaration of Independence and his regard for the War of Independence,
Lincoln defined the virtues that would sustain the nation in a war: justice,
honor, patriotism, and commitment.

Lincoln held out these "virtues of war" as necessary to uphold a national
unity that remained elusive. Lincoln's honor, his duty and commitment as
president, he claimed, forced him to uphold the Constitution and, therefore, to maintain laws that protected slavery where it existed and return
fugitive slaves to their owners. But tragically, his moral stance against slavery, along with his sense of justice and patriotism, would open the wounds
of war and concentrate men and material into the great armed engines of
military might, North and South.

President-Elect Abraham Lincoln raising a flag at Independence Hall, Philadelphia, February 22, 1861. (Library of Congress)

In Lincoln's familial and political life he was perceived as having achieved a certain ethical unity. Lincoln's character evolved in such a way that national values became his personal values and, likewise, his personal values would come to enhance our national values. Yet Lincoln struggled to absorb and maintain a consistent moral attitude against the forces of poverty, migration, death of family members, and separation from loved ones. He imbibed patriotism reading about the Founding Fathers; he learned persistence even when rains washed out newly planted crops; he upheld his honor in a wrestling match when his opponent used dishonest tactics; he claimed justice in defending an Indian in the Black Hawk War. In truth, there was an ethical unity, but expressed in an evolving sense of need to define himself. He strove to make his way in a political world where his perception almost, but not quite, grasped what the Declaration of Independence entailed. That is, even the most profound grasp of those principles could not anticipate what the Civil War and an attack upon slavery would mean. Even the Union victory and the end to slavery did not bring all the blessings of freedom and equality to the freedmen and freedwomen. Nonetheless, in Lincoln's domestic and political life, he always addressed a horizon of union, harmony, oneness as opposed to the forces of disunion, separation, fragmentation.[6]

For Abraham Lincoln, his family's legacy of migration and loss meant he endeavored to embrace a larger, more cohesive stability. The Lincoln family had for generations migrated from East to West in search of land and prosperity. Nonetheless, Thomas Lincoln, Abraham Lincoln's father, accumulated and lost property at a considerable rate, given the numerous land title disputes in Western territories at the time. Thomas married Nancy Hanks, a tall, dark, strong-built woman who endured childbirth and migration in the Western wild. They parented three children, Sarah, Abraham, and Thomas. Thomas Sr. and Nancy had moved three times before they came to the Sinking Spring Farm near Elizabethtown, Kentucky, where Sarah was born in 1807 and their second child, Abraham, was born on February 12, 1809, in a rude clay and log cabin. In 1812, Nancy Hanks Lincoln lost a baby boy, Thomas Jr., who lived only a few days.[7]

Abraham Lincoln rarely spoke of his early life except to say they lived according to "the annals of the poor." After two years the Lincolns moved from the Sinking Spring Farm to Knob Creek, where Thomas leased 30 acres. Opposed to slavery, Thomas joined the Knob Creek Separate Baptist church, which espoused the principles of infant baptism and pre-destination and held to a strict moral code against drinking, dancing, and slavery.[8] Slavery existed in the most intimate relations of Kentucky communities. Abraham later observed how it could attach its tendrils in a family system. He proposed that if 10 men moved into a territory and one man had 10 slaves, the others would accept him in time. As to just how that happened, he explained:

> The slaveholder is a good man in other respects; he is a good neighbor, and being a wealthy man, he is enabled to do the others many neighborly kindnesses. They like the man, though they don't like the system by which he holds his fellow-men in bondage; . . . These ten men . . . live together three or four years; they intermarry, their family ties are strengthened. . . . This is the way in which slavery is planted, and gains so firm a foothold.[9]

Abraham Lincoln's observation on Kansas could have fit the raw backwoods of Kentucky. It would take a determined and objective perspective to detach from the intimacy of slave cultures, an intimacy of inequity. Thomas Lincoln's uncle, Isaac, owned six slaves, and the Berrys, with whom Nancy Hanks lived before her marriage, owned five slaves. Thomas Lincoln did not own slaves. The Lincoln family's model of cohesion was to differentiate itself from the prevailing slave culture but not from its neighbors. Maintaining relationships was important to Abraham; he demonstrated an openness even beyond the easy familiarity with neighbors. Dennis Hanks, a cousin of Nancy Hanks Lincoln, said Abraham, though it was considered rude, spoke first to strangers who came by the farm before his father had a chance to greet them.[10] Abraham needed to prove himself and he liked talking to strangers, those who perhaps brought a new perspective to his hardscrabble existence.

The family settled in primitive forests where young Abraham cleared wood with an axe. Lincoln had one vivid memory of the vagaries of planting at Knob Creek, how all the family's work came to nothing. He said that after he and the boys planted seven acres of corn and pumpkin seeds, rainwater came through the gorges of the hills and into the valley and "washed ground, corn, pumpkin seed and all clear off the field." The final blow came when their landlord, George Linsley, ejected the Lincolns and nine other tenants from the Knob Creek farm.[11] It meant another move, this time across the Ohio to Indiana, where federal land titles guaranteed a more secure property. They were accompanied by Nancy Hanks's relatives, Elizabeth and Thomas Sparrow and Dennis Hanks. They had joined the Lincolns in 1817 when their own land claims proved a legal nullity.[12]

The move to Indiana proved tragic. First the Sparrows died, and then Nancy died of a fever, an epidemic of "milk sickness." Dennis Hanks eulogized Nancy Lincoln as "one of the very best women in the whole race, known for kindness. Mrs. Lincoln always taught Abe goodness—kindness—read the Bible to him—taught him to read and spell—taught him sweetness and benevolence as well."[13] As a boy, Lincoln responded to his mother's benevolence in kind. When wild turkeys lighted by the Lincolns' cabin, Abraham shot one. Yet his empathy with animals was such, he claimed, that it was the last time he ever picked up a gun. In adulthood such strong sympathies provoked memories of family members who died. His sister, Sarah, would die later, in 1827, in childbirth. In adulthood Lincoln wrote a line of poetry about his childhood home as a place:

> Where things decayed, and loved ones lost
> in dreamy shadows rise.[14]

After the death of his wife, Nancy, however, Thomas Lincoln married again, this time to a widow named Sarah Bush Johnson, who had three children. It was Sarah Bush Lincoln who integrated the families and fostered Abraham with loving care and attention. However, where Sarah Lincoln proved loving and protective of Abraham, Thomas Lincoln did not. Between father and son a distance arose as Thomas demanded all of the boy's time in the labor of clearing, plowing, and harvesting. Thomas "slashed" his son when he spent too much time with his books.[15] He perceived his son as lazy. Nevertheless, Abraham persisted, and spent what time he could reading in his characteristic position, lying on the floor.[16]

The ravages of economic instability, paternal harshness, the contagion of "milk sickness," and the presence of slavery might have instilled in Lincoln a sense of himself as nothing, of no account. Instead, those challenges gave him a deep desire to identify with a larger association that could absorb his own imagination and existence. Even then, Lincoln must have thought about justice; he had to ask himself, What does it mean to live as we live? What is the best way to live? His education, though sparse, set him to reading to answer those questions.[17] Lincoln and his sister, Sarah, attended less than a year of A. B. C. schools that taught "readin, writin, cyphering."[18] Nonetheless, it was enough to provoke a keen interest in learning. When available, he attended "blab schools" that emphasized recitation in unison. He worked diligently to spell from *Dilworth's Spelling Book*. Thomas Dilworth's approach to spelling used prayers and a psalter as a basis for learning phonetics and letters. Prayer themes emphasized the importance of community as well as the necessity of obedience to "the law of the Lord." Young students prayed "because no man is made for himself only, but all of us for the mutual he'p of each other, grant that we may ... diligently apply ourselves to our studies." According to the *speller* only the cultivation of virtue enabled youth to excel. Dilworth believed that "a wise man values no possession more than virtue, because it is the fountain of all public and private happiness." Dilworth emphasized: "No man may put off the law of God" and "walk in the law of the Lord, and God will help you."[19] Lincoln learned that the law of God, God's order, demanded solidarity, and virtues upheld that solidarity. A better world awaited those who practiced the cultivation of virtues.

The burden of community lay with the individual, however, and John Bunyan's *Pilgrim's Progress* demonstrated that in life's journey, the virtues must accompany the pilgrim on the road to salvation. *Pilgrim's Progress* warned, for instance, against the advice of the "Worldly Wise" to adjust to worldly values. Rather, one must prefer the cross—to die to the world.

The virtuous, however, are rewarded and are enabled to subdue kingdoms, shut the mouths of lions, stop violence, escape the sword, and be courageous in fight.[20] Bunyan perceived that virtue promised salvation, a better world.

For a child in the wilderness, Parson Mason Weems's biography of George Washington provided Lincoln with an awe of the Founding Fathers. According to Parson Weems, Washington's ambition to serve his country "rendered him superior to all his difficulties." Weems wrote that patriotism, "the cement of nations," is "the first of all Republican virtues" and "the product of an enlightened and virtuous mind." Weems extolled Washington's justice: for never taking pay for his service to country, for his honesty in always paying his debts, and for his commitment to the Republic. He wrote that it was Washington who stressed that "in exact proportion to our union will be our strength, our peace and prosperity."[21] In Weems's estimation, virtue promised a specific end, namely, a prosperous and peaceful union. Patriotism came first, and prosperity followed. In contrast, William Grimshaw's *History of the United States*, which Lincoln also read, warned Americans that without recognizing that "all men are created equal" and without abolishing slavery, peace and prosperity would not move the country to a glorious future.[22]

Yet of all the books that surrounded the young Lincoln, one adventurous tale invoked the excitement of obtaining riches through virtue: the novel *Robinson Crusoe*, by Daniel Defoe. The book may also have implanted the possibilities of making one's own way in the world. Robinson Crusoe "broke loose" from his family, despite the best advice from his father to stay at home. The young adventurer went to sea where he learned to be a Guinea trader but was captured and sold as a slave, but then escaped. After his release from bondage, he had some success in selling his merchandise and invested in a Brazilian tobacco plantation, supported by slave labor. Even with all that, he wanted more and set sail again. This time he experienced a shipwreck on a deserted island where he made a life for himself from his own hands and where he contemplated, "What am I? Whence are we?" From this contemplation he experienced a conversion, a repentance for his sins. Realizing he had nothing to covet, Robinson Crusoe came to the conclusion that he had no desires, lusts, or pride. His only danger was fear of the cannibals who sometimes visited the island. Then, he reasoned, he had no business to attack them unless they attacked him. "Leave them to the justice of God," he thought. Ultimately, he captured one of the cannibal's victims and trained him as a servant. This servant, named Friday, knew the waterways and how to escape the island, which is what they did. His faithful servant prompted

Crusoe to reason, "Blacks have the same powers and capacities as we have." Upon his escape, Crusoe returned to find his plantation prospered and he was a rich man.[23]

For a boy like Lincoln who read deeply and well, there were important lessons to be learned. Some days the young Lincoln "preached" to his playmates those self-same virtues and admonitions he heard in the last Sunday's sermon. For himself Lincoln might have imbibed the lesson that by breaking loose from one's family and limiting circumstances to risk adventure, one could also become rich. Certainly, Lincoln's absorption in mathematics, its logic and precision, gave him the means to exercise the rational control needed for a life of adventure.[24] However, such adventure in *Robinson Crusoe* demanded, for the reflective child, a contemplative, self-critical dimension. Virtue, then, if practiced for itself, lead to prosperity as the life of Washington and *Robinson Crusoe* demonstrated. Thus, within early 19th-century culture lay a paradox: The worldly wise might exercise virtue, an idea foreign to Bunyan's pilgrim. The Republic, itself a paradox as established by the Founding Fathers, promised the liberty to pursue peace and prosperity, whereas justice as defined by the Declaration of Independence demanded equality. A prosperity built upon slave labor headed toward conflict, as a growing sense of injustice began to grip the American conscience.

Lincoln's boyhood occurred during the growth of American nationalism. Jefferson's Louisiana Purchase in 1803 doubled the size of the United States and opened up the West to exploration and settlement. Despite the danger from Indian tribes who populated the territory, the West remained a lure for expansion. A further impetus to push West occurred after the War of 1812. British and French depredations on American neutral shipping prompted the War of 1812. However, when the war ended satisfactorily in the Battle of New Orleans, the postwar period introduced a surge of commercial and economic expansionism. President Madison called for national bank and a protective tariff. Congressional leaders, including Henry Clay, supported a plan that became known as the "American System." The American System enabled national self-sufficiency by supporting northern manufacturing, which in turn imported foodstuffs and raw goods from the South and West. The protective tariff provided revenue for roads, in order for the transportation of goods North, South, and West. The Bank of the United States extended the credit for national projects.[25] The future of prosperity would spread out in a transportation system that included canals and railroads.

Lincoln matured into a world of promise—his desire for self-sufficiency, adventure, stability, and purpose conspired to draw him into the national drive for a prosperous, expansionist union. This then, surely, was the way to live. The first intimation that he might succeed in the world of opportunity came when Lincoln sold wood to buy a shirt of which he was immensely proud. And once when he ferried two gentlemen out to a steamboat, the men each pitched the young fellow a silver half-dollar. As Lincoln later related to William H. Seward, with a dollar in cash, "[t]he world seemed wider and fairer before me."[26] In the fall of 1828, James Gentry entrusted Lincoln to deliver trade goods to the Port of New Orleans. Allen Gentry, the son of the store owner, accompanied Abraham. The young men left Rockport, Indiana, and braved the winter to make a river journey over a thousand miles. One night, a gang of blacks attacked them and their cargo, but the two young men fought them off and delivered the goods to the port.

Later, Denton Offutt commissioned Lincoln to deliver trade goods to New Orleans. Lincoln took his stepbrother John Hanks and his cousin John D. Johnston on the journey down the Sangamon River in south central Illinois to the Ohio River and eventually to the Mississippi and the Port of New Orleans. While passing the town of New Salem, Illinois, their boat got caught on the dam and only Lincoln's ingenious strategy saved the cargo. He transferred the load to another small boat and drilled a hole in their boat that lifted the stern over the dam. Thus lightened, the boat sailed over the dam and impressed the townsmen with Lincoln's ingenuity. His growing strength, his confidence, and his fondness for the main chance increased his restlessness. In 1830 when his father decided to move to Illinois, Lincoln faithfully helped his family make the long trek, but then he set out on his own. When Lincoln appeared in New Salem, a commercial village surrounded by farms, in July 1831 to take up a new life, the village people recognized him as that clever fellow who engineered his boat over the dam. Like Robinson Crusoe, Lincoln extracted a living by the work of his hands and his considerable reasoning power. And it was from reason that he shaped his virtue.[27]

New Salem proved important politically and intellectually. Denton Offutt, knowing Lincoln's honesty and good sense, offered him a job in his grocery store where Lincoln proved an affable if distracted clerk who spent his time in reading the works of Thomas Paine and other enlightened thinkers. He began to question more deeply the Baptist doctrine of his youth. Not only his reading but also his observation of the fragmentation borne of the interreligious rivalries of Christian denominations lead him to religious skepticism.[28]

Lincoln's absorption in his own intellectual development did not detract him from proving his honor and standing among men. Lincoln's reputation for strength and wrestling talent, bragged about by Offutt, drew the attention of a local tough, Jack Armstrong, and his gang, the Clary Grove boys. Lincoln, when he first arrived in New Salem, had voted for Jack Armstrong as constable.[29] Nonetheless, Armstrong challenged Lincoln to a wrestling match. The match ended in a draw, but Lincoln held his honor, the honor of a Southern yeoman—the manly virtues of courage, strength, and determination[30]—and thereby gained the respect of the local men and laid the groundwork for future political support. In the meantime he read law almost obsessively. His friend and mentor attorney John Todd Stuart encouraged him and guided his study. In classical theory the law provided the way to develop virtuous habits in the first place. Aristotle contended that "[l]egislators make the citizens good by forming habits in them." The law was less about rules and more about shaping a moral character.[31] Lincoln would find this a major task of his political life.

His first major challenge to instill discipline and honor in men occurred in 1832 during the Black Hawk War. Offutt's store "petered out" and Lincoln enlisted in the New Salem militia along with the Clary Grove boys. Much to his surprise and delight, the men elected him captain. Lincoln's reputation for outwrestling his men certainly contributed to his prestige. Once, when an elderly, peaceful Indian came into the camp, the men were ready to kill him. Lincoln, however, intervened and defended the Indian. When the men accused Lincoln of cowardice, Lincoln literally rose to his full height in response to the challenge. He gave warning that he was prepared to duel. His moral courage impressed the men. As one witness said, "He would do justice to all although the heavens fell."[32] In this instance, justice to Lincoln meant treating all human beings equally, including Indians.

Returning home after the war, he entered into a partnership with William F. Berry in a general store, a store that failed and left Lincoln with a large debt. He worked briefly as a surveyor but later had to sell his equipment and horse to pay off the debt. His honesty and his military service enhanced his reputation and gave him the courage to run for the state legislature as an anti-Jackson candidate in 1832. He lost by only 15 votes but garnered every vote in New Salem.

Yet, if his increasing rationality and ambition grounded him, his fits of depression unhinged him. He fell in love with Ann Rutledge, a pretty and intelligent young woman already affianced to another, John McNeil, or as he later called himself John McNamer. McNamer sold dry goods but left town after his partner in the business bought him out. He claimed he had to go to New York to settle debts incurred by his father. In the two years of his absence, Lincoln courted Ann Rutledge. When she died in 1835, an acquaintance of Lincoln's, Hardin Bale, claimed Lincoln's friends had to lock him up to prevent "derangement or suicide." Reports were that he suffered melancholy for months afterward.[33] Until the Rutledge affair, Lincoln had not had a romantic attachment. He learned how deep and dangerously unsettling the feelings of dependence could be. Heartbroken, he thereafter attempted to bridle his emotions and shore up his self-sufficiency. Participation in law and politics steadied his equilibrium, but the slavery issue remained to destabilize the political and social order.

Once he regained his emotional balance, he stood for election and in the fall of 1834 won a seat in the state legislature in Vandalia, the state capital. Lincoln's second term proved inauspicious. As a Whig he fought for an extensive system of internal improvements, namely railroads, which would have helped New Salem and Illinois enter into the fast developing American economy. The system was to be paid for by borrowing and by the sale of public lands. Eventually, the scheme proved too expensive and was never fully implemented.[34] Until this point Lincoln had no occasion to balance his ambition for peace and prosperity, with justice. National politics, however, careened close to the divisive issue of slavery.

The slavery issue appeared during Lincoln's second campaign for the legislature in 1836 because of the furor of mob action against abolitionists that roiled the Midwest and the nation. When a resolution against abolitionism arose in the legislature, Lincoln voted against it. The Illinois political dialogue allowed antislavery sentiment to go only so far. Thus, at the end of a session, Lincoln denounced the slavery institution as unjust but argued that "the promulgation of abolition doctrines tends rather to increase than to abate its evils." His caution regarding abolition carried through the tumultuous prewar period. His answer to the unrest was his address to the Young Men's Lyceum in January 1838. Lincoln spoke on the topic "The Perpetuation of Our Political Institutions." He argued that democratic institutions are guaranteed only through reverence for the Constitution and law, for which everyone is to pledge his "life, liberty and sacred honor." If the law maintained justice and one's honor and patriotism upheld it,[35] what did it mean that the law allowed slavery? The choice for lawmakers then remained justice or a fragile peace.

One fateful legislative push of Lincoln's and the "Long Nine," his tall allies in the Illinois House, was a move to relocate the state capital to Springfield. The move detached Lincoln from New Salem and propelled him into a new social dialogue, which in turn advanced his political ambition and tested his commitment to justice. Springfield, Illinois, in 1837 with its few brick buildings and rutted roads appeared unpromising to the young lawyer, Lincoln. Yet he was the partner of John Todd Stuart, a cousin of the socially prominent Todds. Lincoln enjoyed the company of Joshua Speed, a store owner, who gave Lincoln a place to stay and introduced him to the easy company of young men drawn to debate and storytelling. Nonetheless, Lincoln gradually fell into the social orbit of John Todd Stuart and his cousin Elizabeth Todd Edwards, who was married to Ninian Edwards, son of the governor of Illinois. The Todd and Edwards families dominated the Springfield society.

Mary Todd, the sister of Elizabeth Edwards, visited Springfield in 1840. She was pretty, bright, and passionately interested in politics. As she wrote of herself to her friend, Mercy Ann Levering: "This fall I became quite a *politician*, rather an unladylike profession, yet at such a *crisis*, whose heart could remain untouched while the energies of all were called into question.[36]" Mary Todd spoke of the election of William Henry Harrison, whom she favored as a man who could protect "our prosperity." By "our prosperity" she meant her class and the nation's prosperity. Mary Todd was the daughter of Robert Todd, a wealthy banker and civic leader, whose ancestors founded the town of Lexington, Kentucky. Robert Todd devoted his financial interests to promoting the flagging economy of the town that suffered a decline in the aftermath of the War of 1812. Robert and his wife, Eliza, were friends of Henry Clay, whose Ashland plantation lay near the Todd's ancestral home. Mary Ann Todd, born December 18, 1818, lived in comfort and privilege, but she assimilated the family's interest in public service and political involvement. Mary Todd's mother died in 1827, and Robert remarried a year later to Elizabeth Humphreys from a prominent Lexington family. Elizabeth Humphreys Todd brought her own six children to the marriage. Imperious and demanding, "Betsy" Humphreys Todd often clashed with the stubborn and self-willed Mary Todd. Although alienated at home, Mary Todd excelled in her private schooling, especially dramatics.[37]

When Mary Todd visited Springfield, she created much interest among the social set; she was a "belle": Her wit entertained, her beauty captivated, her conversation fascinated. Among the throng of Mary's admirers stood Lincoln, tall, awkward, with prairie humor, political experience, and reticent conversation. Her political acumen and acquaintance with Henry Clay attracted Lincoln. Ninian and Elizabeth Edwards accepted Lincoln as a lawyer in their cousin's law firm, but did not approve of him as a match for Mary. Yet Mary recognized in him the ambition, a keen-edged knowledge of politics, and the easy sympathy with which he concentrated on anyone who spoke to him. The courtship began in the summer of 1840.

However, a break occurred on or around January 1, 1841. Sources claim that both parties flirted with others—Mary Todd with Stephen Douglas and Lincoln with Mary's younger cousin, Matilda. Whatever the cause, Lincoln sank into a profound depression. Ninian Edwards believed that Lincoln, conflicted between his honor and his love, was driven "[c]razy as a *Loon*." Joshua Speed, Lincoln's most intimate friend, certainly understood that Lincoln struggled between his head and his heart. Lincoln once described his rationality by saying "cold, calculating reason" was the solution to all problems.[38] But he could not control a love that, in the case of Mary Todd, absorbed so much of his emotional and intellectual resources.[39] Basically, he could not control Mary Todd. Lincoln's sense of honor could not afford him any leeway to abandon the relationship. Yet he did abandon it.

Lincoln's despondency lasted for months despite entering into a new partnership with Stephen T. Logan and rebuilding his law practice. His friend Joshua Speed suggested a month away at his family home in Kentucky. There, Lincoln reveled in the luxury of plantation living—food, servants, and happy companionship with Speed's family, especially Mary Speed, Joshua's half-sister, whom he teased. For Lincoln, Kentucky was home, and slaves a part of that neighborliness and hospitality. One especially important relationship helped revive his depressed spirit. Lucy Speed, Joshua's mother, talked to Lincoln as perhaps his own mother would have. She gave him a bible as a parting gift. He promised Mary Speed that "I intend to read it [the Oxford Bible] regularly when I return home." He added, "I doubt not that it is really ... the best cure for the 'Blues' could one but take it according to the truth."[40] Despite his misgivings, later in his presidency, Lincoln would keep a well-thumbed bible on his desk.

Estranged but not strangers, Abraham Lincoln and Mary Todd revived their relationship on the field of honor. In 1842, a friend, Eliza Francis, invited Lincoln and Mary Todd to her home, each of them not knowing the other would be there. Once the couple met in Eliza's living room, Eliza persuaded them to be friends. Reconciled, Lincoln sent Mary recent state legislative election returns that showed him a winner in one of them. Such a strange valentine placed the comfortable political sense before the dangerous romantic one. Again feeling secure in their personal understanding, Mary Todd and Abraham Lincoln took political risks. Mary and a friend, Julia Jayne, wrote a letter, signed "Rebecca" in the *Sangamo Journal*, which satirized an Irish Democratic state auditor, James Shield, calling him both a "fool" and a "liar." Mary showed Lincoln the letter

and Lincoln, who as a defender of the banking system also despised
Shield's hard currency schemes, wrote a second "Rebecca" letter. Mary
and Julia, then feeling their power to deflate the vain and pompous
Shields, wrote a third pseudonymous letter. Infuriated, Shields demanded
that the editor reveal the author of the letters. When Lincoln owned up
to all of the letters, Shields challenged him to a duel. Dueling had been
outlawed in Illinois in 1839, but the seriousness of the issue was such that
Lincoln agreed to meet Shields for a duel in Missouri. Lincoln, not as
skilled a marksman as Shields, chose broadswords as his weapon of choice,
a weapon much to his long-armed advantage. The men crossed the
Mississippi to Missouri, but at the last moment the duel was called off.
Perhaps, the absurdity of the weapons ended the affair.[41] Nonetheless,
Lincoln's gallant effort and the protection of her honor must have
impressed Mary Todd. Still reserved, Lincoln needed assurance from
Speed that his own marriage was happy. Speed later claimed, "If I had
not been married & happy . . . [h]e would not have married."[42] Abraham
Lincoln and Mary Todd married hastily on November 4, 1842, before
the groom entertained any more doubts.

In 1846 at the height of the Mexican War, an indignant
Lincoln's personal sense of honor transferred to national honor. Elected
to Congress in 1846 at the height of the Mexican War, an indignant
Lincoln demanded President Polk justify his demand for war on the
grounds that the Mexican government invaded U.S. territory. Lincoln
challenged Polk "to establish whether the particular spot of soil on which
the blood of our *citizens* was so shed, was, or was not, *our own soil*."[43]
Lincoln's opponents ridiculed his argument, and dubbed him "Spotty
Lincoln." At stake for Congressman Lincoln was national honor, ignored
in the lust for Mexican territory. Although Lincoln supported supplies
for the troops, he argued that "the national honor, security of the future,
and everything but territorial indemnity, may be considered the *no pur-
poses*, and *indefinite* objects of the war."[44] Lincoln's hostility to American
aggrandizement of Mexican territory foreshadowed his antagonism toward
the extension of slavery into the Western territories. The Mexican War
aroused his sense of honor, but the issue of slavery had yet to engage
him fully.

In 1848 Lincoln stumped for the election of Whig presidential candidate Zachary Taylor and triumphed in his swing through New England.
When the Whig State Convention met at Worcester, Massachusetts,
Abraham Lincoln was invited to give an address. The night before, the
Governor of Massachusetts Levi Lincoln hosted Congressman Lincoln at
a dinner at his home. Years later Lincoln recalled the scene: "I went with
hay seed in my hair to learn deportment in the most cultivated state in

the Union—and I have never seen such a beautiful table and such fine arrangements as at Governor Lincoln's."[45] Lawyer Edward L. Pierce, later state office holder and biographer of Charles Sumner, recalled that when Abraham Lincoln made his speech the next day at the Whig Convention in Worcester, he referred to antislavery men and said: "They were better treated in Massachusetts than in the West, and, turning to William S. Lincoln of Worcester, who had lived in Illinois, he remarked that in that state they had recently killed one of them."[46] William Lincoln, son of Governor Levi Lincoln, shared the same sentiments with the guest speaker as both abjured radicalism and the violence it spawned. In his remarks Lincoln referred to abolitionist editor Elijah Lovejoy's murder in Alton, Illinois, as one of the most notorious attacks upon an antislavery proponent. Lovejoy's assailants murdered the editor and destroyed his press.

Lincoln impressed Massachusetts Whigs, but abolitionists such as Charles Sumner had refused to support Taylor and already moved apart from the moderate antislavery wing of the party. Sumner wrote to Frances Longfellow, wife of poet Henry Wadsworth Longfellow and a social justice advocate in her own right, that General Taylor had been "forced upon the Whig Party."[47] Lincoln still had not yet grasped the searing import of the slavery issue. After Taylor's successful election, Lincoln left the Congress, and between 1848 and 1854 went back to the private practice of law to earn a living for his growing family of boys. Tragedy stalked him, however, when in 1850 he lost his son Eddie, who died of "consumption."

Lincoln's public life to this point set a cautious course but one aimed at justice. He personally believed slavery was wrong, but that was a stand politically untenable in Illinois or national politics. From his own experience he remembered a vivid example of the horrors of the institution of slavery. When traveling back from Kentucky on a steamboat from his visit with the Speed family, he observed 12 slaves being transported South. They were chained together and he noted, "The negroes were strung together precisely like so many fish upon a trot-line."[48] He had limited solutions for the problem because he adhered to Henry Clay's ideas on the subject. Indeed, Lincoln loved Clay's "deep devotion to liberty" and his "strong sympathy with the oppressed and ... ardent desire for their elevation."[49] He eulogized Clay for his antislavery sentiment and argued that to suppress antislavery sentiment was to "blow out the moral lights around us."[50] Nonetheless, Henry Clay and Lincoln advocated the most conservative options: the nonextension of slavery into the western territories acquired in the Mexican War that ended in 1848 and the colonization of free blacks on African soil. Even more significant in Lincoln's adulation of Clay, he admired Clay's unswerving support of the Union in the Compromise of 1850, ultimately engineered through Congress by Stephen Douglas. The Compromise avoided a war between the states by successfully balancing power between North and South. Under the Compromise, California became a free state, and the slave state of Texas's boundary was set. The territories of Utah and New Mexico were organized with power to legislate. The Compromise also suppressed the slave trade in Washington, D.C. However, the Compromise reinforced the Fugitive Slave Law. The law allowed slave owners to retrieve their runaway slaves even in free states by use of a court order that merely described the fugitive but did not define their status as slave or free. Lincoln supported the law because it preserved the Union. Nonetheless, the Fugitive Slave Law aroused fierce opposition from abolitionists such as Wendell Phillips. Phillips referred to Lincoln as "that slave hound from Illinois."[51] The New England states introduced "personal liberty laws" to offset this federal legislation. Lincoln's moderation did not mean an abandonment of justice; it did mean a pragmatic antislavery commitment. Nonetheless, his adherence to the principle that slavery was morally wrong took courage, especially in Lincoln's own politically divided state of Illinois.

The passage of the Kansas-Nebraska Act in 1854 and its threat to the Union propelled Lincoln back into politics. The Act, largely sponsored by Senator Stephen Douglas, introduced the concept of "popular sovereignty," allowing people residing in the territories to vote on whether or not to allow slavery. Northerners regarded this provision as unconstitutional. In addition, the Kansas-Nebraska Act abrogated the Missouri Compromise Line, which stated that slavery could not be established North of the 36°30' line. Popular sovereignty would allow slavery to move North if the territories of Kansas and Nebraska so voted. Conflict over the provisions of the Kansas-Nebraska Act divided the nation and the Whig party, which broke into northern and southern wings, effectively contributing to the party's demise.

The Republican Party arose as a coalition of antislavery Whigs and Democrats and a reform movement known as the Free Soil Party. The Free Soil Party espoused the nonextension of slavery for the benefit of labor and northern notions of individual liberty. Its slogan proclaimed "Free Soil, free speech, free labor, and free men." With the breakdown of the Whig party, Lincoln aligned with Republicans, and in the summer of 1854 or thereabouts began to organize his ideas on the slavery question. He believed no one doubted that slavery was wrong, except those who had had a "plainly *selfish* way." So he proceeded in a rational way to attain

power and carry the Republican Party's platform on nonextension of slavery to the voters. In 1855 he won a seat in the Illinois State Assembly, but
he had larger ambitions and declared his candidacy for the U.S. Senate.
Under the Constitution, state legislatures voted for U.S. senators. The
Illinois Assembly voted Lincoln a winner on the first ballot but without
a majority. His political friend, Lyman Trumbull, ultimately won a majority on the third ballot and therefore took the coveted Senate seat.[52]

The confidence in his own inner logic and restless ambition that solidi-
fied Lincoln's legal and political career prompted him in 1858 to accept his
party's nomination as U.S. senator again against the incumbent senator,
Democrat Stephen Douglas. In his speech at the Republican State
Convention, where he was nominated for the U.S. Senate, Lincoln maintained that Douglas was not a great man if he upheld the right of slavery to
move anywhere in the Union. He said, "Douglas, if not a dead lion for this
work, is at least a caged and toothless one."[53] Lincoln's remark echoed
John Bunyan's claim that the practice of virtue enabled one to "shut the
mouths of lions."[54]

The Senate race attracted considerable press attention as the candidates
presented a fascinating contrast in appearance and opinion. Douglas, a
short man with an authoritative voice and distinguished, commanding
presence, contrasted sharply with the tall, lean, countrified Lincoln, who
spoke with a high-pitched voice. The debate format tended to focus on
differences between the candidates on the issue of slavery and that difference attracted national attention. The contest would test Lincoln's
commitment to justice.

There were seven face-to-face debates between Lincoln and Douglas in
Illinois. In the first of the debates in Ottawa, Douglas stormed against
Lincoln and his party as "abolitionists" and pressed him to answer questions about such sentiments that Douglas claimed were in the
Republican State Convention resolutions passed in 1854. Lincoln claimed
he had nothing to do with the resolutions passed by the Republican Party
in 1854. Douglas ridiculed his opponent's defense since Lincoln, he said,
was a leader of his party at that time. Later at the debates in Jonesboro
and Quincy, Lincoln would deny that he took part in the state conven-
tions that passed those resolutions.[55] Douglas also demanded if Lincoln
would vote to repeal the Fugitive Slave Act, or would vote to prohibit
slavery in the territories. In effect Douglas challenged Lincoln to repudiate
the Compromise of 1850. Lincoln, not accustomed to *ex tempore* speaking,
stumbled in his replies.[56]

In the second debate at Freeport, Lincoln regained his composure and
laid a trap for Douglas. Lincoln asked the Illinois senator, could "the

people of a United States Territory, in any lawful way . . . exclude slavery from its limits prior to the formation of a State Constitution?" Douglas replied that "unfriendly legislation" might keep slavery out of a territory since "slavery cannot exist . . . unless it is supported by local police regulations."[57] Thus, Douglas conceded that a territory could exclude slavery, thereby losing politically the confidence of Southern Democrats. Lincoln, too, rebutted Senator Stephen Douglas's "popular sovereignty" plan. The objection Lincoln raised to popular sovereignty was that it perpetuated slavery; he argued the Founding Fathers had set slavery on the course to extinction. Moreover, Lincoln foresaw that popular sovereignty would nationalize slavery since there were no legal means to stop its spread, especially since the Supreme Court's Dred Scott decision had precluded that possibility, he observed.[58] Dred Scott, a Missouri slave, sued his owner for freedom on the grounds that his owner had taken him into Illinois, a free state, and into the Wisconsin territory, located above the Missouri Compromise Line. At issue was the constitutionality of the Missouri Compromise. The Supreme Court ruled that Congress had no power to bar slavery in the territories. The decision effectively removed any obstacle to the spread of slavery. The decision inflamed partisan and sectional feelings and made the Lincoln-Douglas debates a forum for the expression of those pent-up emotions.

Illinois reflected national divisions as northern Illinois contained moderate and Republican voters, while southern Illinois held a population of Democratic and largely racist voters. In Jonesboro, southern Illinois, Douglas bated Lincoln calling northern Illinois Republicans "abolitionists," a term of opprobrium in the racist part of the state. The Jonesboro crowd laughed when he told them the Republicans called the repeal of the Missouri Compromise inexpedient. And he regaled them with the story of "Fred Douglass," referring to the famed African American abolitionist speaker and activist, being driven to the debate in Freeport sitting in the back of a carriage next to a white woman. To this the crowd shouted, "Shame!" When Douglas said he had traveled north to Springfield, he pointedly named all the abolitionists he met there. And when he said, "[Salmon] Chase came about the time I left," someone in the crowd shouted, "Why didn't you shoot him?" Douglas replied, "I did take a running shot at them, but as I was single-handed against the white, black and mixed drove, I had to use a short gun and fire into the crowd instead of taking them off singly with a rifle."[59] The retort was met with "great laughter and cheers."[60] Such was the violent banter that precluded any rational discussion about slavery. However, Douglas was desperate at this point since Lincoln had trapped him at Freeport.

Lincoln approached voters in Charleston, southern Illinois, with a frank admission. When an elderly bystander asked Lincoln if he was in favor of equality with blacks, Lincoln replied, "I am not nor ever have been in favor of bringing about in any way the social and political equality of the white and black races."[61] That left Lincoln open to Douglas's taunt that Lincoln said one thing in northern Illinois and another in southern Illinois. It appeared Lincoln was not a man of principle.

Yet, in Peoria, Lincoln made his strongest statement with regard to slavery: "This *declared* indifference, but as I must think, covert *real* zeal for the spread of slavery, I can not but hate. I hate it because of the monstrous injustice of slavery itself. I hate it because it deprives our republican example of its just influence in the world—the insistence that there is no right principle of action but *self-interest*."[62]

Later, in Quincy, Illinois, Lincoln made the issue between the two candidates quite clear when he stated that the difference dividing the men was between those who "think slavery a wrong and those who do not think it wrong." For Republicans slavery was "a moral, a social and a political wrong"; therefore, they wanted to limit its spread. Democrats, Lincoln explained, did not think slavery was a wrong, and Douglas, as the leading Democrat, never avowed whether slavery was right or wrong. At Alton, in the debate that ended the series, Lincoln reiterated his earlier themes: that the real issue between himself and Senator Douglas was an eternal one, "the struggle between right and wrong."[63] Lincoln, despite his moral stance, lost the election. Since state legislatures elected U.S. senators, and Democrats had gained control of the Illinois legislature during the 1858 campaign, the legislature voted Douglas another term as senator. There remained only the plaintive warning that Lincoln gave when nominated for the U.S. Senate by the Republican State Convention in Springfield. He noted,

> A house divided against itself cannot stand.
> I believe this government cannot endure, permanently half slave and half free.
> I do not expect the Union to be *dissolved* ... but I *do* expect it will cease to be divided.
> It will become *all* one thing or *all* the other.[64]

The Lincoln-Douglas debate placed Lincoln in the center of the national conversation. In sum, Lincoln defended the just argument of the Declaration of Independence that proclaimed that all men were created equal, including black men. Slavery, according to Lincoln, violated

the principle of equality and therefore should not spread into the territories. Equality, in Lincoln's definition in 1858, however, did not include
social or political equality.[65] He stepped cautiously into any commitment
to full equality for blacks because his own belief with that of Illinois and
the nation did not support equal rights for "negroes." He believed reason
could overcome the divide. However, events robbed the national dialogue
of reason.

By 1860 Southern opinion was inflamed by the John Brown raid into
the South the year before, ostensibly to start a slave rebellion.
Meanwhile Northern voices decried the Dred Scott opinion that defined
slaves as property protected by the Constitution and subjected runaways
to federal arrest and prosecution. In this hostile environment Lincoln
accepted the distinguished pastor Henry Ward Beecher's invitation to
speak in New York at Cooper Union. The invitation, he believed, would
enhance his reputation among the Northern elite and promote his chances
for the presidency. In this speech Lincoln reviewed his earlier argument
that the federal government could control slavery in the territories.
Only this time he made a thoroughly researched, lengthy historical argument that the Founding Fathers did indeed intend such federal authority.
In addition, Lincoln attempted an appeal for rational moderation with
his Cooper Union address. He appealed to the Southern people: "[I]n the
general qualities of reason and justice you are not inferior to any other people," but he decried their reckless speech. Then he listed all the Southern
grievances against the North from sectionalism to slave insurrection and
refuted them. But he admonished Republicans to "calmly listen to the
South" and stressed the need for patience on both sides. As to the recent
crises, Lincoln denied John Brown was a Republican and suggested the
Dred Scott decision be attacked as a legal document, a document that
failed to prove that "the right of property in a slave is ... affirmed in the
Constitution." He ended his speech with the ringing appeal, "Let us have
faith that right makes might, and in that faith, let us to the end, dare to
do our duty as we understand it." The *New York Tribune*, for one, enthusiastically received Lincoln's first important appeal to a Northern elite
audience.[66]

Yet, Lincoln with his western ways and his habit of addressing the chair-
man as "Mr. Cheerman" offended the sensibilities of certain elites. Lincoln
did not impress some as the embodiment of any national movement.
As Henry B. Rankin recalled, some young, wealthy, and influential men
who took Lincoln to the Athenaeum for a simple supper following his
Cooper Union speech were joined by a few Republican men who "happened to be in the building." Such a casual approach to the

unprepossessing Lincoln meant the men who entertained him certainly did not mean to "flatter" him. A Mr. Nott who had joined the company offered to escort Lincoln back to his hotel, the Astor House. Nott simply took Lincoln to a street car and told him to get off at the "side door of the Astor House." Later Nott would regret his hasty send-off on that February night, because when he looked back at Lincoln sitting alone in the street car, Nott said, "he seemed a sad and lonely man."[67] Perhaps, Nott saw Lincoln's fatigue or his recurrent depression but more likely he saw the loneliness of an ambitious and rational man who could neither control nor predict his future. He had used both conciliatory and uncompromising rhetoric to meet the national crisis. He had lost two senatorial races. What more he could do or say remained unknown. And so he absorbed the pain of it.

Despite his foreboding, Lincoln's stature after the debates with Douglas and his Cooper Union speech made him a national figure and preeminent choice as the Republican candidate for president. His speaking engagements in the West and East did much to ease his self-doubts. Yet he faced formidable opposition in his party with three rivals: William Henry Seward, a former governor of New York and U.S. senator who lead the Republican Party since its inception in 1856; Salmon Chase of Ohio, chief organizer of the Free Soil Party and leading antislavery advocate; and Missouri Judge Edward Bates, who counted upon his strength among conservative Republicans. Seward had already written his victory speech, and Chase hoped the Republican Convention in Chicago would choose him if they deadlocked over Seward. Bates counted upon his assurances of support in the Northwest, New York, Pennsylvania, and some states in New England. In the meantime Lincoln's party workers descended upon Chicago and worked the delegates in his favor. Seward led on the first ballot, but Lincoln gained on the second and finally won on the third. Lincoln's moderation, his adherence to the party's nonextension of slavery, contrasted with Seward's more radical denunciation of the Fugitive Slave Act. Furthermore, Lincoln's biblical, "house divided" speech appeared conciliatory, whereas Seward's Senate speech warning of an "irrepressible conflict" seemed uncompromising. Lincoln appeared less radical than Chase and more strongly antislavery than Bates. Lincoln promised "[j]ustice and fairness to all," by which he meant extending a conciliatory hand to party factions.[68] In the meantime, the Democratic Party split in two with a Northern contingent led by Stephen Douglas and a Southern faction headed by John C. Breckinridge of Kentucky. The Constitutional Union Party, comprised of former Whigs and anti-Catholic Know Nothings nominated John Bell of Tennessee for the presidency of the United States. The division among his opponents gave Lincoln a political advantage.

Lincoln's campaign created great excitement in the Northeast, especially in Worcester, where the aging Elizabeth Trumbull, Levi Lincoln's mother-in-law, lit up all her many windows for the torchlight parades.[69] Lincoln won the election without the electoral votes from a single southern state. His election, however, fueled the secession crisis, as six Southern states—Georgia, Alabama, Mississippi, Florida, Louisiana, and Texas—all followed South Carolina out of the Union. Thus, before his inauguration, Lincoln faced an already broken Union. Four states—Virginia, North Carolina, Arkansas, and Tennessee—bolted the Union once the war began. The border states remained tentatively in the Union. Only a governing principle based on national principles could save the Union. But how to define those values without further fragmenting the Union created Lincoln's dilemma. The national balance between a prosperous peace and the rights of liberty and equality began to tip toward a more just equalization of rights.

In the midst of mounting tensions, on February 11, 1861, Lincoln began to travel slowly east from Springfield toward Washington for his inauguration on March 4. When Lincoln left Springfield, he left his home and the grave of his young son, Edward, to enter a new land of strangers. But at a stop in Lafayette, Indiana, he presented his vision of national cohesion: "[W]e are bound together, I trust in Christianity, civilization, and patriotism, and are attached to our country and our whole country."[70] He stopped along the way in Ohio, New York, New Jersey, and Pennsylvania, where he made a few brief remarks. However, when he reached Philadelphia, he gave his remarkable speech at Independence Hall. The speech contained a new sense of his rational virtues—that honor, justice, commitment, and patriotism now belonged to the fate of the Union. This speech contained all of him, all that he believed and felt in this most perilous of times.

Every national value was at stake that winter day. Lincoln desperately needed a reassurance of democratic purpose and solidarity. At Independence Hall he drew strength from recollecting the wisdom, patriotism, and principle with which the founders conceived the republic and struggled for its birth. He staked his honor on the institution of Union and the protection of the rights in the Declaration of Independence. The audience who cheered his emphatic faith in the Declaration of Independence understood that Lincoln intended to protect cherished national values. As Lincoln observed: "I have often pondered over the dangers which were incurred by the men who assembled here and adopted that Declaration of Independence—I have pondered over the toils that were endured by the officers and soldiers of the army, who achieved that Independence." The crowd applauded because they knew that to commit to the Declaration of Independence meant war in 1775, and it may mean such a crisis again. For Lincoln said, "[T]here will be no blood shed unless it be forced upon the Government."[71]

The deep feeling that suffused Lincoln's words may have been attributed to the moment when he fully realized his fateful path—how far he had to go to avoid war. When he said he would "rather be assassinated on this spot than to surrender" the principles of the Declaration of Independence, he was certainly aware of the assassination plot against him. Allen Pinkerton, head of the Pinkerton National Detective Agency, warned Lincoln's aides that the president-elect faced a very serious assassination plot directed against him in Baltimore, his next stop. Saddened, Lincoln could not believe that such an attempt would be made on his life when he hoped for peace with the South. Lincoln, himself southern born and bred, could not believe that there was "no broadbased support among Southern white people" for union.[72]

Indeed it was a familial delusion, the slave-owning families he lived among in Kentucky, he remembered as living in peace.[73] His virtues, once honed to living in peace, now turned toward saving the Union.

In his inaugural speech Lincoln maintained that the Union was "unbroken" but admitted that slavery divided the country along moral lines of right and wrong. He therefore pleaded the cause of legal justice, that slavery is protected in the states and the Fugitive Slave Law is enforced, however imperfectly. Caught between protecting slavery in the South and defending the right to liberty, Lincoln appealed to national bonds as familial bonds.[74] He entreated the American people to restore "their fraternal sympathies and affections," and to avoid "destruction of the national fabric." In a final plea Lincoln asked his country to remember "the mystic chords of memory stretching from every battle-field, and patriot grave to every living heart and hearthstone" that bound each to this "broad land." However, by his insistence to "hold occupy and possess the property and places belonging to the government," he implied he would use force.[75] As such, Lincoln assumed the place of a national patriarch in the tradition of the Founding Fathers. Francis Preston Blair, former Democratic journalist and slave owner who abhorred the extension of slavery and embraced Free Soilers and the Republican Party, wrote to Lincoln, "Confidence in your honesty and patriotism is now the mainstay of the Union."[76]

Shortly before his inauguration, Lincoln confirmed his rival candidates for the presidency as members of his cabinet.[77] They included William Henry Seward as secretary of state; Edward Bates as attorney general; and

Salmon Chase as treasury secretary. The immediate concern for the new administration was Union, specifically, the fate of Fort Sumter, located in Charleston, South Carolina, which was under threat of a secessionist takeover. General Winfield Scott advised abandoning Fort Sumter and the majority of Lincoln's cabinet cautioned against provisioning the fort. Lincoln rejected outright Seward's advice that the "reinforcement of Fort Sumter would be done on a slavery, or party issue, while that of Fort Pickens would be on a more national, and patriotic one."[78] Fort Pickens in Florida offered a more secure and well-defended position for making a Union stand, if it came to that. Seward believed Southern Unionists would then rally to the Union cause. However, to dissuade Seward, Lincoln dispatched Stephen Hurlburt, an Illinois friend, to Charleston to discover the extent of Unionist sympathy. He found no Unionist advocate.[79] Certainly, Catherine Ann Edmondston, a plantation mistress observing events from North Carolina, had no love for the Union or for Lincoln, whom she referred to as "that wretch."[80] With proof of a dearth of Southern Unionist sentiment and therefore South Carolina's preparedness to attack Sumter, Lincoln could convince Seward, at least, that conciliation with the South lacked hope. Moreover, some radical antislavery activists, such as Maria Weston Chapman, a leading Massachusetts abolitionist, remained indifferent to a Union that included slavery. She held to pacifist ideals and believed only in the immediate abolition of slavery. When urged to write about the nation in peril, Chapman, wrote her sister, Debra, "I don't care anything about it." Meanwhile Debra Weston urged her mother, who was so inclined, to support giving up Sumter.[81]

Before his decision, Lincoln lived in the valley of the shadow of war. Although he had used conciliatory language and insisted that the institution of slavery would not be interfered with in the Southern states, nonetheless, he would not surrender the Forts. In the end, Lincoln moved ahead to reprovision Fort Sumter, a symbol of federal authority. It was a duel. Although both sides chose their weapons, Lincoln selected the place and the strategy, but the South fired the first shot. With the declaration of war, Virginia seceded from the Union. Soon after Sumter, a Baltimore Committee arrived in Washington and asked the president to let the South go in peace. Maryland, along with other border states, remained crucial to the success of the Union cause. Earlier, Baltimore citizens attacked Union troops as they moved South through the city to defend the government in Washington. Lincoln's sense of honor and commitment would not allow such a challenge to go undefended. He said, "You would have me surrender the Government without a blow. There is no Washington in that—no Jackson in that—no manhood nor honor in that."[82]

Washington, D.C. took precedence in the president's concerns for protecting the Union. The city of Washington depended on General McClellan to protect it against Confederate forces located in Virginia and Maryland's secessionist sympathizers. McClellan, the general with "an alarmist tendency" who consistently overestimated the enemy's numbers and refused to fight without huge reinforcements, exasperated Lincoln.[83] Dangers without and within plagued Washington. The White House resided in the midst of a catastrophic humanitarian event—the influx of runaway slaves and their containment in refugee camps around the city. Washington was geographically and culturally a Southern town, albeit a backward one, lacking sanitation, water, and an orderly local government. Although the slave trade had been abolished in 1850, the Fugitive Slave Law allowed slave catchers and local marshals a lucrative business in catching and returning runaway slaves. Yet, former slaves crossed into Washington and worked as servants and in all manner of low-wage work. Lincoln supported such contraband work because the army, especially, had need of laborers. It was only when General Butler rebuffed a Southern planter who demanded his runaway with the explanation that such persons were "contraband" that some protection was loosely applied to the fugitives. And on April 16, 1862, the bill for Washington, D.C. emancipation passed into law. Yet the emancipatory law had not abrogated the Federal Fugitive Slave Act. Contrabands then came under military protection but were placed in either private service or in tenements, the so-called Duff Green's Row, where they lived in poverty. When smallpox broke out in July, families were removed to the camps in the city where the situation proved desperate. Lincoln was well aware of "the good deal of smallpox" that existed in Washington. And Lincoln's goodwill gesture to transport poverty-stricken colonists on the Isle of A'Vache, off the coast of Haiti, to Washington further threatened crowding in the camps.[84]

The Freedman's Aid Association, African American churches, and Northern missionaries contributed relief in the form of clothing and teachers. Mary Todd Lincoln ministered to hospitalized soldiers only after she recovered somewhat from her grief caused by the death of her son, Willie, who died on February 20, 1862. By November 1862 she visited New York to advance her humanitarian causes, among them the plight of the contrabands.[85] From New York she wrote to her husband and noted that her seamstress and friend, the ex-slave Elizabeth Keckley, had been working for the Contraband Association of Washington and was authorized to collect for them. Mary Todd Lincoln noted that Mrs. Keckley said that "the immense number of Contraband in Washington are suffering intensely, many without bed covering and having to use any bits of carpeting to cover themselves.—Many dying of want." The president's wife then continued, "Out of the $1000 fund given to you by General Corcoran, I have given her the privilege of investing $200 ... in bed covering." Mrs. Lincoln prodded her husband with the words, "I'm sure you won't object. The cause of humanity requires it."[86]

Lincoln, of course, had fashioned his career on "the cause of humanity," in justice seeing the dignity of all persons. During a speech at a Republican Banquet in Chicago in 1856, Lincoln rallied the party to adhere to the "central ideas of the Republic" with the passionate declaration, "We *can* do it. The human heart *is* with us—God is with us. We shall be able ... to declare ... that all *men* are created equal."[87] But because political circumstance and national racist sentiment prevented immediate emancipation, all he could offer was compensated emancipation and colonization as a solution to the slavery problem. And yet it was the same Lincoln who admonished his friend Joshua Speed writing about the time they witnessed a slave coffle, a train of black men fastened together like animals: "You ought to appreciate how much the great body of the Northern people do crucify their feelings, in order to maintain their loyalty to the constitution and the Union."[88] His own crucified feelings quite naturally reflected the sense of one who has existed in a divided family or, nationally, in a "House divided."

President Lincoln had no choice but to lead the fight against his own in the South. Mary Todd Lincoln's brothers, George, Samuel, David, and Alexander, enlisted in the Confederate cause. David and George gained notoriety for their cruelty toward Union prisoners. Mary Todd Lincoln suffered much derision for her Southern family's action during the war. President Lincoln, nonetheless, treated members of the Todd family with respect and due regard for their circumstances. For the widow of Captain Charles Todd of Shelbyville, Kentucky, killed at the battle of Murfreesboro, Lincoln wrote to Governor Andrew Johnson to inquire if Captain Todd's remains were in the hands of his family.[89] And Lincoln was especially fond of Emilie Todd's husband, Benjamin Hardin Helm. Knowing that the young lawyer and former soldier needed money for his growing family, Lincoln offered him a commission and position as paymaster in the Union army. Grateful yet torn, Hardin joined the Confederacy. Rising to the rank of general, Helm lost his life at the battle of Chickamauga.[90] To aid the grieving family, Lincoln granted Mrs. Robert Todd (Mary Lincoln's stepmother); her daughter, Emilie, the widow of General Hardin Helm; and Emilie's three children a pass through the Union lines north to the neutral state of Kentucky.[91] Later when Lincoln heard disturbing rumors of Emilie Todd Helms's disloyal conduct, he added a precaution to his orders, namely, that if she was guilty of disloyal acts, "[d]eal with her for current conduct, just as you would with *any other.*"[92] Later Emily Helm would plead for special favors from. Lincoln, which caused Mary Lincoln great embarrassment.[93] Family demanded respect, but questions of disloyalty entailed an impartial justice.

Routinely, however, Lincoln intervened to help the erring, the distressed, the grieving. Compassion annealed the tensions of separation and fragmentation that burned within him. His pardon and aid, often given with fatherly feeling, nonetheless, emanated from his position as commander-in-chief. Family concerns became matters of state. For example, he pardoned a boy of 18 in ill-health who was dishonorably discharged, and he pardoned two young lieutenants because he did not want their careers "to be ruined for slight causes."[94] To help "a distressed girl," Lincoln personally wrote to Hon. Senator James F. Simmons for information about the girl's missing father who fought for the Union in the Peninsula Campaign. The girl's brother had also died in the same campaign.[95] Lincoln's friend and congressman from Illinois, William Kellogg Jr. petitioned the president to reinstate his son as a West Point Cadet. The young man had resigned on demerit. Lincoln understood that "[t]his matter touches him [Kellogg] very deeply—the feelings of a father for a child. . . . I can not be the instrument to crush his heart." Accordingly, Lincoln overrode General Totten's decision and reinstated the cadet.[96] And when Major General John A. McClernand charged Major General Henry W. Halleck with "contempt of superior authority and with utter incompetency" for placing Major General U. S. Grant in charge of the Memphis Expedition instead of himself, Lincoln, already burdened by concerns of the Todd relations, replied, "I have too many *family* controversies (so to speak) already on my hands, to . . . take up another."[97]

While it was humanitarian concerns that sorely tried his compassionate efforts, the political energies newly awakened by the war affronted his administration. On August 30, 1861, General John C. Fremont issued a proclamation liberating slaves of Confederate owners in Missouri. Lincoln well knew that Fremont's act sent shock waves through the border states. Any vision of holding together border states' Unionists, War Democrats, and the factions in his own party appeared at risk. The president admonished Fremont, "I think there is great danger that . . . the confiscation of property and the liberating slaves of traitorous owners will alarm our Southern Union, and turn them against us—perhaps ruin our rather fair prospect for Kentucky." In response to Fremont's proclamation, James Speed of Kentucky sent a telegram to the White House

suggesting that "the foolish proclamation of Fremont . . . will crush every
vestige of Union party in the state."[98] Fremont wanted a direct order to
countermand his proclamation. And on September 11, Lincoln replied
that he saw no general objection to the proclamation as it referred to
circumstances on the ground but he objected to the provisions that contradicted congressional acts regarding the confiscation of property and the
liberation of slaves. Lincoln's action as commander-in-chief, to countermand Fremont's proclamation in Missouri, did much to salve Kentucky's
anxiety about the liberation of slaves in its state. Such was the delicate balance of moral right and legal necessity, justice and commitment, that
forced Lincoln to defer liberation.

Lincoln's purpose was quite plain—to save the Union; his pragmatism at
this point defined his politics. Those who received the benefits of this decision were slave holders. The rationality of Lincoln's act ran counter to what
legal scholar Michael J. Sandel argues is the purpose of politics: "The purpose
of politics is nothing less than to enable people to develop their distinctive
human capacities and virtues—to deliberate about the common good, to
acquire practical judgment, to share in self government, to care for the fate
of the community as a whole."[99] Lincoln's dilemma strained his sense of
honor and patriotism, his commitment to the recognition of the humanity
of the slaves and justice, their right to equality, as stated in the Declaration
of Independence. But few individuals in the Civil War accepted the
virtue of regarding all persons, especially slaves, as having the capacity to
deliberate "the fate of the community as a whole." In one sense, in the recognition of common humanity, the Union cause lacked virtue. But Lincoln,
politically vulnerable in the by-elections, debated within himself and with
the members of his government how to escape the dilemma.

Congress had passed the Confiscation Act in August 1861, and meanwhile Lincoln as president considered the effect of the confiscation of slave
"Property." He suggested taxation to support the refugees from Southern
states and even considered acquiring new territory in which to colonize
the former slaves. By his March 6, 1862, Message to Congress, Lincoln
returned to his appeal for gradual, compensated emancipation, an issue
he had emphasized in his campaign. His sense of the good of "the community as a whole" was that "gradual, not sudden emancipation, is better for
all."[100] And on April 16, 1862, Lincoln agreed that Congress had the right
to abolish slavery in the District of Columbia and he said, "[T]here has
never been, in my mind, any question upon the subject, except the one
of expediency." He especially approved the "principles" of gradual emancipation and colonization contained in the Senate bill for the District of
Columbia.[101] And when General Hunter on May 9, 1862, proclaimed

emancipation under martial law in his military district of Georgia, Florida, and South Carolina, Lincoln countermanded the general's order within 10 days, again urging instead that Congress take up gradual compensated emancipation. Nonetheless, Lincoln did maintain that under some indispensable necessity, he reserved the power as commander-in-chief to deal with emancipation.[102] Thus, in a concentrated period of time, between March and May, Lincoln evolved a tentative consideration regarding the emancipatory power.

Charles Sumner, however, never hesitated in pressuring Lincoln to commit to justice for the enslaved black population. In the summer of 1861, Sumner wrote to John Jay, distinguished diplomat, and implored him to "visit Washington at once and press upon the Presdt. the duty of Emancipation *in order to save the country.*" Jay told Sumner to have patience, something Sumner could not tolerate. Rather, he anguished that the president "is honest and slow." Depressed by abolitionist anger that insisted he denounce the government, he rallied, feeling it was better to lead than repudiate the administration. He believed that with emancipation "the terrible strife will be over." Less than a year later, in the spring of 1862, Sumner had cause to hope when Lincoln's Secretary of War Edwin M. Stanton told him that a decree of emancipation would be forthcoming in a matter of two months. When the two months evaporated with no sign of an emancipation document, Sumner admitted the president was "hard to move." He had been urging Lincoln to promulgate emancipation on the Fourth of July, "telling him he could make the day more sacred and historic than ever." To which the president replied, "I would do it if I were not afraid that half the officers would fling down their arms & three more States would rise."[103]

Also hoping to encourage his impulse toward emancipation, a Quaker delegation known as Progressive Friends met with Lincoln and acknowledged that the president had no constitutional basis for emancipation, but they hoped for a declaration, nonetheless. Lincoln's sharp response was: "If a decree of emancipation could abolish slavery, John Brown would have done the work effectually."[104] William Barnard, a member of the delegation, then sympathized with the president's burdens but hoped he would free the slaves under divine guidance. Lincoln replied "very impressively" and said according to an account:

He had sometime thought that perhaps he might be an instrument in God's hands of accomplishing a great work and he certainly was not unwilling to be. Perhaps, however, God's way of accomplishing the end which the memorialists have in view may be different from

theirs. It would be his earnest endeavor, with a firm reliance upon the
Divine arm, and seeking light from above, to do his duty in the place
to which he had been called.[105]

Lincoln may have felt a deep and compassionate duty or call for emancipation, but just as he had done with every defense he made in his legal
career, he reasoned out every conceivable consequence before issuing the
Emancipation Proclamation. He tried to reason with the border states,
whose representatives met with him on July 12, yet the representatives
proved unwilling to compromise on compensated, gradual emancipation.
Lincoln had no options left but to do justice. With his reasoning infused
with determination, he found fault with Congress's Second Confiscation
Act, which urged the confiscation of rebel slave property. Lincoln
demurred, because he believed Congress had no power over slavery in
the states.[106] If Congress could not act, the president must have felt the
imperative to do so. His commitment met one last obstacle. On July 22,
1862, Lincoln read to the cabinet his preliminary Emancipation
Proclamation, which although couched in legalese did say that "all persons
held as slaves within any state or states . . . shall then, thenceforward, and
forever, be free." The members divided on method, but ultimately all but
Blair approved. Yet Seward advised waiting until a Union victory on the
battlefield before issuing a public declaration. [107] Later that day Lincoln
issued a memorandum concerning the recruitment of blacks in the military, to wit: He had no objection to recruiting them from disloyal owners
or with the consent of the loyal owners "*unless the necessity is urgent.*"[108]

In the meantime without a military victory, Lincoln had to defend his
seeming lack of initiative on the slavery issue. When an Indiana delegation offered two colored regiments to the Union army, Lincoln demurred,
citing fear of slave insurrections and the delicate nature of Kentucky's alli-
ance. To Horace Greeley he wrote of his "*official* duty" and emphasized:
"My paramount object in this struggle *is* to save the Union, and is *not*
either to save or destroy slavery."[109] And once again pressured by
Christians, this time a group from Chicago, to proclaim an end to slavery,
Lincoln, exasperated, said that he had thought about this issue for
"weeks . . . even . . . months" and emphasized that it was his "earnest desire
to know the will of Providence." He continued, "*And if I can learn what it is
I will do it.*" But he explained he had to study "the plain physical facts of
the case [to] ascertain what is possible and learn what is wise and right."
Then impatiently he exclaimed, "What *good* would a proclamation of
emancipation from me do, especially as we are now situated? I do not want
to issue a document that the whole world will see must necessarily be

inoperative, like the Pope's bull against the comet!"[110] Perhaps, the saddest episode of Lincoln's dilemma caught between justice and commitment to the possible, was his meeting with a "committee of colored men." In his attempt to persuade the men of the necessity of colonization, the president said: "You and we are different races. We have between us a broader difference than exists between almost any other two races. Whether it is right or wrong I need not discuss, but this physical difference is a great disadvantage to us both."[111] Lincoln gave voice to the realities of white racism and thus the limitations of emancipation, his cause of justice.

When McClellan achieved a bloody victory at Antietam, Lincoln offered his preliminary Emancipation Proclamation on September 22, effective January 1, 1863. In it he promised to recommend to Congress compensated emancipation and colonization for slaves in those states not in rebellion. The president as commander-in-chief ordered all slaves in rebellious states or parts of states "forever free" and commanded the military not to return fugitive slaves.[112] Celebrations erupted in all the major cities in the North. A cheering, happy crowd serenaded the president at the White House.[113] Nonetheless, abolitionists lamented the limitations of the Emancipation Proclamation. Maria Weston Chapman wrote to her sister-in-law, "The Emancipation Proclamation does not go far enough. Black soldiers would save our army and black citizens our Republic. Everybody's mortified."[114] Lincoln himself knew that the slavery issue had not been utterly resolved. He wrote to Vice-President Hannibal Hamlin after the issuance of the preliminary Emancipation Proclamation:

> It is six days old, and while commendation in newspapers and by distinguished individuals is all that a vain man could wish, the stocks have declined, and troops come forward more slowly than ever. This, looked soberly in the face, is not very satisfactory. We have fewer troops in the field at the end of six days than we had at the beginning—the attrition among the old outnumbering the addition by the new. The North responds to the proclamation sufficiently in breath; but breath alone kills no rebels.[115]

And in his Annual Message to Congress, Lincoln made one last plea for unity. In it he differentiated between the familial and the body politic: "Physically speaking, we cannot separate. . . . A husband and wife may be divorced, and go out of the presence, and beyond the reach of each other, but the different parts of our country cannot do this." Then he argued for compensated and prolonged emancipation, if only the slave states would agree. He foresaw that such emancipation might take until the new century. And he again invoked colonization as another solution to the slavery problem. In the end he warned that national honor was at stake. He said, "Fellow-citizens, *we* cannot escape history. . . . The fiery trial through which we pass, will light us down, in honor or dishonor, to the latest generation."[116]

The final Emancipation Proclamation issued on January 1, 1863, and rewritten by Lincoln as commander-in-chief, emancipated "all persons held as slaves within any state . . . the people thereof shall then be in rebellion against the United States, shall be then, thenceforward, and forever free." He specifically detailed the parts of Louisiana and Virginia that were exempted from this order. By the final Emancipation Proclamation, however, Lincoln had moved specifically toward the recruitment of black men into the army "to garrison forts, positions, stations and other places and to man vessels," that is, to bear arms. Lincoln maintained the proclamation to be "an act of justice."[117] Contemporaries debated whether the Emancipation Proclamation was an act of necessity as Joshua Speed thought at one point,[118] or justice, as Congressman Henry Wilson believed. Wilson ventured his opinion:

> Mr Lincoln is a man of *heart*—aye as gentle as a woman's and as tender—but he has a will as strong as iron. He therefore loves all mankind—hates slavery—every form of Despotism. Put these together—Love for the slave and a determination—a will that justice, strong and unyielding shall be done, where he has got a right to act . . . no man can move him.[119]

Wilson was alluding to the election of 1864 when it appeared Lincoln would be defeated because of the Union's continual losses and pressure for peace negotiations with the South. Wilson concluded that not even the pressures of political defeat forced Lincoln to disavow the Emancipation Proclamation. Wilson remembered the president said, "I will not modify, qualify nor retract my proclamation."[120]

Such tender testimonies did not square with events as Charles Sumner interpreted them. In the summer of 1863, Sumner wrote to Lincoln that "everywhere [is] consternation that the Proclamation can be forgotten or abandoned. For myself," he wrote, "I have seen but one way from the beginning, and that way becomes brighter as we proceed. It is by doing justice to the black man. Then we shall deserve success."[121] Lincoln himself did not interpret even the 1863 proclamation as a final word on emancipation. Writing to General John Schofield concerning gradual emancipation in Missouri, June 1863, Lincoln said, "I can not know exactly what shape an act of emancipation may take." He meant if gradual emancipation were temporary and future slavery prohibited, he would not object to it in the case of military necessity.[122] Lincoln conveyed the same sentiments to General Stephen A. Hurlbut with regard to Arkansas. His words are somewhat tenuous, probably because he awaited a legal decision on the proclamation. He said:

> The emancipation proclamation applies to Arkansas. I think it is valid in law, and will be so held by the courts. I think I shall not retract or repudiate it. Those who shall have tasted actual freedom I believe can never be slaves, or quasi slaves again. For the rest, I believe some plan, substantially being gradual emancipation, would be better for both white and black.[123]

Lincoln's apparent ambiguity must be seen in the light of national racism, constitutional restraint, and military necessity. The president's caution in delivering a wholly abolitionist measure may have been thought reasonable in light of the devastating anti-draft riots in New York City in 1863. Aimed at the black population, Northern urban mobs reacted against the fight for Union transformed into an abolitionist cause.[124] Yet, by November 1863 when he had issued the Emancipation Proclamation and the tide had turned in favor of the North at the battle of Gettysburg in July, Lincoln could once more state his commitment to the Declaration of Independence. In his Address delivered at the dedication of the Cemetery at Gettysburg, Lincoln reminded the gathered crowd, "[O]ur fathers brought forth on this continent, a new nation, conceived in Liberty, and dedicated to the proposition that all men are created equal." Perhaps, Lincoln felt that "the world will little note, nor long remember what we say here" because the cause of equality still remained an open question.

By March 1864, he wrote to Governor John J. Cresswell of Maryland, not prioritizing either immediate or gradual emancipation. He simply said, "My wish is that all who wish emancipation cooperate."[125] Lincoln moved to aid local forces in quelling the New York riots and attempted to smooth transition in a border state.[126] Attempting to clarify his policy, he wrote to Albert G. Hodges, a prominent lawyer in Kentucky, stating he was "naturally anti-slavery," but that his oath of office to protect and defend the Constitution prevented him from acting upon his own opinion. He reiterated that his prevention of military emancipation or the arming of black soldiers evolved because he did not believe those policies at that time were an "indispensable necessity." He said the turning point for him came when the representatives to the border states refused to accept compensated emancipation in the wake of an indispensable necessity. Thus, he chose emancipation and to employ black recruits. He admitted he remained uncertain after a year of trial, but that since no international or national sentiment rose against it, he was satisfied with the facts of his decision. But he said he did not attribute this to any inherent wisdom on his part, but rather, "I claim not to have controlled events, but confess plainly that events have controlled me."[127]

Despite his growing confidence in the way events had worked to his advantage, he still had the problem of loyalty in the conquered southern states. In December 1863, the president proclaimed Amnesty for those Southerners who participated in the rebellion but would take an oath of loyalty. Upon taking the oath, all property, except slaves, would be returned. Abolitionists seethed that Lincoln appeared to back step. Wendell Phillips continued speaking out against Lincoln, especially for his calls for amnesty, and at one point, declared his intention to seek the president's impeachment. Maria Weston Chapman took a more moderate position and felt that bullying should be left to others.[128]

However, abolitionists defined their desires and strategy, the real engine of reform was Union victory. That became clearer to the administration in the early months of 1864 as Lincoln discussed a more comprehensive military plan with Grant. Thus advised, Grant outlined a coordinated military campaign against Lee's army. He directed General George G. Meade, commander of the Army of the Potomac, to follow Lee's army. Grant then wanted General William T. Sherman, commander of the Western Theater, "to move against Johnston's army, to break it up and to get into the interior, inflicting all the damage you can against their war resources." Before Grant's ambitious plan went into effect, the Union suffered a series of stinging defeats, most tragically the infamous murders of hundreds of black soldiers who had surrendered to Confederate forces at Fort Pillow, Tennessee, and Poison Spring, Arkansas. The sacrifices of black Union troops did not move the Congress to offer equal pay until 1864 despite the plea of abolitionist Frederick Douglass to the president. Convinced that only victory would guarantee safety and liberty to the black population, Lincoln determined to pursue that end with renewed energy and dogged determination.[129]

Justice and compassion had steered Lincoln's determination in the final year of the war. Yet Democrats and some Republicans who sought peace negotiations urged Lincoln to drop his proclamation and, thus, the abolitionist aim of the war. Although Lincoln had little hope for his reelection since the army had not delivered a decisive victory, he replied to the Republican Party that he approved of a plank in the party platform in favor of a constitutional amendment to prohibit slavery "throughout the nation."[130] As to the army on whom he pinned the hopes of liberation and Union, Lincoln wired Grant at his headquarters at City Point, Virginia, and reinforced Grant's determination to hold his position. The president said, "Hold on with a bull-dog grip, and chew and choke, as much as possible."[131] In the meantime the president evaded those who clamored for peace and the abandonment of black regiments. He argued that to disband the regiments was to return the men to slavery; then the Union would have to fight "two nations instead of one."[132] Democrats inured to presidential assurances intensified their demands for an end to the war and nominated McClellan for president, who pledged himself to a negotiated peace. Within days, Atlanta fell and Lincoln's hopes and his presidency were restored as he won a second term.

Lincoln's great work, however, had not ended. The abolition of slavery by the Emancipation Proclamation remained tenuous in the face of the war's end. Questions might have been raised as to the proclamation's legality, whether it referred to subsequent generations born into slavery, for instance. The Thirteenth Amendment, which abolished slavery everywhere in the United States forever, passed the Senate by a two-thirds majority in the spring of 1864. But the House of Representatives, on a strictly partisan vote, failed to pass the amendment by a narrow margin. Lincoln and his allies went to work on moderate Democrats and border state Unionists. By the promise of patronage, federal offices and favors, political and personal, the Thirteenth Amendment passed the House by the slimmest of margins.[133] Lincoln's hope of liberation had survived him. Lincoln vowed he would rather be assassinated than surrender the national values in the Declaration of Independence. And he died according to his promise.

In the Civil War, national values as Lincoln defined them, justice, honor, patriotism, and commitment, became the virtues of war. Lincoln would not allow a peaceful secession; there was "no honor in that," as he told the Baltimore delegation. His patriotism, his loyalty to the integrity of the Union, led him to war. Yet virtue requires discernment. In his public life his notion of patriotism, of loyalty to the Union, meant a duty to uphold the law and the Constitution. Such loyalty, however, conflicted with his sense of justice, his commitment to the rights embodied in the Declaration of Independence. In the Lincoln-Douglas debates, Lincoln attested to his hatred of slavery; nonetheless, he refrained from the idea of African American social and political equality. As president, he abided by Secretary of State Seward's advice to withhold the Emancipation Proclamation until a Union victory. He acted prudently despite intense pressure from abolitionists and his commanders in the field who had issued their own liberation documents, which Lincoln rescinded. American racism, both in the North and the South, precluded any earlier move toward racial equality. In addition the fate of the slave-holding border states, whether they would remain loyal to the Union, hung in the balance. The Thirteenth Amendment, however, obtained the permanent abolition of slavery in the United States. And Lincoln used every means necessary to secure that constitutional amendment. He attained the greatest good possible in the most intense and straitened of circumstances.

Lincoln's virtues, framed in childhood by reading, maternal education, and the discipline of work, trained him in the habitual acts of justice, honor, patriotism, and commitment. The instability of migration and family deaths secured in him a desire for a larger sense of belonging. In his early years he worked out his identity and what kind of life he would lead for himself and others. Virtue gave Lincoln a certain clarity. His wrestling match with the Clary Grove boys enhanced his honor and status, and his protection of the Indian in the Black Hawk War gave him a reputation for justice. As Lincoln moved from New Salem to Springfield, he gained "practical wisdom"—the ability to discern among the powerful, how to use power. As a legislator, Lincoln hedged his principles, condemning slavery but criticizing abolitionists. He held to patriotism and prosperity, the cement of his expanding nation, but used every lever in his power to contain slavery where it existed. Only the great separation of North and South gave him the opportunity to effect an inclusive Union of white and black peoples. That is, Lincoln initiated a process toward peace and prosperity with justice. In his inaugural speech, he appealed to the "mystic chords of memory" and to "every heart and hearthstone." Unity, however much desired by Lincoln, did not necessarily translate into the moral language of the national family.

2

❖

Honor and the Moral Imagination
of Confederate Family Politics

I could not love thee, Dear, so much,
Loved I not honour more.

—Richard Lovelace, To Lucasta

Traditional sentiments of honor resonated with mid-19th-century Southern notions of virtue, even though, as noted by historian Bertram Wyatt-Brown, the ethics of honor competed with evangelical and Primitive Baptist moral norms until the Civil War. Old South honor referred to the ritual defense of personal, familial, racial, and sectional pride against the fear of public humiliation. The code of honor in effect ranked men in the social hierarchy. In contrast, obedience to God in the formation of conscience and consequent guilt ensured a holy life of Christian self-principle. Thus, Wyatt-Brown concludes that the Civil War completed an uneasy merger of Christian and secular ethics that yielded a pious code of honor as Southerners reacted violently to Northern moral criticism of slavery. He argues that the code of honor cut a broad swath across class, generation, and religion.[1]

Yet, Wyatt-Brown's work fails to answer a key question: if honor ultimately subsumed all ethical persuasions, then why and how did an individual develop the moral imagination to challenge or subvert that largely masculine code?[2] Perhaps one's perception of oneself within the various

Southern family patterns shaped one's ethical choices. Close analysis of family styles of harmony and conflict, in addition to questions important to the individual,[3] reveals broader categories of ethical norms than recent studies of the code of honor may indicate. For instance, a Confederate family's moral vision, whether enlightened Jewish Orthodox, traditional Roman Catholic, Protestant Baptist, or morally ambivalent, also determined Southern ethics regarding the war.

For Southerners, the choice for or against war with the North involved an individual's peculiar relationship with the family's moral vision. Indeed, the very development of selfhood engaged this outlook.[4] That moral imagination applied to one's choice for war or peace involved not only political and social influences, but also an internal moral process that turned back upon itself to its origin—the family. Although one member might deviate from an otherwise harmonious family's wishes, the web of dependence exerted a powerful influence nonetheless, with a language all its own that invited deeper investigations of shared values and moral assumptions.[5] In the case of internal family conflict, of generational friction, the Civil War politicized personal issues. Ideology, sectional interests, and politics played out publicly in a contest already privately debated. That does not make the political stakes in the Civil War reducible to petty personal squabbles or Freudian narratives. But it does emphasize the way in which conflict and values within a particular family structure raised the moral stakes and demanded the definition of moral direction and sense of justice.

Moral culture may be understood not simply in terms of ritual and behavior, but also, according to philosopher Charles Taylor, in terms of the object of one's love.[6] What moves an individual, what constitutes notions of respect, dignity, and the meaning of a full life, are the questions that help an individual develop an identity by deciding what is important. That identity then calls for a commitment to the chosen good. The development of self in tandem with moral vision assumes that one is a self only among other selves. And the sense of self is always changing according to the narrative of the life lived. That is, one exists within a context of questions, and the questions determine the direction of the life.[7]

Consider what this meant in the lives of Major Alfred Mordecai of North Carolina and Dr. George William Bagby of Virginia. These men represent two different moral perspectives and, therefore, two distinct processes of moral imagination. Yet, the wartime decisions of both ultimately rested upon their family's moral culture. Major Mordecai, a favored son in a harmonious family, assimilated its enlightened Orthodox Jewish ethics. As an observant Jew, the question of how to live a righteous life defined him. A distinguished U.S. Army ordnance officer, international consultant on weapons technology, and commander of the New York Watervliet Arsenal, he faced a crucial decision in 1861: should he retain his army post and fight against his Southern homeland or resign and join the Confederacy? When he resigned from the U.S. Army and retired to private life, his Southern family reviled his choice and pitied his fate. Yet, Alfred Mordecai placed the family's moral standards both above family interest and his own military sense of honor.

George William Bagby, anything but a favored son, lived with a domineering father in a fractured family and developed an ambiguous set of values. The Civil War only exacerbated his moral uncertainty. A medical doctor by training, he nonetheless had great ambitions for a journalistic career. The Civil War forced him to choose between honest coverage of dramatic political events and the fire-eating brand of incendiary journalism. He wrote in both veins: polemical fodder that inflamed the South's decision for war against the North, and objective criticism that contributed to the South's dissatisfaction with the administration of Jefferson Davis. The contrast in moral choices between the two men reveals a difference in individual perceptions of family moral patterns, righteousness versus rigidity, that enabled them to challenge or undermine the prevalent Southern code of honor.

Alfred Mordecai, born in 1804 in Warrenton, North Carolina, the son of Jacob and Rebecca Myers Mordecai, early proved himself a scholar in a scholarly family. In 1808, his father founded the Warrenton Female Academy, a renowned institution that emphasized progressive education in the classics and sciences for young women. Five of the eldest children from Jacob's first marriage, to Rebecca's sister, Judith Myers, contributed to the success of the school, which lasted a prosperous decade, until the family moved to Spring Farm, outside of Richmond, Virginia.[8] The academy proved a key element in the formation of family unity.

Jacob and especially his eldest daughter, Rachel, taught according to an enlightened Anglo-Irish guide, *Practical Education*, based on Enlightenment principles. This educational text was written by the celebrated Richard Lovell Edgeworth and his novelist daughter, Maria.[9] A correspondence initiated by Rachel Mordecai with Maria Edgeworth in Edgeworthstown, Ireland, opened a half-century of communication between the families, including a visit by Alfred in 1833 to the Edgeworths.[10] Alfred and all the younger children from Jacob's second marriage experienced this progressive home schooling, which demanded moral patterning, dialogic method, and a liberal ideology.

The Edgeworths counseled the "education of the heart," the inducement of "useful and agreeable habits, well regulated sympathy and benevolent affections"; that is, a warm yet disciplined heart devoted to the practice of virtue.[11] Such practice instilled virtues of benevolence, honesty, self-reliance, self-control, and industry. The Enlightenment virtue of benevolence fostered an obligation to the broader social order. Family members practiced charity and retained a patriotic loyalty to the nation. Instruction in science and mathematics honed observation and enhanced inductive skills. Moreover, scientific methods also guided a rational approach to experience that proved invaluable in training the emotions. Nonetheless, the Edgeworth family remained a benevolent patriarchy that involved paternal control over sons' and daughters' careers and marriage choices.

The Mordecai family revered egalitarian values by educating both women and men. In addition, they respected individual rights by holding democratic family conferences. Yet, the Mordecai siblings honored traditional patriarchal values and sought their father's permission to marry. The father also remained the authority on matters of religion and morals. As a family, the Mordecais easily absorbed the democratic ideology of the early-19th-century "Republic of Men" that obscured a paternal hegemony. Enlightened ethics and Orthodox Judaism thus contained assumptions of hierarchy that contradicted democratic principles.

As Orthodox Jews, the Mordecais kept a kosher household, observed the High Holidays, reverenced the *hashem* (the name of God), and maintained a faith in Providence. Orthodox notions of holiness or perfection far exceeded the demands of republican virtue. The Hebrew belief in a transcendent, holy God, whose ways could not be known or understood, demanded obedience and called all believers to holiness. The people covenanted to God followed his way and not the ways of the idolatrous. The covenant promised God's providential care in return for his people's total giving. Moreover, the prophetic tradition demanded a high ethical standard of righteousness: justice, humility, and service to the poor. Following the precepts of the Torah required a sanctified life.[12]

Mordecai biographer Emily Bingham has noted that the family defined themselves in terms of a covenant, as a "little faithful band of love and duty," devoted to mutual protection, religious and intellectual liberalism, and bourgeois domesticity. Only later in mature years, according to Bingham, did individual members, pressured by issues of class and religious assimilation, challenge family cohesion.[13] Inner-family contradictions notwithstanding, they retained the principled ethic of enlightened Jewish Orthodoxy.

Alfred Mordecai, a talented scientist and technician, demonstrated an integrity woven of the two strands of objectivity and Orthodox Jewish self-giving. His principles can only be understood by his interpretation of the resources found in his upbringing. But the Mordecai family did not share his interpretation. In 1861, Alfred resigned his commission in the U.S. Army but refused his family's and the Confederated government's pleas to take up the South's cause.

The family's moral vision shaped Alfred's education and character. His father and elder brothers and sisters favored Alfred among the six young children of Jacob Mordecai's second marriage. Alfred's sister Ellen, 14 years his senior, who taught him, considered him one of the best students in the school and believed that the boy would be conscientious "when he [got] over his foolishness."[14] The family evidently had a disciplinary problem with the young teenager. Alfred later apologized to his brother Solomon, who also trained him, writing, "How ungrateful I have been to be the means of knowingly inflicting pain on you instead of endeavoring by all means in my power to relieve you from the cares and anxieties with which you have been perplexed on my account."[15] Ellen expected Alfred to learn sympathetic understanding. He did so later in the context of self-criticism.

Alfred's brothers and sisters instructed him in the classics: French, mathematics, science, history, literature, and geography. His education included the Jewish catechism and Maria Edgeworth's *Moral Stories*. As a boy, Alfred enthusiastically followed the campaigns of the War of 1812; the war had a special significance since Mordecai and Myers family members in Norfolk took refuge with Jacob's family during the British blockade of the Virginia coast. Alfred then followed Napoleon's exploits in Europe. Appraising his son's talents and interests, Jacob decided to send him in 1819 to the fledgling U.S. Military Academy at West Point for a scientific education.[16] He may also have been encouraged to do so since a Jewish cadet had graduated in the academy's first class in 1802.[17]

Reorganized in 1817 by Superintendent Sylvanus Thayer, West Point emerged as a premier scientific and technological institute. There, Alfred's growth clearly showed that the development of self and moral vision were clearly intertwined.[18] Inspired by Thayer's vision, the young Mordecai applied himself assiduously to his engineering studies, embraced Thayer's concern with international military and technological developments, and imitated his values of rectitude and honor. During his first year of study, he placed second (out of 91 students) in mathematics, studied French in his spare time in order to read French military texts, and followed the academy's honor code that one's word was one's bond. Distinguished as first in his graduating class, Mordecai earned Thayer's invitation to teach at the academy. His outstanding scholastic record determined his course as an engineering officer.[19]

Alfred rose steadily in the military as an ordnance officer. He commanded arsenals at Frankford, Pennsylvania, Washington, D.C., and Watervliet, New York, and served as assistant to the secretary of war and to the chief of ordnance. He published the *Digest of Military Laws* (1833) and served on the Ordnance Board, which contributed to the antebellum technological revolution in the U.S. military. And like his mentor Thayer, Mordecai was sent to Europe and the Crimea to study European weapons systems. His reports and his experiments that resulted in publications for the Ordnance Board proved invaluable in the improvement of weapons technology. Through this work, he earned an international reputation.[20]

The Mordecai family took pride not only in Alfred's academic achievements but especially in his character. Ellen remarked, "He surpasses my highest expectations . . .; he is the pride of our father's heart."[21] Rachel wrote, "Alfred always reminds me of Miss E[dgeworth]'s Orlando—so wise, steady and sedate."[22] His mother, Rebecca, likewise approved: "His mother's Blessing ever rests on his head; and like the patriarchs would extend to the utmost bounds of everlasting Hills."[23] With Alfred's marriage to Sara Hays in 1836, he entered into an observant, well-integrated Philadelphia Orthodox family. Sara's mother, Richea Gratz Hays, was the sister of Rebecca Gratz, a celebrated philanthropist and activist in the Philadelphia Orphan Society.[24] Although Alfred did not remain an observant Jew, he retained the meaning, value, and intent of his early practice, even when he found himself far from his family.[25]

Stationed in the North, the young officer still remained connected with his family. One summer moonlit night in 1836, as he sat by an open window, Alfred wrote to his young niece that he was thinking "how each of the widely scattered family was spending this same lovely evening."[26] Later, he urgently requested aid from his sister when he was recalled to active duty soon after his daughter, Emma, died and his wife lay ill. He felt a special bond to his younger sister, also named Emma.[27] Alfred always clung to a Jewish notion of the importance of family. The Civil War, however, tried both his faith and his commitment to family.

Prior to the war, Alfred kept to Northern conservative opinion and company. He supported the Whiggish *Boston Courier* and hoped the *Albany Argus* would condemn abolitionist John Brown's Harpers Ferry raid. He believed a Republican defeat necessary to "save our goodly fabric [nation] from ruin."[28] Alfred saw no security in a united South; rather, he supported a politically untenable alternative, a reconstructed Union without resorting to war. His thoughts went back to his family's classical training as he recalled a conversation between Pyrrhus and his counselor before the Roman campaign: "How much easier and better it would be to sit down now in peace, than to purchase it with the horrors of revolution and civil war!"[29]

In January 1861, Alfred still disdained any "extreme course" by the South. Amid the rising tensions, however, his concern lay with his family, and he discussed with his brother Samuel the possibility of a journey south to visit them. In April, he did reach Richmond and visited his mother, but he apologized to his brother George for not stopping in Raleigh to visit him because a storm delayed the trip and, in any case, the shelling of Fort Sumter prompted his immediate recall to the New York arsenal. Even after Sumter, Alfred considered wise North Carolina's cautious approach to secession.[30]

His conservative views precluded any abolitionist sympathy. He could hold stringent moral principles yet support the institution of slavery because Enlightenment ethics and Jewish Orthodoxy maintained a paternal hierarchy. Jacob Mordecai's family owned a few slaves, and Alfred once commented to his niece as he observed a "nigger gal" who just scoured his room at the Frankfurt Arsenal in Pennsylvania, "Don't you know how much I enjoy the sight of her in this land of white niggers."[31] He criticized peace plans that he felt undermined slavery and feared that, in Lincoln's cabinet, "unmixed abolitionism will rule."[32] Given Alfred's sympathies, the Mordecai family hoped he would join the Confederate Army. As his brother's confidante, Samuel explained to the family, "Under no circumstances will [Alfred] be placed in conflict with his native land and that of his dearest connections."[33] At the same time, the Mordecais worried about Alfred's domination by his Northern wife's "petticoat appeals."[34] Certainly, Alfred's long-term residence in the North and his wife's influence contributed to his refusal of offers from President Davis and other high-level officials to join the Confederacy.[35] Nonetheless, such influences played upon deeper religious and Enlightenment ethical sentiments.

The Mordecais realized their worst fears when Alfred resigned his commission and vowed to retire to private life in Philadelphia. They received the news just as Alfred's nephew, Edmund Myers, and a number of other nephews joined Confederate ranks and 17-year-old Alfred Mordecai Jr. of West Point joined the Union Army. Samuel blamed Alfred's "weakness" in submitting to pressure from his in-laws.[36] Rebecca attempted to appeal to her son's family loyalty: "Be still useful to yourself, to your family and to your native state," she wrote, while assuring him that the family neither judged him harshly nor felt alienated from him. She knew how to twist the anguish in his heart, however, when she implored Alfred to withdraw his son from active combat. "Let it not be said that he applied a torch to your mother's habitation."[37]

The family's deep disappointment, however, never equaled the vehement criticism directed at Alfred in New York. The *Troy Daily Times* doubted his loyalty and argued that all military personnel who resign ought to be arrested and then placed on parole. In Major Mordecai's case, the paper insinuated that he transferred designs for a "bullet machine" to the Confederacy when he visited Richmond in April.[38] Alfred wrote a defense of his conduct that accounted for all of his time in the South, including the visit to his mother in Richmond. Furthermore, he argued that his identity as a Southerner compromised his position as commander of the Watervliet Arsenal. Therefore, instead of resigning, he had requested a less active duty. In the most forceful terms he argued, "If any one imagines that I could persevere, for an indefinite time, in forwarding warlike preparations which were intended to be used against the homes of my mother, brothers and numerous relatives in the South, he gives me too much credit for philosophy."[39] The *Daily Times* called him a traitor for requesting lesser duties, thus deserting his country in its hour of need. It claimed that true patriotism held country above family.[40]

A career soldier, Alfred invested mightily in advancement and promotion. His identity rested in his honor as a U.S. military officer; Alfred swore he never betrayed that trust. Given his untenable dilemma, he made a rational choice to resign. Enlightenment Jewish Orthodoxy informed his course of action neither to betray his office nor fight against his family. In the *Daily Whig*, he argued his case as a Southerner and a family man. Alfred's decision rested solidly on his family's basic moral directive, namely enlightened self-discipline applied to total self-giving. Yet, the Civil War revealed contradictory tendencies within the family ethos. Democratic principles of equality and independence imbibed in his family clashed with the close-knit style of his Orthodox kin. Alfred emerged as a singular individual, apart from his family's interest but not from its ethical core.

For Alfred, the military code of honor rested upon Jewish righteousness. He could not give up either his military honor or his family honor unless he served a higher purpose. His was a primal ethic, the Jewish spirit of righteousness that existed before Indo-European notions of honor.[41] Confronted with the choice between honor as community-derived and honor as God-directed, Alfred chose the traditional path of justice and humility, leaving all to the Divine will. He considered it just to reject betrayal of his Southern family and his military commission. Initially,

Alfred Mordecai. (West Point Museum of Art)

he gained nothing but poverty. From 1861 to 1864, he tutored a few students in mathematics. Alfred's moral code went beyond the strict military ethic of honor that demanded duty to nation above family. Rather, he observed the Orthodox way, which demanded everything. Toward the end of the war, his prospects brightened. From 1864 to 1866, he worked in Mexico as assistant engineer of the Mexico and Pacific Railroad. Thereafter, his friends obtained for him an appointment as secretary of the Pennsylvania Canal Company, a subsidiary of the Pennsylvania Railroad Company.[42] Upon Alfred's death, in 1887, at the age of 83, his eulogist acclaimed his righteousness: "The name and character of Major Alfred Mordecai should be deemed worthy of mention and regard; for the lessons of the youth were the source of strength in the man, and in old age gave that peace of conscience, which made his simple greeting almost a benediction."[43]

In sum, Mordecai exemplified the early-19th-century enlightened family norms that supported "rational orthodoxy."[44] Such standards survived into the Civil War era. A product of a small town, Alfred's character afforded him the initiative to shed his provincialism and with it a narrow sense of community and honor. In addition, his habit of "well-regulated sympathy," benevolence, and dependence upon Divine Providence conditioned him for the sacrifice of his honor. But the rational and religious ethic that guided Alfred Mordecai's family norms unraveled in the later Victorian decades, replaced by evangelical enthusiasm and romantic idealism.

Nonetheless, the growth of Southern towns and urban culture spawned a skepticism that competed with waves of evangelicalism. George William Bagby, born in 1828 in the vital market town of Lynchburg, Virginia, was raised among a new generation of educated men for whom money and ambition vied with piety and honor.[45]

Bagby earned a medical degree but abandoned his practice for a journalistic career. Hired by the polemical newspapers *Charleston Mercury* and *New Orleans Crescent* as a Washington and Richmond correspondent before and during the Civil War, Bagby found it increasingly difficult to make a living without bending to distorted notions of truth. On the eve of the Civil War, he joined the community of fire-eaters who felt the South's honor at stake. Yet, he went against the code of honor in criticizing the Davis administration. His diatribes against both the North and the Confederate government arose from an inchoate anger, given vent without a well-defined moral framework.

The genial writer-physician and politician, known as "a Virginia Realist,"[46] produced romantic views of the past and had little faith in large systems, whether of religion or government. Trained in scientific rationality, he very nearly came undone through his passionate prejudices. Although he tried desperately to mold his life to his will, his life often demonstrated a depressed passivity.[47] After the Civil War, his curious mix of verisimilitude and myth found a loyal Virginia audience with his popular Old South essays. Until then, he had not found himself.

George William Bagby, the only son of merchant George Bagby, never felt himself to be a favored son. On the contrary, after the death of his mother, Virginia, when he was eight years old, his father sent him to a series of "old field schools" in Buckingham and Prince Edward counties and to the plantation of his uncle, James Evan, in Prince Edward County.[48] The plantation served as a refuge, and the schools proved a beneficial separation since his father had an "evil temper" and berated the boy for his less than stringent morals. This attitude may have had some effect on the ambivalent moral values young George developed.[49] His father held to a fierce evangelicalism with an emphasis upon sin, repentance, and a strict moral code. Although he loved his children and wrote affectionate letters, his insistence that his son imagine the horrors of martyrdom and the death of sinners must have frightened the child.

The elder Bagby wrote to his six-year-old son of the martyrdom of a little girl who refused to recant her Christianity before Roman officials, explaining: "They drove a stake in the ground and chained her little hands and feet to it and then built a great fire to burn her up." Moreover, he wrote that two wicked boys drowned in a millpond.[50] Wicked children were those who did not love their father: "You are in danger every day. You may soon die,"[51] he threatened. George Bagby presented a cruel and punishing image of God and of paternal authority. It is no wonder his son developed habits of deception and deviousness.

Letters from the master at Edgehill Academy, in Princeton, New Jersey, where the teenage George attended school, noted the boy's evasion or subversion of the rules. He did not speak the truth, his teachers complained.[52] George's actions pained his father, who warned: "No son prospers who insults authority of Father and Mother. God has inseparably connected the happiness of the child with his obedience to his parents."[53] Secretly, young George indulged in sexual fantasies tinged with guilt. He drew caricatures of himself as a demon racing toward a young woman. He depicted priapic demons boiling a man in a pot.[54] His father only saw his son's laziness, his lack of gratitude. Gradually, young George fell into depression. Despite his unhappiness, he excelled in school, so much so that his father cautioned that he placed too much trust in his intellectual powers, offering constructive advice to think through and not parrot his studies.[55] George William Bagby inherited a legacy of love and fear, and this ambiguity propelled him into adulthood.[56]

In 1846, soon after his father remarried, George entered the University of Pennsylvania Medical School, where he gained a reputation for skill and accuracy.[57] The bouts with depression continued, however, and his father noted, "You are your own tormentor," and advised him to seek divine help.[58] Despite the young medical student's moods, he graduated and set up a practice in Lynchburg. Four years later, James McDonald, the editor of the *Lynchburg Virginian*, encouraged him to start a new career in journalism because the physician loved words, reading, and writing and claimed reporters as his closest friends.[59]

Bagby's journalistic apprenticeship in Lynchburg included more than professional training. Fellow newspaperman Thomas Jellis Kirkpatrick endeavored to help him sort through the questions the physician-journalist entertained concerning a moral life. Between 1850 and 1853, they corresponded and wrestled with the larger questions of God, sin, and moral responsibility. When Bagby became a writer, Kirkpatrick worried that now he had "unwholesome influences to create prejudices which are unreasonable and highly injurious."[60] He sympathized with Bagby's aspirations but likened them to his own vainglorious desires, warning, "We must have fixed, enduring and long-cherished aims."[61] Despite his qualms, Kirkpatrick several times offered to help Bagby obtain a post in his hometown or publish in his columns. The two bachelors probably lived together until Kirkpatrick married. Kirkpatrick observed that denial of secret depravity leads to pride and criticism of others.[62] Friendship and an evangelical conversion emboldened him to offer guidance to Bagby and provide honest criticism of his moral ideology. Kirkpatrick sensed that his friend was morally adrift.

Bagby insisted that moral evil did not exist, that it proved inconsistent with God's perfection. Kirkpatrick replied that God's justice demanded that hell existed as an answer to the consequences of moral evil: If hell did not exist, then neither did the difference between good and evil. According to Kirkpatrick, lusty desires corrupted the body, and only a force of will could prevent the disastrous consequences. He believed that Bagby's denial of sin was the result of a "lazy, voluptuous idealism" that led to deceitfulness.[63] Bagby's notion of manliness did not include power-lessness, and he believed that Christian notions of God's justice included a wretched notion of the moral order. In his view, the idea of justice con-demning people to hell was repugnant. Kirkpatrick reminded him that human beings existed as free agents and could not exist as such without the choice between good and evil. But, in the end, where did the truth reside? What beliefs could these two men share? Kirkpatrick suggested, "There is truth in love."[64]

Clearly, Bagby entertained ambiguous moral assumptions in direct opposition to his father's rigid moral theology. Kirkpatrick's fears that such indifference to right and wrong would open his friend to all the vicissitudes of passion and prejudice proved prophetic. On the eve of the Civil War, George Bagby faced challenges that tested his moral strength.

The Civil War set families and generations apart, including the Bagbys, father and son. Their differences had increased as the younger man matured politically. The father remained a steadfast Whig in a Whig town, his party loyalty determined by his business and religion. As a merchant and trader in Lynchburg, an urban-commercial center fueled by the canal and railroad arteries that stimulated manufacturing and a dynamic market system in western Virginia, the senior Bagby honored Henry Clay's American System, which supported such economic growth. As a Presbyterian, his Puritan ethic of hard work and conversion of heart spurred his quest for financial security and peace of mind.[65] The younger Bagby first intimated his father's interest in antimercantilist, strict-constructionist, states' rights ideology when he attended the Democratic convention in Baltimore in 1844. His visit coincided with his first taste of freedom before entering medical school. His father, meanwhile, cheered the Virginia Whig partisan John Minor Botts and glowed at the defeat of "locofocos," the hard money Democrats, in 1848. He later decried the decline of the Whigs in 1857 when party losses began to mount in local elections. His Whig loyalty remained on the eve of the Civil War as he gathered his fellow Presbyterians in January 1861 in a prayer for the Union and the success of reconciliation with the North through the Crittenden Compromise, a Southern proposal by Senator John J. Crittenden of Kentucky to divide the territories between North and South at the 36°30' line.[66] Only the outbreak of hostilities forced him to change his mind. The elder Bagby's faithful partisanship made him fearful for his son's association with Democrats. In 1859, the father remarked that he knew "not how an honest true hearted man could be a Democrat."[67] Democrats, he believed, reveled in the corruption of political spoils.[68]

As the political scene darkened in the late 1850s, the younger Bagby's newspaper, the *Lynchburg Express*, folded because it could not rival the influential Whig paper, the *Lynchburg Gazette*. He then moved to Washington in 1857 as a correspondent for the *New Orleans Crescent*. While there, he observed the Democrats flounder and the Republicans gain strength. In 1859, he moved to Richmond, where a more financially secure opportunity opened as librarian of both the Richmond Library Association and the Virginia Historical Society. But he also continued to pursue journalism as a freelance writer for local newspapers and for the *Charleston Mercury* and *New Orleans Crescent*, both highly partisan secessionist papers. In 1860, he served as the editor of the *Southern Literary Messenger* in Richmond and ventured out on the lecture circuit.[69]

George William Bagby represented the new generation of politically minded men who emerged in Virginia at the time of the constitutional convention of 1851. During the decade preceding the Civil War, they paid no attention to the nuances of Madisonian nationalism and increasingly pitched everything into the increasingly vehement demand for states' rights.[70] Bagby's correspondence, both personal and political, took on the same heedless cast. For example, John Hampton Chamberlayne, Bagby's future brother-in-law who later joined the Confederate Army as an artillery captain, railed against Kentucky senator John J. Crittenden's peace efforts in Congress, saying that Crittenden and his like should be banished from this generation: "Gray heads are good when things are as they have been; but they cannot direct revolutions."[71] Stephen Davenport Yancy, a young firebrand who later joined the Confederate army, wrote to Bagby in January 1861: "I am emphatically opposed to any disgraceful compromise. . . . I would prefer to see blood flow like the cataract of Niagara and chaos reign supreme over this once happy and prosperous country."[72] Bagby himself wrote to Virginia congressman John Esten Cooke, with whom he remained on friendly terms, remarking, "If you . . . let Virginia stay in this Abolition hole of a Union, I'll disembowel you on sight."[73] The congressional delegation wavered on secession until the state constitutional convention of April 1861, when Virginia joined the Confederacy.

The South resisted the intemperate call for disunion in 1828, 1833, and 1844. In those years, Robert Barnwell Rhett Sr. emerged as a leading secessionist orator, and he later inspired his son, the editor of the *Charleston Mercury*, as well as a radical journalistic cadre.[74] When Robert Barnwell Rhett Jr. took over the *Mercury* and pursued a temperate climate of unbiased journalism, the South embraced his editorship. But with the outbreak of hostilities, Rhett's paper reverted to vituperation, lies, and distortion. This fueled Bagby's polemics in the early years of the war. In print, he surmised that it would fall to South Carolina to make the state "fatter with Yankee gore than the plains of Manassas."[75] He dismissed Lincoln as "a poor dirty stick" and purported to demonstrate that Yankee newspapers showed the "unutterable depravity of the Northern people."[76] In addition to such "patriotic gore," Bagby traded in rumor and innuendo. He conspired with Rhett in January 1861 to supply the *Mercury* with a letter from a "gentleman" who attested to the claim that Hannibal Hamlin, Lincoln's vice president, was a descendant of a mulatto.[77] The claim, wholly fictitious, raised a firestorm of racial hatred in the South.

Yet, when Bagby joined the Confederate Army in 1862, serving for a year until poor health forced him to resign, he observed favoritism, inefficiency, and incompetence. During this time, he wrote sporadically for newspapers, but afterward he emerged as an unreserved critic of the Davis administration and army field operations.

Bagby's open criticism of the government proved too much even for the hard-hitting *Mercury*. Rhett censored Bagby's correspondence and advised him that criticism was a casualty of war. Rhett acknowledged, "Truth is hard to get."[78] Nonetheless, he said, "Our affairs are now in such a condition that it is necessary to *sustain* the courage of the people; and criticism, unless plainly and palpably beneficial, does more harm than good. . . . People cannot always stand too much truth." To make the point even plainer, Rhett asked Bagby to "try and shape your correspondence in accordance with these views, the truth but not all the truth at present."[79] Again, the editor negated many of his writer's criticisms of the president. "I would never attack him [Davis] except upon public matters and with

George Bagby. (Virginia Historical Society)

infallible proofs," said Rhett.[80] Chastened but not silenced, Bagby persisted in telling the truth in the *Mercury* and in other newspapers.
He excoriated rich millers who monopolized transportation and profited
handsomely from the war, kept a close eye on rumors of European loans
for the Confederacy, criticized Davis's favoritism in his military appoint-
ments, and pleaded for the relief of black refugees.[81] In one unfortunate
incident, he accused an officer of financial fraud but later, to avoid a duel,
recanted his allegations.[82] Bagby felt compelled to report unvarnished
truth. Yet, his prejudice against the South's enemies would not allow
complete objectivity.

Since Bagby held an ambitious code of ethics, his ambition and determination made him prey to duplicity and falsehood. He joined the
Mercury's reckless course on the eve of war and painted Northern
opposition in exaggerated and distorted poses. He conspired with Rhett
to play the race card and further embittered sectional hatred. As a radical
journalist, he seized the moment and joined forces with the fire-eaters
who used the code of honor as a cover for a weak administration, a secessionist administration that radicals upheld at any cost. The *Mercury*'s

anxiety stemmed from the dubious image of the newspaper in Southern minds. Southerners only succumbed to the Rhetts' extremism during the Civil War. Earlier, the Southern population was not so taken with their brand of secessionist rhetoric. The newspapers quickly folded after the war. Bagby himself came to rebel against the extremism of the *Mercury*. His brief war experience allowed him to distance himself from Rhett's yellow journalism. In the course of distancing himself from polemical journalism, he attained a degree of emotional maturity, individuation, a separation from the destructiveness of his earlier connections.

As he struggled with the truth and slowly began to grasp it, there was one person who understood his anguish. Lucy Parke Chamberlayne, daughter of the distinguished physician Dr. Lewis Webb Chamberlayne, founder of the Medical College of Virginia, and Martha Burwell Dabney Chamberlayne embodied character, strength, perseverance, and an intelligent insight into politics. Dr. Chamberlayne died in 1854, and the family sold their estate, Montrose, in the first year of the Civil War. Lucy ensured a family income by enlisting in the Confederate Civil Service as a clerk in the Treasury Department, where she was celebrated for her savvy understanding of bureaucratic personnel.[83] When Bagby courted Chamberlayne in Richmond during the fall of 1862, she wrote, "I hope ever to remain pure and loyal—wanting to be your wife—the keeper of your honor and your love."[84] They married in February 1863. Lucy Chamberlayne provided the moral framework, the emotional harbor for the critical and impulsive writer. Their marriage proved happy, and they raised a large family. Nonetheless, their postwar separation due to Bagby's job search took a toll on the couple's well-being.

Hard times came after the war and prevented Bagby from obtaining a correspondent's post in Washington. He could not earn a living even as both associate editor of the *Richmond Whig* and contributing editor of the *Richmond Examiner*. Moreover, the *Southern Literary Messenger*, which he edited, paid only $300 a year. So, in May 1865, Bagby went to New York looking for a newspaper that would hire him. But he received a cold reception from former Northern friends, and when his hardships continued, he fell into depression and despair. Desperately, he wrote his wife: "Mother, you have spoiled me and I feel lost without you. There is no [world] away from you . . . and no friend but you. Pray always for me that I may be guided aright. . . . I am crying."[85] The very next day, he wrote again, in the same anguished tone: "I think of Virginia [their daughter] as I lay up here alone with the bible. . . . Truly you are my mother the only mother I ever knew and I honor you as such."[86] Later, he admitted he cried on his sofa and pleaded, "Come to me mother."[87] By the end of July, Bagby had only

Lucy Parke Chamberlayne Bagby. (Virginia Historical Society)

$1.25 in his pocket. After his emotional breakdown in New York, he retreated to Richmond and the safer realm of domestic care and pleasant memory. By Christmas, he was able to launch a Southern lecture tour redolent of Old South memories.[88] Thus began a new writing career.

For two men, the decision for or against war played out in family dynamics, the individual's interpretation of his inherited moral vision. Alfred Mordecai, an esteemed son in a warm, cohesive family, practiced the precepts of enlightened virtue and Jewish Orthodoxy. His "education of the heart," which resulted in disciplined character and habitual virtue, prepared him for his critical trial, submission to a higher purpose. Mordecai remained loyal to the values that structured his family's cohesion. Faced with the dilemma of acting in accord with military honor or personal integrity, he chose the latter, not to fight. Justice, according to the Mordecais, demanded that he fight for the Confederacy. But Alfred upheld the family principle of sacrificial trust in Divine Providence against immediate family interest.

George William Bagby fashioned himself in conflict with his father. He rebelled against his father's strict moral standard, which demanded submission to an all-powerful God and an overweening parental authority. Yet, Bagby never developed a consistent alternative set of values. Although he joined the radicals in defending the South's conception of honor against Northern criticism of slavery, he came to undermine wartime yellow journalism by attacking the Davis administration. Bitterness and rage filled the hollows of his heart. Until Lucy Chamberlayne promised to keep his honor and he discovered in his emotional breakdown in New York that he needed her for stability, Bagby could not love "honor more." With her support, he then continued with greater confidence to present his ambiguous vision of fact and myth, heartily approved by his Virginia audience.

These two case studies only suggest a course of investigation into the complex pattern of Confederate moral culture, which included a pattern woven of Enlightenment ethics, skepticism, and Jewish Orthodoxy, along with traditional notions of honor and evangelicalism. While historians point to the wealth of family narratives that influence partisan identities, they do not acknowledge the role of the family's moral vision in the development of the Confederate self. And the individual's interpretation of that moral vision undeniably played a crucial role in secession and war.

3

---•❖•---

The Appleton Family's Practices
of Justice Tested in the Civil War

[W]e become just by doing just acts.
                                    —Aristotle, Nicomachean Ethics

With malice toward none; with charity for all, with firmness in the
right, as God gives us to see the right, let us strive on to finish the
work we are in.
                        —Abraham Lincoln, Second Inaugural Address

The Civil War presented an unprecedented work of justice, to preserve the
Union and emancipate slaves. Lincoln in wartime defined national principles of justice in universal terms, and called upon the nation to engage in
the varied and particular works of justice in service to those principles.[1]
Ordinary citizens, as well as the government, had to agree on the terms
of Union and bear the consequences of abolition and war. Harry S.
Stout, in *Upon the Altar of the Nation*,[2] cites many examples of politicians,
clergy, and citizens who weighed their support of national war aims in
terms of just war principles and acted accordingly. Stout also makes the
case of those, such as the generals, who violated just war principles.
Historian James M. McPherson noted that those who fought for the
North or the South believed they fought to preserve liberty and

republicanism but interpreted those principles differently.[3] However, why individuals supported or did not support idealistic war aims may well have depended on their practice of justice—that is, justice as a learned habit that eschews self-interest.[4] If justice may be defined as giving everyone his or her due, or seeking to redress injustice,[5] then that motive, it may be argued, arises from versions of fairness or what is good and right as experienced in childhood or learned in adult experience. This chapter aims to show that the issue of justice in the Civil War, rather than merely an ideological choice, proved a culmination of lived experience and moral development most readily demonstrated in the family.

Context is important when discussing either moral or political ideology. Consider the shift to a familial context, as in this case study of members of the Appleton family of Boston. Nathan Appleton Sr., Frances Appleton, and Nathan Appleton Jr. expressed notions of justice rooted in, respectively, entitlement, empathy, and friendship. Each took different paths of action. Individuals may use constitutional or moral principles, such as just war, to judge the state's war policy, but, more broadly, citizens also apply lived standards of justice—that is, norms fashioned from the more reflective experience of their own lives.[6] During the Civil War, national justice rhetoric suggested, but did not determine, family consensus or paths of action.

Nathan Appleton Sr. was a financier and textile manufacturer who married into the prosperous family of Maria Theresa Gold and had four children by her: Thomas Gold, Frances, Charles, and Mary. After the death of Maria Theresa, Appleton married Harriot Sumner in 1839 and had two children by her: Nathan Jr. (also known as Nate) and Harriot (or Hattie). This chapter examines the attitudes and actions of Appleton, Frances, and Nathan Jr.—the family members who fully engaged in reckoning with the causes of justice in the Civil War. (Charles died in 1835; Thomas Gold, a *bon vivant*, lived a largely expatriate existence and only occasionally commented on political issues; Mary married and lived in England; Hattie, who married during the war, expressed few opinions about it, although she corresponded with her brother, Nathan, during the conflict.)

Appleton upheld the status quo that protected his financial interests and allowed him to continue his humanitarian endeavors. Frances adopted his humanitarian concerns early in life and, therefore, reform minded, supported the Union but despised the Fugitive Slave Law. Her husband, Henry Wadsworth Longfellow, and his friend, Senator Charles Sumner, encouraged her views. She ultimately supported the war. Nathan Jr. remained ambivalent about the rightness of the war, bound more by his friendships and a masculine code of duty than by any ideal. He served in the Union army, energized by his newfound independence. The Appletons give evidence that, in times of national conflict, families internalize public definitions of justice but reform and reshape them, according to patterns of dialogue and debate understood in childhood and adult experience as a good life.[7]

Appleton family members differed among themselves as to the meaning of justice and Union. Their actions in support of, or against, the war's stated ends presupposed a consideration of their own circumstances. Each engaged in a unique inner dialogue that intersected with a constitutional crisis. Thus, the cause of Union, if viewed from inside the family, may reveal a more elusive aspect of justice. Family members reacted differently to the injustice of disunion and slavery. Yet, each individual maintained a wish for a good that may be described as "a fulfilled life" and thus were concerned, in the end, with just institutions that provide "a good life for all." Participation in reform movements, encouragement of free labor capitalism, and the exhibition of manly courage in the face of war were integral to each according to his or her desire to live well and define what constituted good character, virtue, and civil rights. Nonetheless, from that perspective, they disagreed among themselves about the definition of Union, the justness of the institutions that upheld the government, and the limits of freedom and equality. For Civil War families, discerning a desirable way of life preceded support for any coherent system of government.[8]

For Nathan Appleton Sr., "a good life" meant financial control of the textile industry, and justice meant government protection of textile manufacture. Yet, as he claimed, he was not simply concerned with the pursuit of wealth. His notion of equity consisted of high wages for workers and adequate protection of the disabled and disadvantaged. The Appleton family contributed to a number of causes, including missions to the Indians and aid to freedmen. However, the tension between Appleton's humanitarian (antislavery) views and economic interests grew stronger during the advent of the war. As the crisis progressed, Appleton's actions favored economic, rather than humanitarian, solutions.

Appleton accumulated his great wealth in textile manufacturing by dint of his business acumen, managerial ability, and renowned integrity. For all of his wealth, however, he dressed simply and sometimes carelessly. He appeared born with his focus on enterprise. His birth is recorded on October 1, 1779, in New Ipswich, New Hampshire, to Deacon Isaac Appleton, a farmer with Puritan bloodlines. Samuel Appleton, of Suffolk, England, arrived in New England, where he held a grant of lands, in 1635. The Appleton family, nonetheless, traced its mercantile heritage to the 15th century.[9] Appleton learned about a diligent work ethic on the farm and quite naturally took up a mercantile life his brothers had built. But, first, Nathan learned the importance of generosity. His father's concern for his neighbors remained legendary in New Ipswich. Streams and the Souhegan River coursed through the town. No doubt, the young Nathan recognized early the water's importance and utility for farming and milling. Isaac noted Nathan's abilities and sent him to the New Ipswich Academy, then to Phillips' Academy, in Exeter, and Dartmouth College. But by the age of 15, Nathan Appleton entered into a commercial enterprise with his brothers.[10] The business traded dry goods with England. His shrewdness in anticipating financial cycles during disastrous commercial failures established him as a successful and responsible businessman. Nathan attributed business failure to "a want of attention . . . or a want of knowledge in the proper principles of book-keeping."[11] It also helped that he married Maria Theresa Gold, the daughter of a moneyed family, in 1806, a move that only enhanced his status. Hard work and industry paid dividends in establishing that status, thus influencing his perception of the necessity of "moral character" as the foundation of the economy.

When Francis Lowell reconstituted the highly prized British textile machinery in his factory at Waltham, Massachusetts, and embarked on textile manufacturing to rival England's, he invited Appleton to invest. The venture resulted in the foundation of the city of Lowell, Massachusetts, then a model not only for manufacture but also for fair wages for textile workers. At Appleton's urging, the construction of Lowell would include support for the "moral character" of the labor force—that is, the building of a church and the addition of supervised dormitories. Regarded as temporary workers, the mostly unskilled, unmarried farm women received higher-than-typical factory pay. Later, the Lowell firm would lower wages according to labor supply and demand and workers would protest against longer hours. Appleton's idea of equity for textile workers operated only within the confines of the market system. However, the experience of the market system did not dim his conviction that "human labor is the only source of wealth."[12] By exertion of labor, workers might own property and "rise to any position in society."[13] His opinion, generally shared, however, conflicted with the reality of the terrible effects of economic depressions. Nonetheless, Appleton could claim a social consciousness, since the mills operated as joint-stock companies; their incorporation allowed not only limited liability, but also a responsibility, along with the state, in the building of roads and care for orphans. In addition, he and the Associates, the entrepreneurs who cornered the textile market, established the Massachusetts Hospital Life Insurance Company, a profitable venture that donated one-quarter of its profits to the Massachusetts General Hospital. As he later stated in his memoirs, integrity is uppermost in the morality of a merchant and thus he claimed, in all honesty, that he never had been devoted just to money-making.[14] With the success of Lowell, Appleton opened his own mills at Pittsfield with capital from his father-in-law, Thomas Gold. The business failed, but Appleton sat on the board of directors of numerous other mills, exercising considerable control over the textile industry.[15]

To protect the industry and free trade, he took a seat in the state legislature, known as the General Court of Massachusetts in 1815 (and held it until 1827). Politically influential, he ran for Congress and was elected in 1830 and 1842. Concerned for the health of his son Charles and the welfare of Charles's children, he declined national political office for more than a decade between his tenures in office. However, when elected, he naturally argued for the protective tariff, against the vehement opposition of Southern congressmen. The South attacked the protective tariff, considering it "at war with the eternal principle of justice"[16] because the tariff on manufactured goods increased the cost of living for producers of raw material. In reply, Appleton dismissed the quid pro quo and coolly suggested that merchants who sold the textiles, not the manufacturers, were to blame.[17] Appleton reminded the South that William Lowndes of South Carolina first promoted such a tariff in 1816 as a measure to bind together the country in the "mutual relation of producer of raw material and the manufacturer of it."[18] At one point, against the protests of the South, Appleton made his case in Congress, backed by a packed audience of textile manufacturers. Such "lobbying" may have appeared to the South as a blatant maneuver to dominate the entire machinery of government for the protection of one region's industry.[19] Manufacturers, with Appleton as their champion, would not accept the Southern complaint that an impost on British woolens hurt the production of cotton since it squeezed England's manufacturers' ability to pay in specie for raw cotton. Although Appleton recognized the scarcity of specie, a condition that would erupt later in the Panic of 1837, his solution was for greater production of cotton to supply New England cotton producers. The key to greater production was free labor, he argued. Appleton then linked the protective tariff to high factory wages, a condition, he claimed, that spurred great industry. Again, his argument on the tariff, backed by special interests, reiterated his assumption of equity within a market system. Nonetheless, his support of the cause of free labor as productive of wealth challenged the Southern notion of wealth in land and, coincidently, the institution of slavery. His insistence on his point of view provoked Southern talk of rebellion, a condition he rejected as "fanaticism." He questioned whether the South would prosper apart from the Union.[20] Yet, he pleaded with Southern congressmen, "For Heaven's sakes, pause!"[21]

The tariff question represented the first salvo in the Civil War, and because the tariff involved labor issues, debates over slavery intensified the crisis. Unlike some of his Northern colleagues, Appleton had firsthand knowledge of the South. His impressions, drawn in broad outline on a business trip, sketched a violent society overshadowed by fear and poverty. Southerners' chief pleasure, he wrote, consisted of shooting—in duels and hunting. Fear of insurrection dampened the 1804 Christmas holiday in Savannah, he noted ominously. A hurricane had ruined the cotton, rice, and tobacco crops and left the planters in debt.[22] Appleton, the merchant, regretted that circumstance. In January 1805, Appleton witnessed a slave auction, a "horrid sight."[23] He wrote to a friend about how one feels on the subject: "[W]e naturally resent the pain or hardship of others."[24] He sympathized with the countless numbers subject to the Middle Passage.[25] Nonetheless, his solution to the continuance of slavery remained: "Slavery will end when slaves have no value. Why argue in the abstract?"[26] Appleton's notion of distributive justice was the sharing of wealth or goods among the most productive. Moreover, Southern cotton production held no counter to the interest of Northern textile manufacturing, in Appleton's estimation. His concept of justice did not contain any notion of equality among human beings.[27] In a deeper sense, he expressed an ambivalence about slavery that suggested he believed slaves by nature were unequal to whites.

Throughout the sectional crisis, Appleton remained antislavery and anti-abolition. He opposed slavery because he supported free labor. Nonetheless, Appleton blamed William Lloyd Garrison and British emancipation adherents as provocateurs for their insistence on slaveholding as a sin. More sober men viewed slavery as a political institution and not within the purview of the clergy, who made slavery a moral issue, Appleton argued. Sin was something between the individual and his or her Maker, a situation best left alone, he felt. He refused support for the abolitionist position on the annexation of Texas, a slave nation.[28] By 1850, the slavery issue had inflamed partisanship to the extent that former Massachusetts Whig governor Edward Everett warned Appleton that leading Southerners desired "a separation."[29] Although the Massachusetts delegation supported the Compromise of 1850, Appleton saw it as putting manufacturing in a "state of repose."[30] During the heightened period of tension, Appleton contributed to the Liberia Emigration Society, but he would not aid emigration to Canada. He asserted that the climate of Canada was not conducive to ex-slaves. He wrote to Rev. M. M. Dillon, "I very much doubt whether they [ex-slaves] are capable of reaching any high degree in civilization or Christianity." He raised two questions for the abolitionist clergyman: How to compensate slave owners for loss of slaves, and "what happens [nationally] when blacks outnumber whites?"[31] Clearly, disruption of the economic status quo threatened Appleton's status, identity, and racist assumptions. Implicit in a rationalist conception of economic justice is the notion of hierarchy. Compensation to the slave owners meant they retained an economic upper hand. Appleton's personal integrity and humanitarianism fostered justice as entitlement, to secure what was legitimately his and to honor the legitimate entitlements of others. Thus, despite his humanitarianism and vision of a prosperous working class, the wealthy few apportioned resources and opportunities. His oligarchic economic rationalism did not carry a notion of full equality.[32]

As the crisis deepened, Appleton pleaded in vain with his Massachusetts fellow citizens to halt their march to disunion. In the winter of 1860, Appleton lamented the prospect of "this powerful glorious nation in the midst of unparalleled prosperity shattering itself into fragments and all out of an impractical idea, a nonentity [abolition] connected with the institution of slavery."[33] He referred to the abolitionists as that fragment of Massachusetts society that, unfortunately, acted as firebrands thrown among the combustibles of the Missouri Compromise and the Kansas-Nebraska bill. With the political parties fragmented by the crises of the 1850s, the abolitionists were free to argue slavery in the abstract. Nonetheless, he believed the body of opinion in Massachusetts still held to the Constitution and Union. He could not believe the South would prosper as a separate nation. Despite decades of Southerners' heated complaint, Appleton held to his opinion that the South's greatest advantage lay as a producer of raw material. He ignored the question of who produced it. In the face of secession, Appleton asked, "What could be more advantageous than the intercourse between South Carolina and Massachusetts?"[34] Furthermore, he dismissed as "overrated" the Southern argument that the cotton economy would uphold the confederacy of Southern states.[35] His views amounted to defense of the status quo, which favored his interests and the stability of the market.

At his summer home in Nahunt, Massachusetts, in 1858, toward the end of his life, Appleton had time to reflect upon his life's values or what comprised a good life. He initiated a correspondence, subsequently published, with W. E. Heygate, an Anglican cleric who debated the merits of

Unitarianism, Appleton's faith. In that debate, Appleton explained that God created the world "with the purpose of producing the highest degree of happiness in the creatures of this creation."[36] At the head of this creation was humankind, endowed with extraordinary powers of reason and free will. Appleton's claim may have been magnified by his insistence that his religious party held "the most intelligent and high-minded portion of this community."[37] Heygate argued that God created in humanity both an intellectual and a moral sense. He said, "We do not know what justice, love, holiness are by the intellect, but by affections towards and of justice, love, holiness, which are implanted in us by God."[38] Appleton replied, "Why should I believe what is contrary to my reason? What are known to be facts cannot be denied."[39] Appleton refused to place a moral sense over reason, since he believed that one's senses or passions and affections might lead to belief in only what gave individuals pleasure. As to evil, Appleton maintained that its existence is the unfortunate choice of humans endowed with free will.[40] The good life, according to Appleton, amounted to a happy life, the rationalization of all areas of action and behavior. Free and rational choices, the check upon deficiencies, would promote "the good life for all" and protect against evil. In sum, he dismissed moral sensibilities—that part of consciousness that made humans human. Reason was both the means of his success and his moral shortsightedness. His consistent rationalization of behavior made control of an industry possible, and his insistence wholly on facts blinded him to the moral dimensions of slavery. He held to a quid pro quo conception of justice, a calibration of economic interests and political entitlements. If slavery produced economic benefits, then why disrupt the economy? If the Union protected economic entitlements, why disrupt the Union? Nonetheless, he was not blind to the devastating consequences of disunion and a war to protect the Union.

Nathan Appleton and his family were congregants at William Ellery Channing's Unitarian Federal Street Church. Channing preached a more nuanced version of rational faith. His understanding of the good life involved a more particular "self-culture" than Emerson's more egoistic and individualistic notion of the term.[41] "Self-culture," wrote Channing, is "the care which every man owes to himself, to the unfolding and perfecting of his nature."[42] Conscience that evolved from a God-given power, a meditative center, gave force to character. Such a conscience acknowledged evil in the world, struggled against it, but recognized that it can never be eradicated. Channing stressed self-criticism as a necessary counterforce to ego or any worldly chauvinism. He supported the reform causes of labor and antislavery, as did Appleton. Politically, he embraced the gradual abolition of slavery, since the cultivation of conscience, he rather naively assumed, sufficed to enable reform. Channing differed from Appleton in that he remained critical of slave owners because they did not use their God-given power to see the slaves as human beings. Nonetheless, Channing disavowed the abolitionists who divided the world between the forces of good and evil and tended not to see their own failings.[43] Channing's ability to see slaves as human beings and rational creatures who had the power of "self-culture" went beyond Appleton's reductionism because Channing's nature embraced a "power within."[44]

Channing's influence on the Appleton family cannot be exaggerated. Yet, his message spoke powerfully and much differently to Frances Appleton, Nathan Appleton Sr.'s daughter born in 1817. Frances had the model of her mother, Maria Theresa Gold Appleton, who, although a stout Calvinist at heart, sat in awe at Channing's sermons. Frances, or Fanny as she was called, imbibed the reform-mindedness and contemplative attitude of Channing and her father's humanitarianism. Fanny, so much the daughter of privilege—intelligent, serious, self-assured—lived at a depth only fully appreciated by her admirer, Henry Wadsworth Longfellow. Although her early schooling prompted a love of dancing and French, her later sympathies turned to reform. At 15, she announced her interest in public affairs. She joined a sewing group to sew for "the poor Irish" and attended a church meeting to listen to arguments for the rights of the Cherokee Indians. She dined with a young Cherokee chief there and, impressed by his eloquence, sent him to her father to deliver a letter supporting the Indians' cause. At the same time, she never lost interest in literature and the arts. Fanny was fond of her mother's cousin, the author Catherine Sedgwick, who must have inspired some of her literary sensibility. Although Fanny retained the bearing of her class, she disdained balls and society events. On a tour of England, she regarded as boring her visit to the Court of St. James, except the opportunity to observe the new queen, Victoria, whom she described in unflattering terms. Fanny looked elsewhere for meaning. In addition to Channing's influence, her father's sense of social responsibility surrounded her. Fanny spent vacations at her father's model village, Lowell. In comparison, she criticized the conditions at Niagara factories, such was her eye for social justice.[45] For Fanny, the good life meant the formation of good character and encouragement of just relations. Her actions were based on assumptions of a common humanity that lead to greater freedom and equity for all, especially the poor and the dispossessed. Her introspective notion evolved from a passionate sympathy to a deep turnabout in social and religious convictions.

Fanny's life unfolded in quiet breaks—the first, in sorrow, in the deaths of her mother and brother. In 1833, Maria Theresa Gold Appleton died. On her deathbed, she exhorted her children to follow her religious example. Appleton, attending a session of Congress, was unable to reach home before his wife died. Sadness in the Appleton family doubled when Appleton's son, the 20-year-old Charles, died two years later. Fanny wrote, "We are desolate . . . [the] survivors are anxious for each other."[46] In 1835, Appleton took his grieving family—his daughters, Fanny and Mary; his son, Thomas Gold; and an ailing nephew, William Appleton—on a European tour to assuage the pain of loss. It turned out to be a fateful choice. Another Bostonian, Henry Wadsworth Longfellow, also grieving the loss of his wife, crossed paths with the Appletons in Interlaken, Switzerland. Longfellow joined the Appletons for drives, walks, German tutoring lessons, and rowing on the lake. He fell in love with Fanny, but, when he proposed, sometime later, she refused him. Her grief; her distraction by yet another death, that of her cousin William, who died on the tour; and Longfellow's boorishness in tutoring contributed to her refusal. Later, she commented on what she considered his naiveté. She said, "Longfellow does not understand the state of the world."[47] To relieve his grave disappointment, Longfellow wrote *Hyperion: A Romance*, which expressed his feelings about his romance but disguised the characters involved. Of the hero, he wrote, "He acted more from impulse than principle . . . yet underneath the poetry . . . there was good . . . a layer of common sense."[48] Of the female character, he wrote, "She is my heroine . . . she is not beautiful but intellectual." He described her as possessing "a calm, quiet face, serious . . . but light of soul with deep and luminous eyes." He vowed he would carry the wound of her refusal with him always.[49] Fanny was stunned and horrified that Longfellow would make her a public figure. Longfellow, a romantic poet, longed to cast his fortune with Fanny, a woman of feeling and uncommon sense. Although he visited the Appletons at times, he and Fanny did not come to an understanding until 1843, seven years later.[50]

During the lonely period when he remained apart from Fanny, he struck up a close friendship with Charles Sumner, a young and brilliant Harvard-educated lawyer. Longfellow and Sumner belonged to the Five of Clubs, a group whose fellowship excited literary and political discussions. Longfellow wrote to his cousin George Washington Greene, "Charles Sumner is a very lovely character—simple, energetic, hearty, poetic and no nonsense in him . . . holding his burning heart in his hand."[51] Longfellow, equally passionate, explained to Sumner, "I like to feel deep emotions."[52] For a period of time, Sumner stayed with Longfellow, while

Sumner lectured at Harvard in Judge Story's law classes during the judge's absence. After that, there were visits and jaunts to meet authors and politicians.[53] Sumner, who tended to approach the law in a more literary fashion, became a sometime editor and critic of Longfellow's work.[54] Appleton welcomed Sumner into Boston's Unitarian and commercial circles. Harriot Sumner Appleton, Appleton's wife, and Charles Sumner were cousins. The young lawyer's practice included many Boston capitalists.[55]

As Sumner and Longfellow developed their political views, Fanny underwent a second rupture, an emotional change of heart. With deepening interest, she read Dante, which Longfellow taught and later translated, and she read Longfellow's poetry. She had reached a spiritual breaking point. At Christmastime, Fanny experienced a religious conversion that gave her new life, new strength, so much so that she could understand death as a happy experience. She saw "visible things as more real [and] . . . all things transfigured." The sadness that she had endured lifted; she felt "really alive" and, in the spring of 1843, welcomed Longfellow into her life. Love and death presented Fanny with the same challenge to give one's all to an uncertain destiny. After her conversion, nothing remained the same, including her fear of commitment to Longfellow.[56] The couple married in 1843 and lived in the historic Craigie House, which Nathan Appleton bought for them. Appleton helped remodel the house with all the modern conveniences, including a shower.[57] Craigie House held the five Longfellow children and, with the cultured couple, became a lively social center for literature, politics, and the arts.

Longfellow may have well suited his father-in-law, since the Harvard professor and well-known poet was a Conservative Whig, pro-tariff, anti-slavery moderate who never condemned the South. Longfellow had ties to the cotton South; his sister, Mary Longfellow, married a cotton broker from New Orleans. However, Longfellow moved more toward radicalism as his friendship with Sumner deepened. While Longfellow made fun of nonviolence advocates, transcendentalists, utopianists, and those "nonsectarians who debate what is a sect,"[58] Sumner ventured into activism; he joined reform causes for the blind, the immigrant, the imprisoned, and the enslaved. In Sumner's choice of reforms, Channing exerted much influence. However, by 1844, Sumner turned more radical in his antislavery and antiwar stances. Sumner eschewed Channing's theism and instead adopted a progressive humanism that believed "man is capable of improvement" and can change the environment. He veered from Channing's interpretation of self-culture and acted under the notion that the whole human family—not simply the individual—must be the object of reform. Yet, as a moral idealist, he accepted the notion that a reformer had first

The Longfellow Family, 1849. (Longfellow House-Washington's Headquarters National Historical Site)

to purify self and then act for the public good. Then, all would join in a "moral blockade," as Channing urged. Sumner encouraged Longfellow to publish his *Poems of Slavery*. Longfellow claimed, rather defensively, that his poems on slavery were mild and not incendiary, as his critics claimed.[59] Sumner patiently led Longfellow along the radical path. On July 4, 1845, with the Boston militia displayed in all its pomp, Sumner gave an antiwar, anti-Texas Annexation speech in which he said, "In our age there can be no peace that is not honorable; there can be no war that is not dishonorable."[60] Longfellow supported him.[61] Nathan Appleton wanted no public outcry against slavery, since President Polk moved to lower the tariff and conciliate the South. Sumner joined the antislavery Conscience Whigs, who excoriated Appleton for placing self-interest above principle.

In doing so, the Whig Party split between the Conscience and Cotton, or merchant, Whigs. Sumner termed cotton manufacturers "the Lords of Lash and Loom." Open hostility characterized the Sumner and Appleton factions. Longfellow, caught between them, warned Sumner not to come to dinner when Appleton was to visit.[62]

Both Fanny and Henry Longfellow believed that a good life meant more than their comfort; a good life meant a political consciousness with a principled sense of justice. But it was Fanny, with her strong sense of empathy for the impoverished classes, who reinforced the couple's notion of justice. When, newly married, Fanny visited New York City, she observed with disgust that so much waste existed and that everything was turned into a profit. Ironically, the capitalist's daughter had a keen eye for greed. Because her sympathy more often lay with the oppressed, she expressed compassion for the poor in the cold New England winters and was moved by the plight of British shirtmakers. Fanny understood the new economic reality better than those social reformers who ignored the plight of workers.[63] And the unfortunates condemned to death also aroused her sympathy; she abhorred the death penalty.[64] And when she read of a rape in the newspaper, she remarked, "When will they [male jurors] recognize the moral murder as great a crime as the physical?"[65] As the political parties debated war with Mexico, she read William H. Prescott's history of the conquest of Mexico, which reinforced her hatred of war. She characterized war as "glory in butchery." A flash of realism entered her thoughts when she compared the human condition of war to Lowell's plans for his (and her father's) city; she characterized as idealistic Lowell's belief that communitarianism held the wave of the future. Nonetheless, she hoped for peace. In their visit to the Springfield Arsenal, Fanny remarked that the guns reminded her of the "organ pipes of death." She spurred Henry to write peace poems that became "The Springfield Arsenal" and contained Fanny's metaphor.[66] Even to her new in-laws, she anxiously wrote, "How do you feel about the annexation of Texas?"[67] She joined the League of Universal Brotherhood against war. Fanny listened to Channing's admonition that only by purification of self or self-criticism could anyone form a judgment about others' social or political opinions. Like Channing, she did not join the abolitionists because they denounced the Union, thereby making a wholesale condemnation of the nation and the Constitution.[68] Yet, in her desire for purification, she resembled Sumner.

By 1848, the Longfellows and Sumner identified with the Free Soil Party. Henry Longfellow supported the party as an antidote to the weakness of Congress, calling it "ridiculous. The North would make many concessions, if not for the backbone of Freesoilers." Fanny felt Whigs did not do enough about slavery. She wanted the federal government on the side of freedom.[69] Sumner descended into a dispute with Appleton on whether or not cotton manufacturers had engaged in a conspiracy to suppress the Conscience Whigs. Appleton vehemently denied such a charge, claiming there was no evidence to support it. Longfellow, irenic by temperament, detached himself from such bitter politics. He chose instead to act as a hospitable, sympathetic friend whose home remained ever open to the lonely, increasingly isolated Sumner.[70] By 1851, the Free Soilers, Conscience Whigs, and even Democrats in the state legislature, disgusted by the Compromise of 1850 and Daniel Webster's part in it, helped to elect Sumner to the Senate to replace Webster, who advanced to Tyler's Cabinet. Sumner, mordant by temperament, escaped any celebration of his election by fleeing to the Longfellows. Longfellow assured Sumner that South Carolina's threats of secession were not serious. Appleton, ever sympathetic to compromise, saw Sumner's election as "the most fatal blow to ... popular suffrage that [had] been inflicted."[71] Fanny wrote to her father that the plight of runaway slaves, who under the Fugitive Slave Act had no legal recourse to plead their case, contributed to Sumner's election. She knew, she said, that his election "does not cheer you."[72] The Longfellows, although devoted to Sumner and supportive of the antislavery position, still took part in civic demonstrations of unity and maintained dialogue with Conservative Whigs and supporters of the Compromise of 1850. Henry and Fanny attended President Taylor's reception; Longfellow himself dined with Webster and talked with Benton and Clay. Nonetheless, after speaking to members of Congress and the administration, Longfellow realized the seriousness of South Carolina's threats.[73]

When Longfellow addressed his friend now in Washington, "O Soul, Sweet ... Beloved," Sumner wrote back with sadness, the "quiet days are gone."[74] And, indeed, they were, since Sumner began his tumultuous career in the Senate. Fanny approved his maiden speech on antislavery but anxiously awaited Sumner's attack on the Fugitive Slave Law that had roiled Massachusetts. She referred to the Fugitive Slave Act as "human game laws."[75] Longfellow gently urged Sumner to speak against the hated Fugitive Slave Law by saying, Fanny hoped Sumner "will soon have a chance to speak on the Fugitive Slave law. I tell her to be patient. Neither the hour nor the man will fail."[76] He did not fail; Sumner spoke against the Fugitive Slave Law on July 27, 1852. However strong Sumner's declaration on antislavery in 1852, he could not call himself an abolitionist; rather, he referred to himself as a conservative reformer who would not overturn either the Constitution or the legal system. His vision of emancipation merely meant the retention of a peasant class in the South and compensation for slaveholders. Henry Longfellow, invested with the same caution as Sumner, wrote to James M. Legare of South Carolina, "My heart has a Southern side to it, and I am sure yours has a Northern. We could speak to slavery *sans peur et sans reproche!*" Despite Longfellow's chivalric overture to Legare, the Longfellows enthusiastically cheered Sumner's speech for repeal of the Fugitive Slave Act.[77]

Uncle Tom's Cabin, published in 1852, aroused the reading public between the passing of the Fugitive Slave Act and the Kansas-Nebraska Act, which repealed the Missouri Compromise and, therefore, threatened to advance the spread of slavery into Northern territory. Fanny Longfellow praised *Uncle Tom's Cabin*. She remained thoroughly incensed about slaves' condition and later protested the "Nebraska wickedness."[78] Sumner, in his most eloquent and damning prose, castigated the 1854 Kansas-Nebraska Act as a "gross violation of a sacred pledge" and accused the Southern "slaveocracy" of a conspiracy to dominate the powers of government. Any concession to the South *sans peur et sans reproche* remained out of the question. Longfellow consulted with Sumner on whether the situation was as serious as it seemed. Sumner wrote back that the series of events made him "almost ill." Parties fractured with the Kansas-Nebraska Act. Fanny rejoiced that the Free Soilers met separately from the Whigs. She found the Whigs tepid in their response to the spread of slavery. The Free Soilers, however, attacked the cotton manufacturers for their neutrality on the slave question. Meanwhile, her spouse participated in the partisan conflict.[79] He lectured friends on the Nebraska question and applauded Sumner's courage, despite the threats against him. "He [Sumner] will do his duty," Longfellow assured his friends. As the Kansas-Nebraska Act inflamed Northern abolitionist ire, the Anthony Burns incident turned even prominent Boston conservatives against slavery. Burns, a fugitive slave who lived in Boston, was captured and, notwithstanding demonstrations and violent mob actions, was marched under guard to the Boston harbor, where a ship awaited his deportation to Virginia. His arrest demonstrated the determination of President Franklin Pierce, Longfellow's classmate at Bowdoin, to enforce the Fugitive Slave Act. The level of outrage spurred the passage of personal liberty laws in Northern states.[80] The Longfellows did not participate in any public demonstration; rather, their compassionate concern remained wholly about the fate of Burns.

Sumner observed the actions of pro-slavery forces in Kansas that took control of the polls, set up a fraudulent pro-slavery government, and sacked the opposing, but illegal, Free Soil government in Lawrence. Long identified as a moralist, uncompromising in his stand on "higher law" (law higher than the constitutional protection of slavery), Sumner took an injudicious step, encouraged by Longfellow, and engaged in a personal attack. In his virulent Senate oration enumerating the "crimes against Kansas," Sumner named Senator Butler from South Carolina as consorting with "the harlot slavery," among other insults. To avenge his cousin's honor, Preston Brooks caned Sumner bloody and senseless on the Senate floor.[81] In shock and anger, Longfellow wrote of such Southerners and called them "traitors."[82] Sumner, recuperating after a long convalescence, replied and stated baldly the future direction of the country, "Freedom and slavery [are] face to face."[83]

John Brown assumed the improbable face of freedom in 1860 and won the heart of Fanny Appleton. His daring but doomed raid into Virginia to promote a slave uprising won him Northern supporters awed by his martyrdom, his hanging, for the cause. First electrified by a Wendell Phillips speech on antislavery and convinced by the abolitionist preacher Henry Ward Beecher's antislavery sermon-letter, printed as a pamphlet,[84] Fanny could accept radical means to end slavery. She regarded Brown's attack as foolhardy. Yet, she praised him for his Puritan "Covenanter spirit"— that is, belief in a God-given mission to a chosen community. She admired "the strong stuff of a Yankee farmer" and compared it to "the cowardice and fear" of the slave states. What they feared, she thought, was "a great invisible force," by which she meant the power of freedom and righteousness. She referred to Emerson and then to Wendell Phillips, who called Brown a saint.[85] At this point, Fanny's notion of justice stemmed from empathy with the slaves, her hatred of the Fugitive Slave Act, the fear of the spread of slavery, and her acceptance of Brown's intervention on behalf of the slaves. The "Covenanter spirit" meant acceptance of war, and Fanny knew it, but she only reluctantly acceded to the inevitable. The New England esprit touched a deep generational chord.

The Longfellows, as Free Soil partisans, moved with their supporters to the Republican Party and Lincoln. At Lincoln's election, Fanny ruefully noted that "the capitalists in New York got up a business panic to counter Pennsylvania's vote in our favor." Clearly, Fanny did not identify with her father's business interests and happily counted herself in the antislavery column. Still, she refrained from supporting outright war. She rejoiced in the Republican torchlight parades, "the rivers of fire," convinced that Republicans marched for order and discipline. Unhappily, she regarded her uncle William Appleton's indifference to slavery in his congressional election campaign.[86] In the great "crescendo of events," Fanny hoped there would be no war. Furthermore, the Longfellows did not agree with the abolitionists who favored disunion. Yet, the couple hoped the Republicans would stand firm and not compromise, regardless of South Carolina's secession. Fanny remained unconcerned about secession and believed that, outside the Union, South Carolina's would be "a piteous fate." In that, she agreed with her father. Nonetheless, she hoped the Southern states would come to their senses, but, if not, she had confidence in the North's resources.[87]

On April 1, 1861, Fanny, still cautious about the resort to war, wrote her impressions on the day war began, "War is upon us. Virginia seceded but the North and West are aroused to patriotism. All parties wish to protect the government. Volunteers are pouring in. It is likened to the enthusiasm of '76. There is the cruel necessity of war because our cause is self-defense."[88] Fanny added her growing alienation from the South; she wrote, "The South is alien to me more than the British." Her condemnation of the South expressed itself as more like sadness and disappointment than hostility.[89] She struggled with the North's participation in war, "Still I abhor war wherever or whenever produced, and trust this will be a short one." On the question of a peaceful secession, Fanny felt she would rejoice if the president cut the seceded states off without a fight. Yet, she reasoned, the president "must do his duty." She wrote plaintively, "It seems like a dream to be living in such days."[90] In the end, her sense of principle emboldened her to conclude: "Painful as it is it is better than the past apathy when we yielded principle and power to these corrupt men until they believed they could make us slaves. The North is aroused for liberty and an intense love of country. I am proud to live at such a time ... so sublime ... [when] a prosperous people risk[s] all for an idea of right."[91] She praised her own people, who stood on principle "after our long dream of self-indulgence." For all of Fanny's righteous conviction, she held the war against the rebels—not the Southern people.[92] And she, born to a monied class, distanced herself from wealth and privilege.

As the hostilities progressed, she hoped the blockade would prove that the war would follow only a defensive course. She disapproved of New York's clamor for more aggressive action. Her only option, she thought, was prayer that God would shield the right. The war had moved to a more uncomfortable place, where the reality before her had turned from principle to reckless pursuit. Slowly, she accepted a pragmatic view. She reasoned that the United States could not endure military despotism on the

Southern border controlling the Gulf and extending into Mexico and, if provoked, invite foreign protection. Thus, the Southern Navy had to be stopped.[93] She understood that the U.S. government had to change foreign public opinion because, she knew, the war had come down to "civilization versus barbarism."[94] Longfellow, who had followed Sumner's prewar course, affirmed Sumner in his war aims. On July 5, 1861, he wrote to Sumner, "The war seems to be assuming vaster and nobler proportions. The great question Freedom or Slavery is coming out clearer and clearer."[95]

Justice, for Fanny Longfellow, meant a life lived for reform, of promoting the good. All her "preunderstandings,"[96] her compassionate regard for the oppressed, played out in her convictions about justice. She could not live a good life with unjust institutions that upheld the Fugitive Slave Act and abrogated a "good life for all." She entertained pragmatic political concerns but ultimately yielded to an intuitive sense about the good, the necessity of a war for Union. Hers was not a choice propelled by "status anxiety";[97] she had far more empathy for the plight of workers than her father did. It was as if she lived justice as a virtue that protected the unity of family and state. She embraced familial and political divisions between her father and Sumner with love and tact. Yet, she very reluctantly yielded to the necessity of war. Hers is a more complicated view of war than her husband's. Nonetheless, her view and Henry Longfellow's support for Sumner's aggressive war of words and idealization of the cause led to the same end, the war for Union and, later, freedom—a tragic war of unrelenting savagery.

National and personal tragedy joined when Fanny died in a fire. She had been writing letters and, the family said, by accident dropped the wax on her dress and it went up in flames. Fanny ran to Henry, who tried to wrap her in a rug to smother the flames, but was unsuccessful. She died the next day, at the age of 44. Longfellow's hands were badly burned and took months to heal. In his grief, he spoke of leaving for the South of France in the spring of 1862.[98] When Longfellow himself died, his family found a poem in his desk that, better than anything, expressed his deep, profound, unyielding sorrow at his wife's death. In the "Cross of Snow" he wrote,

> There is a mountain in the distant West
> That, sun-defying, in its deep ravines
> Displays a cross of snow upon its side.
> Such is the cross I wear upon my breast
> These eighteen years, through all the changing scenes
> And seasons, changeless since the day she died.

Fanny's grief-stricken father, Nathan Appleton Sr., died only days after his favorite daughter. According to Nathan Appleton Jr., had his father lived, he would have been grieved had he known of the hard words his former Southern business associates and friends hurled at the North that led to bloodshed.[99] Nonetheless, his heir, Nathan Jr., the son he had with his second wife, Harriot Sumner Appleton, relished the fight. Unlike his father, Nate showed little aptitude for business and, in contrast to his half-sister, no passion for reform. Rather, he displayed a certain ambivalence about the war and a youthful lack of introspection. His childhood diary, which he kept from the age of seven through adolescence, revealed an inventive fellow who liked to draw and build structures, and who, although occasionally naughty, said his prayers, read his Bible, and went to church with his grandmother.[100] An adventurous boy, he records riding a "velocipede"[101] and taking off with a friend to see some confiscated gambling equipment.[102]

As a child and teenager, Nate remained isolated from an understanding of the national crisis that surrounded him. For the youth, a good life was pleasure, pure and simple. At the age of 10, he observed the inauguration of President Franklin Pierce as a grand national event. Nonetheless, he focused more on the absorptions of youth—a tour of the New York mansions on Fifth Avenue, a visit to Christy's "Negro entertainment."[103] At his Boston dancing school, he noticed how "jolly" it was to be in the company of pretty girls. At the same time, he recorded zeros on his Latin lesson and algebra test.[104] On one occasion, he studied French long and hard, missing out on the family's social evening with the Peabodys. That distressed his mother. She believed he worked too long on his lessons, and she told Nate to tell his teacher, Mr. Demprock, that it was "a shame to impose such a lesson on [the class] now." Mr. Demprock replied to Nate that he "was very much obliged for my mother's opinion but he should keep his own." Nate noted, rather sullenly, that Mr. Demprock's reply was "rather saucy."[105] He endured the preaching at chapel and resented his "stupid, nasty school."[106] His attitude is typical of Victorian adolescent males' ease in rebellion against authority figures, such as teachers.[107] And, indeed, his mother indulged him. Nonetheless, he studied his Latin and eventually won a second prize for his translations of *The Dialogues of Lucian* and *The Aeneid*. And, slowly, the critical issues of the day dawned upon him. By 1858, he imbibed the slogan "Liberty and Union."[108] And, yet, that same year, when he accompanied his sister, Hattie, and family friends to hear an antislavery lecture, he reviled the talk as "beastly."[109]

Despite his early failures, Nathan persevered in his schooling and received congratulations from his friend G. D. Wells on how he, Nathan, got into Harvard.[110] Nonetheless, Nathan's interests in divertissements continued in his college career. Another friend looked forward to playing billiards with him and, in addition, counseled him that "money should have no *weight* in the affairs of the heart!"[111] Perhaps his friend alluded to Nathan's close friendship with his cousin, Carolyn Le Roy Appleton, who appealed to his heart and his sense of status. As a typical college student, money from home assured his place. "Don't forget the money," he wrote to his father. Sports, fine sermons in the chapel, exciting theater, and good books held his interest in college. He was 16 years old in 1859.[112]

Nathan's sense of justice emerged as he read accounts of the unjust conditions at the textile mills of Lawrence, Massachusetts. Surely, his father's attitude toward labor sensitized Nathan's notion of justice. His father's idealistic terms for laborers—high wages and decent conditions—vanished in the 1850s, as speed-ups, injuries, and wage reductions caused strikes among textile workers. Nathan recorded "the Lawrence Massacre," as he called it, at the Pemberton Mills in Lawrence, Massachusetts. The Mill collapsed around quitting time, five o'clock, under the weight of extra-heavy machinery and poor construction. Hundreds of operatives, including women, children, and emigrants, were trapped inside and died. Later that evening, in the efforts to locate survivors, a lantern tipped and set the site ablaze. Nathan Appleton Sr. was, of course, an original investor in the Lawrence Mill, renamed the Pemberton Mill when it was sold to George Howe and David Nevins in 1857.[113] Days after the Mill strikes, Harvard students massed to protest police interference in their right of assembly. The students contended that "such extreme measures led to violence" and, further, that the students were "actuated by no rebellious spirit." They were indignant that they "should be submitted to surveillance of armed men," who forced obedience "at the muzzle of a revolver."[114] Despite their best reasoning, the students were afforded a lecture by Dr. Dewey on "the insubordination of the young."[115] Nathan remained aware of labor strikes and avidly recorded student strikes at Harvard.[116] College ties heightened Nathan's sense of loyalty and broadened his scope of justice.

In the midst of his studies, romances, and athletics at college, in 1860 he took up a more serious pastime—target practice. The intent, as his friend Robert Winthrop put it, was "warlike."[117] Nathan's roommate, E. H. Kidder, wrote to him in February 1860 and apprised him of the situation in Wilmington. He said,

All the people feel here that their rights are in great danger. The rejection of the Crittenden compromise by the Republicans, has done a great deal to further the cause of secession. It is my firm belief that many, who would not have been willing to accept the compromise, make it one of their chief arguments for secession. . . . There is . . . one point about which almost *every man* agrees, namely to resist any attempt to coerce [the South].[118]

Nathan did not ignore the political crisis. As a moderate Whig, like his father, he abhorred disunion. Nathan happily marched in the torchlight parade for presidential candidate Bell. But, to his circle of young men, the torchlight parades provided heady amusement. Nor did the ominous rumblings from the South deter Nathan from indulging in infatuations and engaging in sports: boxing, sculling, cricket, and billiards. And he took up smoking, despite his mother's misgivings. She might also have had worries if she had known that Nathan's comrades had ended up in the lockup.[119] Nathan's own behavior warranted college discipline when he threw trash out his window and hid liquor in his room. Mortified, his mother wrote to him, "You know how I feel about a public and I can only say you ought to be more circumspect in your conduct—why throw anything out of a window? You were never taught that at home."[120] Nathan wrote back with sophomoric condescension,

> Dear Mawther, I received this morning your epistle. I pitched rubbish out my window—that was one indictment . . . the other . . . was ordering 12 bottles of ale for my room from the apothecary. These circumstances show you how childish the faculty are. But a public does not amount to much, so don't feel concerned.[121]

Nathan's condescension reveals young men's aversion to women's influence over them and the distance men placed between men's and women's spheres.[122] Naturally, Harriot Sumner Appleton felt great concern when the president of Harvard mentioned Nathan's conduct to Nathan Appleton Sr. She chided Nathan Jr. and told him to "make good resolutions and *keep* them for the future."[123]

Nathan did have a serious side. In his quiet moments, he meditated and went to meetings with the Quakers.[124] By the beginning of 1861, Nathan recognized the critical political situation of secession. He had visited Washington and heard congressional debates and secession talk at Willard's Hotel. When Nathan returned to campus, he reported that "many leading Southerners have left Harvard and gone South."[125] E. H. Kidder from Wilmington, North Carolina, again warned him, "The seceding states are *determined not* to come back into the union," and added,

"If I was going to remain at home I think I would join the artillery Company."[126] At the start of hostilities, Kidder telegraphed Nathan, "Ask President to excuse my absence."[127] A number of Southern men quietly slipped away from Harvard to enlist in the Confederate army. These young men said goodbye to one another with ritualistic stoicism, each determined to find personal freedom in their choice. In spite of his close friend's determination to fight for the South, Nathan drilled on campus with his fellow students in the hopes of fighting for the North. Presentations of swords to Union enlistees in "brilliant uniforms" demonstrated military splendor on campus. To prove class Unionist loyalty, Nathan instigated the hanging of American flags in every window of the "Old Mass" dormitory. His proudest moment, however, came when he volunteered, at the governor's request, to guard the Boston Armory. In preparation for military service, which he very much desired, his studies at the college included lectures on recent innovations in weapons, military use of the telegraph, and naval engineering. And a good deal of fraternizing of Harvard students with the Irish 28th Massachusetts Brigade turned Nathan's mind to the fight. Nonetheless, for all of his yearning and enthusiasm, his mother refused to allow him to enlist until he finished college, in 1863. His mother's veto carried weight because, when Appleton died, in 1861, he left Nate with a small fortune, but under his mother's control.[128]

Immediately after commencement, in 1863, Nathan applied to Governor Andrew of Massachusetts for a commission in the Light Artillery; he had studied such weapons management in college. He was then commissioned a second lieutenant in the Fifth Massachusetts Battery on August 31, 1863, and assigned to the 5th Corps of the Army of the Potomac. His military career began after the Battle of Gettysburg, when the tide had turned in favor of the North. He admitted the rank and file did not relish welcoming a rich, inexperienced, young man into its command. Yet, he remembered his first night in camp at Beverly Ford, Virginia: "supper al fresco under the tent fly ... mild autumn air in our faces, sentinel at his post, horses reigning and kicking at the picket post, graceful groups of soldiers, the white tents of the different regiments, evening bugles." For Nate Appleton, the sweet knowledge of personal independence heightened his senses.[129] Nevertheless, as he matured, he reported with pleasure that the army was "a splendid school for control of one's spirits." His note of sobriety may have signaled his mother that he had learned discipline or that he had not engaged in soldierly vices—such as drinking, gambling, and whoring.[130]

Nathan's company engaged in only brief skirmishes with the enemy, but he, nonetheless, observed in his letters home the rotting horseflesh, skulls, and damaged horse carts from previous battles around Beverly Ford and Bull Run. The subtext of his letter—that in his manly duties he risked horrors—could not have escaped his family's notice.[131] In the five months before he engaged in a major battle, he had time for reflection. In addition, his growing closeness to his men gave him a fleeting sense of injustice. He wrote to his mother that he received $249.20 pay for two months of service, but that the (white) Infantry received $20 for the same time period. But, he added, "why philosophize?"[132] Nonetheless, he entertained moral musings one evening, when the Army of the Potomac took possession of a camp in which the Confederate officers, having retreated in haste, left behind their papers and memorabilia. Nate entered an officer's quarters and went through the man's things: religious papers, a prayer for the Confederate cause, and an obituary of a young officer. Then he observed,

> What confused ideas of right and wrong on both sides, war causes, and you suddenly pull up with the thought Why should I think that I am in the right, with all my enthusiasm and education? It is sickening to think that you are tossing slugs of lead at human beings, and setting yourself up as a target, because people have mistaken ideas, and this too 1800 years after Christ preached peace, good will.[133]

When Nathan wrote his misgivings about war, he had not yet been tested in battle. Despite his doubts and his earlier loyalty to the Constitutional Union Party, Nathan expressed an admiration for Lincoln. Shortly after Lincoln's Proclamation on Amnesty and Reconstruction, on December 8, 1863, Nathan wrote to his sister, "Old Abe's Proclamation is manly. What an old brick he is, after all. Our men are getting quite interested in this 'reenlisting business.' "[134] For Nathan, the war experience filtered his political perspective in a decidedly masculine way and made the Union cause "manly." Later, in his 1871 memoirs, Nathan erased all doubts about the Northern cause and injected a more ideological view of the war. He wrote that the war "was one of the most uncalled for and terrible attacks against right that can be found in history, largely fomented, I believe, by an unscrupulous or misguided few, who worked upon the passions of the white masses."[135]

In February 1864, he came into his inheritance and believed it was much better for him to start out in life "plainly" than to flaunt his immense inheritance.[136] Yet, he impatiently awaited the end of the war, when he could "go to Europe, and eat pates, and wear white cravats, and get married and build pretty cottages by the sea."[137] Perhaps, at this point, justice meant the cause of Union and its promise of a better civilian life.[138] All idle musings ended with the spring campaign in May 1864, when he participated in the battles of the Second Wilderness and Spotsylvania. Nightmare scenes of the wounded in the field hospitals, the incessant sounds of musketry, moans of the dying, and cries of the horses burned in his brain. He acknowledged he harbored a persistent fear of injury and then, with his worst fear realized, on May 25, 1864, he suffered bullet wounds in his arm. He resigned from active duty and, after a convalescence, sojourned to Europe.[139]

During this hiatus, Nathan again considered his future. "The question . . . is how can a rich, educated and patriotic person best do his duty to his conscience, his family, his country and himself?" he wrote to his sister. He considered politics, but "pride and conscience egg me on," he admitted to her. Not encouraged by the war news, he relayed from Hamburg, Germany, the opinion that "as far as fighting goes they [the South] have earned their independence and almost wonder that Europe does not give it them on the score alone, but I find that the people in Europe do not believe in the justice of the Southern cause." European public opinion further underlined Nathan's ambivalent sense of justice in the Union cause. His mother chided him for his restless wandering and sent him glowing news of Savannah's surrender. But Nathan did come home and reenlist, for his mother's sake as much as his own. She wished him to march into Richmond.[140]

He rejoined his old regiment, the artillery brigade of the 15th Corps, on April 1. Two days later, he exulted in victory. Breathlessly, he wrote his sister Hattie, "The fight and thrashing which we gave the Rebs on the 1st was the most complete I ever saw in Virginia as we captured two thirds of the whole force which Lee sent out to hold Virginia." On April 10, he witnessed Lee's surrender. He said, "I saw a strange sight at the Court House this morning Genls Grant, Meade and our Corps Commanders in pleasant confab with Longstreet, Gordon, Heath and their Staffs." The strangeness of the peaceful meeting contrasted with the scenes of destruction around him. He observed "the road in some places being filled with dead horses and mules abandoned artillery wagons, and ambulances, officers' trunks and rebel military documents" scattered about. His final hope from the battlefield was that old wounds would heal and that the Southerners would be treated as countrymen. He even wished Jefferson Davis and his cabinet would escape unharmed. For all his ambivalence, Nathan fought for the Union cause and, with his Corps, was immortalized in *The New York Herald* newspaper of April 4, 1865, the same day Lincoln landed in Richmond.[141]

Nathan remained true to his class ideas of a good life. Happy in his command, he prided himself on his men's acceptance of his aristocratic background. Doggedly, he slogged through the Wilderness Campaign. In a sense, he embodied the classic assumption of virtue that the man who possessed courage would not be unjust.[142] Duty, conscience, and his mother's urgings brought him back from Europe to witness the surrender at Appomatox. In manliness, Nathan Appleton Jr. learned courage, and in courage he served justice.

In the Appleton family, justice had several meanings that influenced their interpretation of Union. Nathan Appleton Sr., a rationalist, invested in a good life as an honest and humanitarian capitalist who lived with government institutions that protected his business interests. He believed maintenance of the market system would ensure "a good life for all." His notion of justice foreclosed any declaration of war between producer and supplier. Appleton's view of justice implied a very tangible quid pro quo; he perceived that, with war, individuals and society would not get what they deserved, what they were entitled to, in a society that engaged in peaceful economic pursuits. In apprising the causes for the war, he took a long view. He noted "faults on both sides." But the first aggression, he argued, was clearly the North's—that is, William Lloyd Garrison's denunciation of the Constitution. Aggrieved by abolitionists, the South took defensive measures, most notably the tariff struggles of 1831–1832. Religious and moral notions of slavery as sinful or immoral abstracted a political and economic issue best left to the states, according to Nathan Appleton Sr. The resultant crisis attacked the Constitution and Union.[143] His stringent notion of legal justice did not include "a good life" for the slave. He saw no benefit in war with the South. Indeed, he grieved at the overwhelming price the nation would pay. And he was right about the level of disorder and destruction. His is also a distributive justice, in which the deserving few prosper. The productive and ambitious free laborer deserved a better life, too. The unfree laborers did not deserve the same regard; they had proven less productive and, therefore, less deserving. Appleton, although sympathetic to their plight, simply did not identify with the slaves; they were not within his "moral community," a community of equals.

Appleton's daughter, Fanny, perceived the injustice of slavery and maintained a principled attitude, combined with an underlying empathetic identification with the plight of the slaves. It allowed her to apprehend a political notion more congruent with the "other," rather than those of her own privileged class. She consistently lived "the good life," questioning instances of injustice, whether they were economic, sexual, or political. She valued justice as a virtue and held political discourse to a high standard, equal justice for all. There was nothing self-serving in Fanny's response to the key justice issues of the day. She perceived them with "practical wisdom." For her, abolition and Union meant the ability of all to develop their own unique capabilities and talents and to coalesce those talents in a reunited community.[144]

Nathan Appleton Jr., who genuinely embraced privilege, nonetheless responded to duty and enlisted in military service. Indifferent to institutions, except when they restrained him, he had only the vaguest notions of "a good life for all." Military service presented a larger experience of common bonds. He exulted in "the good life" of a peaceful camp but then experienced the horror of battle, with its dire comradeship. Law did not rule the field of battle, and only the virtue of courage gave it meaning. Nonetheless, he supported the Union cause that protected his way of life. Yet, like the new and still disparate Union, Nathan Appleton Jr. was a man unknown to himself.

There are treatises about justice and the cause of Union in the Civil War. Yet, the works of justice remain concrete, human, and complicated. Some, like legislative service, reform activity, and military duty, strike a public audience; others, such as letters of conciliation to Southern friends, domestic conversations about slavery and abolition, and support for those engaged in public service, constitute the social web of justice without which the state could not have acted in justice. The Appletons, drawn into conflict both public and domestic, nevertheless experienced the human context of justice that a good life in common demanded a price for just institutions.

4

❖

Patriotism and the Twin Loyalties
of African American Families

What country have I?

—Frederick Douglass[1]

Frederick Douglass's question of loyalty and belonging to the nation dramatically challenged black patriotism before and after the Civil War. Patriotism means devotion to country and the protection of its interests. Yet, with the outbreak of the war and the possibility of freedom, traditional notions of loyalty and belonging suddenly took on new meaning for contrabands. Former slaves asked themselves to whom they belonged, where they belonged, and what they owed one another. These questions represented intense dilemmas for African Americans. To whom they belonged posed legal questions of paternity and marriage in cases of separation by sale. Where they belonged was unclear also, given that former slave families' migration to freedom was often stymied by poverty and political powerlessness. And as to what they owed one another, former bondsman Elbert Head testified that, in June 1865, in Georgia, "there was a whole *nation* of us set free and none with homes."[2] He grieved for his fellow displaced African Americans and identified with their plight. To him, "nation" meant "us"—a suffering, aggrieved people, a nation within a nation. Yet, within that "nation," change already had taken place. African American families had formed in individuals the moral and political values that culminated in the passionate fight for justice in the Civil War.[3] In the postwar era, African American loyalty, tried by racial prejudice, survived in the fight for economic and civil rights.

Scholars contend that African Americans' loyalty consistently expressed itself in relation to the principles of freedom and equality. The proudest boast of slave or freedman was that his forebear had fought for freedom in the American Revolution. Historian Benjamin Quarles insisted, "The Negro's role in the Revolution can best be understood by realizing that his major loyalty was not to a place or a people but to a principle."[4] The cause of freedom in the slave quarters, according to recent historians, characterized both the War for Independence and the Civil War. Elizabeth D. Samet, a historian of citizenship, noted that in the Civil War, "black men fought for principle," lest they be thought "beasts."[5] According to historian James M. McPherson, black recruits in the Civil War fought for the freedom of themselves and their families, but, by 1864, they fought for the Republican government.[6]

The Civil War experience of black people clearly depicts the innate ambivalence of patriotism as a dilemma of greater and lesser loyalties. In September 1864, Private Spotswood Rice assured his children held in bondage, "I will have you if it cost me my life." The father promised that the general who led the white and black soldiers up the river to Glasgow would return his children to him.[7]

In a divided nation, the North claimed freedom for slaves but mostly exhibited indifference to equality. Although African American men fought for the Union, the Union devoted few resources to the protection of their families, thus proving a dilemma for black soldiers. Scholar Alasdair MacIntyre notes that patriotism, loyalty to a country, if it could be defined as a virtue, is only "one of a class of loyalty-exhibiting virtues." Other classifications include loyalty to family, spouse, kin, and friends. He cautions of the danger that such loyalties will be confused with universal morality. He believes that, ultimately, particular and universal moral beliefs would clash. Indeed, MacIntyre argues that the patriot's choice between national claims and particular communal morality "turns out to be a permanent source of moral danger" because the choice is irreconcilable.[8] Yet, historian Melinda Lawson argues that, in the North, a rational, principled, contractual, national identity evolved, but one with "an indefinable feeling" of religious, political, and cultural unity.[9] Patriotism and family interests conjoined even more strikingly among freedmen and freedwomen. Contrabands forced to choose between universal principles of freedom and equality and the particular obligations to family and community, however, opened new dimensions of patriotism and changed the direction of the war.

The development of African American attitudes toward patriotism may be traced to the circumstances of war, but also to the values held and the virtues expressed in their familial and community culture. Primarily, of course, emancipation broke the bonds of slavery. Consequently, survival depended on survival of the family. The sheer magnitude of former slaves' desire for reunification of family, the stability of traditional African-inspired family and kin networks, and the adoption of proto-kin ensured that survival.[10] A good example of how families regarded kin and adopted non-kin or proto-kin may be understood from historian George Rawick's description of African American integrative familial notions. He wrote: "The slave community acted like a generalized extended kinship system in which all adults looked after all children and there was little division between "my children for whom I'm responsible" and 'your children for whom you're responsible.' "[11]

During and immediately after the Civil War, African American loyal identity proceeded in four stages: adaptive familial and communal relations, patriotic military service, military protest, and migration and resettlement. In the first stage, the familial and communal elements of loyalty included an evangelical religion that stressed the necessity of community and freedom, a folklore that encouraged debate and self-protection, an adaptive family structure that supported inclusiveness, and familial work patterns that necessitated cooperation. All the elements of slave culture cohered to produce an interdependent system of obligation and trust coexisting within a white-dominated slave system.

Adaptive family patterns attest to the evolution of broader loyalties among blacks. Generations of historians attest to the stability and inclusiveness of black families. Herbert G. Gutman argued that black families oppressed by separation and harsh conditions nonetheless established long slave marriages, two-parent households, and an extended kin group that included fictive kin.[12] That slaves, whose families may have been disrupted by sale, then chose their fictive kin from among their community proves the ever-increasing need to extend loyalty and, therefore, stability among blacks. Ira Berlin notes that many slaves could relate their great-grandparents' lineage[13]—thus proving extensive cohesion through generations. Eugene D. Genovese, who argued for a paternalistic slave culture with mutual dependence and obligations between blacks and whites, nonetheless held that, by emancipation, a "remarkably stable family base" existed in a unique slave culture.[14] The crushing effects of war, although they raised horrific problems for families, did not alter black determination to reunite family members, to protect family from government-imposed hardship, and to revere the sanctity of slave marriages.[15]

Southern white evangelicalism wielded a double-edged sword within slave culture. Christianity encouraged spiritual freedom and individual autonomy dedicated to the will of God. This religious teaching countered the docility and servility demanded by the slave system. However, evangelicalism, preached from a master's perspective, could also portend a meek acceptance of circumstance. Examples of both existed in the history of Southern slave culture. Obviously, newfound spiritual freedom and identity did not cohere with masters' demands of total deference. And servility brought with it, often enough, humiliation and oppression. The 19th-century slave community then offered expressions of both discontent and suffering in prayers for freedom within a safe hush harbor. Kept within that world were the African traditions and rituals of ecstatic visions, magical practices, ring shouts, and dances. Although open to Southern white religion, slaves made it their own and practiced a syncretism that augured judgment upon the slave owners' society.[16] The combination of religious practices contributed to complicated loyalties.

Perhaps the most profound influence of Southern white evangelicalism upon slave religion was the experience of conversion. When "the time of trouble" began for the converts, their loyalty to the Union prevailed because of their faith in the God of Deliverance. God promised in conversion testimony: "I am Almighty God, I will be closer to you than a brother."[17] Moreover, the divine promise remained, "The soul that trusts in God need never stumble or fall."[18] Trust seemed ever more necessary, since liberation opened new chapters on harrowing and difficult trials. African Americans underwent suffering for the sake of freedom for themselves and their families. The conversion experience extended beyond slave visions and prophecies. Conversion involved a long and brutal process, one that culminated in the Civil Rights Movement.[19] The black "nation" only slowly gained human and civil rights in a society that largely excluded them. Freed people persevered despite the warnings of self-interested Southerners who gave them a choice. A preacher said, "Do you want a home or life as an animal?" His hearers admitted, "We raise hands but didn't want the South to win."[20]

Conversion of heart also intensified identification with one's own community. One convert related her journey through hell, which culminated in her prophetic vision: "I came to the building and saw God and all the prophets and they all came around and when I laid my hand on the altar of God they laid their hands on mine. They all bowed and said,

'Amen.'" Such heavenly election only increased her self-definition and confidence to spread the gospel. A voice declared to her, "many shall hear and believe," thus sealing her election and sanctifying her community relationships.[21] Emotional and visionary, the conversion experience bound the convert to others by an ethic of love. One slave who related her conversion story said she had gone to heaven and there she was told she "was one of the elected children." She then entered her "Father's welcome home" and saw "a host of children . . . sitting around a table" who bowed to her. When she left heaven, she testified that she "was all new." In her joy, she said, "I began shouting and praising God. I loved everybody and every creeping thing."[22] Her vision of heaven involved "a host of children" who included her in the divine feast at the table of the Lord. The vision of heaven as a community of love and praise transferred to her earthly condition, where love permeated her relationships. Nonetheless, the community, when assembled in church, became increasingly segregated. Mixed churches did exist, often as precautions, in order for white control over black congregants. However, with the advent of black preachers and the growth of black populations in urban areas, African American churches increased. Here, too, licensed black preachers felt the weight of white oversight.[23] Yet, the aspirations for freedom could not be suppressed.

Conversion narratives also spoke of freedom from sin as inner freedom. The voice of God told one convert, "Whosoever my Son sets free, He is free indeed."[24] A visionary claimed she saw God "when he freed my soul from Hell."[25] Thus, dreams told of a spiritual deliverance that easily translated into a belief of freedom from slavery. The theme of deliverance welded conversion testimony into mutually acceptable strains of religious belonging. For black evangelical converts, a significant minority within plantation culture, an apocalyptic vision defined their sense of freedom. Slave congregations sang:

> Didn't my Lord deliver Daniel?
> Deliver Daniel, deliver Daniel?
> Didn't my Lord deliver Daniel?
> And why not every man?[26]

Freedom always remained a slave's desire. Lewis Clarke, a fugitive slave from Kentucky, vehemently expressed what lay hidden in the slave's life. "He daren't tell what's in him," said Clarke. Furthermore, he explained, "If a woman slave had a husband and children, and somebody asked her if she would like her freedom? Would she tell'em, yes? If she did, she'd be down the river to Louisiana, in no time; her husband and children never

know what become of her. Of course, the slaves don't tell folks what's passing in their minds about freedom." For Clarke, freedom was his inheritance, he supposed. His father had fought in the Revolutionary War, but
the system had denied him his birthright.[27] Despite a kind master,
Jonathan Thomas stated, "I had from childhood a great wish to be free."[28]
The Union cause of freedom prompted stirrings deep within the slaves'
own spiritual and psychological sense of self.

Black folklore included morality and trickster tales. Such tales suggest
that the slave culture both promoted the positive values of honesty, hard
work, and faithfulness and sometimes tolerated the negative values of
lying, cheating, and stealing. Trickster tales, amoral in content, proposed
that power evoked against a stronger adversary meant survival. These tales
also taught boundaries: Slaves did not steal from slaves. And they alerted
would-be victims.[29] If these contradictory values existed in slave cultures,
then it may be argued that slaves held conflicting views of loyalty within
slave culture. African American patriots who upheld the Union may have
had a desire to protect the community and/or a desire for revenge against a
hated adversary. Such anger, often deflected by military discipline and
federal authority, nonetheless, upheld the Union cause.[30]

The classical definition of virtue was that which engendered human
flourishing.[31] Any character value within slave culture was tested and
measured by the degree of human flourishing it promoted. Loyalty to the
slave community preserved its very existence and contributed to the continuance of its vibrant culture. The primary locus of loyalty arose, quite
naturally, in the family. Among blacks, there was no doubt to whom one
belonged. Slaves lived and worked among family units. Georgia plantation
mistress Mary Telfair hired out husband and wife George and Coombra to
A. N. Urquhart. And, later, she proposed sending the couple, along with
Juddy, Coombra's mother, to William N. Habersham. She wrote, "I will
be glad to accommodate you with servants on moderate wages." She
offered Juddy, the cook, "excellent tempered, a woman you can trust her
with the keys," at six dollars a month. Coombra, the chamber maid, who
was in a delicate condition, Mrs. Telfair hired out for five dollars a month.
George, whom she described as "not smart but steady," was to receive eight
dollars a month. The three workers retained one dollar each of their earnings.[32] However, death of the slave owner threatened the stability of the
slave family, causing even the disruption of generations of slave families,
as in the case of Jennie Hill, whose family lived on the Fray farm.
According to a transcription of Jennie Hill's words: "Her father and
mother were owned by Aaron Fray, a small landowner in Howard county,
near Boonville, Missouri. His slaves consisted of this couple who had

served the Frays before him, the 11 children of which Mrs. Hill was the oldest, and an uncle of Mrs. Hill's who was also an old servant in the family."[33]

Despite the long and faithful service of the entire Hill family, however, upon the death of Aaron Fray, the will bequeathed members of the Hill family to separate members of the Frays.[34]

The threat of sale or separation, more likely on small farms, such as the one on which Jennie Hill labored, evoked anger and the pain of loss. Slaves recounted the memories: "My husband is torn from me and carried away by his master"; "Master gave one of my sisters to his daughter." Susan Boggs related her tragedy, "A son of mine—the only son I had—was sold for a thousand dollars."[35] The threat of sale, which most often loomed larger over more profitable male slaves, made relatives even more precious. In the state of anxiety where the threat of sale loomed ever darker, the mother–child bond proved most tenacious.

As the danger of sale and separation persisted, families regrouped and maintained loyal ties. Family members made up the work team. Caroline Ates noted, "[O]ne of my cousins wove the cloth" on the plantation. Julia Bunch said, "My mother was head weaver." Others, not so fortunate, worked in the field or at any odd job. As Sarah Byrd attested, "My mother was a full hand." And, for 64 years, a daughter said, her mother worked as a "Washer and Ironer."[36] In the wake of separation, remaining family accounted for stability, a consciousness of belonging to a group, no matter how truncated. Often, mothers and children accounted for a family dyad, as male hands offered the most promising sale. In that case, mistresses might simply have preferred women and children as slaves.[37] Anna Baker testified to the tenacity of the mother–child bond. Anna Baker's mother, who escaped sexual assault in the fields, kept on running. She found a decent family to serve away from her owner but slipped back several times to visit the children. With freedom, she returned to claim her children. The owner consented to surrender all, except the child, Anna Baker. Her mother, according to the daughter, "went back and got some more papers and come show dem to Marse Morgen, and he say, 'G_ _ D_ _ _, take dem all!' She come out of de house to get us and at first I was scared of her case I didden know who she was. But she put me up in her lap and loved me and I knowed den I loved her too."[38] Anna Baker belonged to her mother—blood ties proved strong, even in the breach.

Slave mothers often had their children underfoot. One daughter remembered, "My mother was cook and her children stayed right with her; and her house was right in the yard. They built her two rooms. All her children was just nachul pets around the house."[39] Slave women used various strategies to keep their children from sale, including training them in valuable work skills. Linda Anne Pendergrass's mother trained her in her own semi-skilled work. Pendergrass testified, "I'se nussed since I was a little gal. My ma made me make teas to cure folks' colds and ailments. She made me fetch her water and towels and other things while she wait on de sick folks. Dat's de way I was broke into nussing."[40] Because owners made all slave women responsible for carding and spinning of cotton, the work devolved upon maternal households. Under duress, slave mothers ran an efficient workplace. Emmaline Heard explained that "her mother had to card bats at night so that the two older sisters could begin spinning the next morning."[41]

Families honored hard work and faithfulness in order to survive. Such values strengthened family ties and the practice of loyalty. Slaves also assimilated non-kin or proto-kin who held an affinity and relationship most dear to those in bondage. A slave woman, Dora Brewer, spoke of seeing "Sis Sophia" thrown across a log and beaten until whelps appeared and " 'Brer Frank' came in for his share of the lashings,"[42] too. Suffering made slaves brother and sister; loyalty stretched across blood lines and made for a more inclusive sense of belonging. But belonging always pertained to family, no matter how defined. The most intimate ties, because they were adaptive, prepared slaves for the larger associations of loyalty. The family, no matter how battered, assimilated a code of cohesion that enabled individuals to move beyond self and family and identify in classical associative terms or circles, toward extended family and toward "neighbors or local groups, fellow city dwellers and fellow countrymen."[43]

Studies of resilience in child development note that the "attachment relationship" proves fundamental to family in an "adaptive system"—that is, a warm and supportive relationship can offset adversity. However, repeated risks to some individuals may cause psychological damage. The family and community that provide adolescents with gradual decision-making training do much to encourage interdependence, a sense of reciprocity.[44] Slave families introduced and trained members to the work and family ethos of slave culture. Such training nourished a sense of political understanding—that is, problem solving—and of interdependence, the building block of loyalty.

Marriages, though long lasting, were vulnerable to break up by sale. Some slaves never forgot the pain of enforced separation; the marital memory remained. When sold by an infuriated plantation mistress, Mollie Simpkins recalled her deepest wound: "I wuz sold 'way fum mah husband en I neber se'd 'im 'gin."[45] Memories of such acts of injustice further reduced loyalty to the master. Yet, for some slaves, freedom meant shedding their former slave partners. That informal divorce existed suggests that the process of sorting out who belonged to whom remained crucial in the development of patriotism. Clergy regarded informal divorces as lacking respect for self and others. One clergyman noted that such self-regard would most effectively be instilled in liberated slaves by enforcing "the marriage relation among them" and, in addition, by "putting them in relations where they will be inspired with self-respect and a consciousness of their rights, and taught by a pure and plain-spoken Christianity."[46] Although well intended, such clerical regard ignored the intense sense of belonging slave marriages engendered. Before the war, Susan (Sukey) and Ersey wrote to their master, Beverly Tucker, not to force them to leave St. Louis and their husbands. They pleaded, "As we had been here a long time and had become much attached to the place (our husbands being here) and as we hated the idea of going to Texas, Mr. Jones [who was to accompany them to Texas] was kind enough to let us remain till March." The supplicants made their reasons plain. "We can't bear to go to Texas with a parcel of strangers—if you were there we should go without saying a word, but to be separated from our husbands forever in this world would make us unhappy for life. We have a great many friends in this place and would rather be sold than go to Texas."[47] Historian Donald Shaffer notes that formal and informal marriage customs existed among former bondsmen and women. Informal marriage customs existed because, he argues, they "believed their lives together consecrated the marriage."[48]

For some, the U.S. flag, with its guarantees of protection and support, meant legitimacy for their marriages. Women testified to Pension Bureau agents that they married soldiers "under the flag" and that that established a greater legitimacy than a slave marriage.[49] Moreover, contrary to reports from observers who saw a causal attitude toward marriage and family, former bondsmen strove to keep their marriages and, by definition, their families intact against all odds. The case of Louis Jourdon is perhaps not exceptional in its heroism. One of ten children, he was sold, with his family, to a slave trader about five years before the war. He and his two brothers wound up in New Orleans. He remained on the plantation of a Dr. Martin until the age of 18, when a battle fought near Paincoutville prompted him to join the soldiers and travel to Thibodaux. Married with four children, he stayed for a while with his family in a contraband camp. When the mistress of his wife took her back to the plantation, Jourdon followed to visit, but then was captured by Confederates and forced to dig ditches. Finally, he escaped from the Confederates and went back to New Orleans to enlist. He was not discharged from the Union army until February 1867. He married a second time.[50] Enlistment endangered black marriages and families already vulnerable to separation and sale. Regosin and Shaffer emphasize the casualness of slave marriages and indifference to families, and they cite Jourdon as an example.[51] Yet, Jourdon remained in touch with his brothers and visited his wife and family at great risk. He advanced the Union cause as he strove to keep his family together. Given the odds, 50 percent, that former bondsmen had of reuniting with their families, Jourdon's decision appears more tragic than irresponsible. It is within the tragedy that the ambiguity lies with regard to loyalty. Unable to repair the separation of families or no longer able to endure enforced slave marriages, ex-slaves began new lives and families. Loyalty shifted and, with it, a more complicated and expansive set of obligations resulted, as Regosin and Shaffer's examination of the Pension files demonstrates.

The attitudes toward marriage and family suggest that slaves made their own choices of marriage partners and of who belonged to whom. Their separate culture and independent judgment fostered a second stage of moral development—adoption of the Union ideologies of freedom and equality. Former bondsmen insisted upon the necessity of black men fighting for the cause, even though, initially, racial prejudice prevented them from enlisting in military service. Harry Jarvis escaped to Fort Monroe, Virginia. Jarvis asked General Butler if he could enlist. Jarvis said General Butler answered, "It warn't a black man's war." Jarvis replied, "[I]t *would* be a black man's war 'fore dey gets fru."[52] Certainly, an observer in the *New-York Tribune* knew ex-slaves desired to fight. He reported runaway slaves who wished to be armed and described their bitterness. Deprived of decent food or clothing and, in some cases, cruelly treated, men ached for revenge on their masters. In 1861, before Negro recruitment commenced, a reporter dispatched his view of recently released slaves. He wrote, "I have known of several instances where slaves asked for arms to fire on their own masters ... I have known where slaves assisted in the capture of their masters."[53] Free blacks who migrated to Washington, D.C., offered their services to the government. They were rebuffed by the secretary of war, who stated flatly, "[T]his Department has no intention at present to call into the service of the Government any colored soldiers."[54] Robert Smalls, a hero, who piloted a Confederate steamer to Union forces, claimed many other slaves desired to fight for liberty. In 1863, he surmised there would be "ten or fifteen" regiments in Charleston alone if blacks could enlist.[55]

By September 1862, the Preliminary Emancipation Proclamation legally authorized the recruitment of black men. And between the Emancipation Proclamation of January 1, 1863, and the end of the war, nearly 200,000 black men had enlisted. The Civil War then did become "a black man's war," with black men wanting and willing to fight for equal protection and freedom. Christian Fleetwood, an educated freedman, enlisted in 1863 to end slavery and the discrimination he and all blacks suffered.[56] That former bondsmen fought for their own freedom and the freedom of all Southern captives is plainly evident. A sergeant in the 107th Infantry said that he fought "to break the chain and exclaim Freedom for all."[57] Port Hudson, Milliken's Bend, and Fort Wagner, to name a few black engagements, may not have produced Union victories, but they proved, against racist assumptions to the contrary, that black men were, indeed, aggressive and determined fighters. After the battle of Port Hudson, black volunteers' first engagement, *The New York Times* enthused, "It is no longer possible to doubt the bravery and steadfastness of the colored race when properly led." The article hinted at the fact that white leadership proved weak in the string of military encounters that used black troops. However, black resolve remained steady, especially after the Fort Pillow massacre, in which Confederate General Nathan Bedford Forrest's troops killed surrendering black and white troops.[58]

Enlistment, however, meant great risks to preserve family. When Samuel Ballton heard talk of the war and liberation, "his young heart was fired ... and the thought of liberty for his sweetheart and himself was uppermost in his mind."[59] After his escape from enforced labor on Confederate works, he made his way eventually back to his wife's plantation and proudly announced, "Rebecca, I'm going to take you to freedom with me."[60] He then led his wife, her mother, and two other slaves to freedom. With his wife ensconced in Alexandria, he worked for a while and then traveled, in 1864, to Boston and enlisted in the Fifth Massachusetts Cavalry. His regiment was given the honor of being the first troop to enter Richmond on April 3, 1865. One of his officers raised the U.S. flag on the courthouse.[61] Octave Johnson of Louisiana took similar risks to join the Union effort. It was his community, however, that enabled him to enlist. Overworked and threatened by a cruel overseer, Johnson escaped into woods and thereafter collected a group of 30 fellow slaves to keep alive and away from the hounds. Slaves on his plantation supplied the runaways with matches and necessities. Sometime later, Johnson escaped to Camp Parapet, where he worked in the Commissary Office and then enlisted.[62]

Unidentified African American Union soldier with wife and two daughters. (Library of Congress)

The temptation to escape from slavery and family may have prompted some men to enlist, but the burning desire to change their way of life meant sacrifice rather than complete self-interest. Solomon Bradley witnessed the torture of a slave woman by a master. After that, he prayed the Lord would release his people from bondage. He enlisted to fight for liberty. He said, "I could not feel right so long as I was not in the regiment." Bradley's slave family was sold and he never saw them again. He married for a second time, in October 1862, and enlisted in the 21st Colored Troops on August 27, 1863. Promoted to sergeant, he died of typhoid fever on October 22, 1864.[63] Enlisted men believed the government had the duty to liberate their families still in bondage in the far reaches of the South. Joseph J. Harris, in Florida, begged his commanding general to cross the Mississippi into Louisiana and free his father, mother, and brothers, along with their wives and children. Some men did not ask permission and simply raided plantations, plundering and removing their families.[64] Lucy Chase noted that, in order to protect contrabands, black troops invited 400 of them into the Union army's Norfolk camp. There, Chase saw a mother and daughter reunited; the daughter had been separated from the mother as a baby.[65]

The actions of black troops in emancipating slave families and thus bringing about incidences of reunion among long-separated family members demonstrated the tension between loyalty and justice: loyalty to family and the just struggle for liberty. Some marriages dissolved with emancipation, and tragically, for great numbers of former bondsmen and bondswomen, emancipation could not eradicate the loss of family members by separation and sale. Certainly, African Americans' loyalty was to a principle of freedom.[66] But freedom included freedom to create, protect, and raise a family without ownership by whites—a new principle of bonding. Loyalty to family, however, strained loyalty to the Union when the government proved insufficient to protect those self-same black families.

The third stage of black patriotism emerged with protests in the military to protect their families. In this stage, the recruits recognized that their ordinary familial commitments created a sounder basis for a moral existence than an abstract loyalty that promised equality but practiced inequality. When enlistment of black men after 1863 became Union policy, so did federal discrimination and abuse of recruits. Black men in the army endured unequal pay, lack of promotion to commissioned ranks, and in some cases, impressment. Black soldiers were promised equal pay on enlistment, but that proved false. Black attempts to change the country's discriminatory military policy placed a greater personal burden on individuals and certainly marked their actions as virtuous. Segregated into black regiments, black men found a certain solidarity in the ranks that supported protests. And some of their noncommissioned officers provided leadership and support. Then, with a measure of hope, recruits had reason to protest successfully.

Black sergeants, the highest rank afforded to black men, proved their mettle in battle and in protest. Christian Fleetwood is a case in point. Ambivalent about enlistment, but driven by a desire to end slavery and racial prejudice, he joined the army. Fleetwood, a Baltimore shipyard clerk and journalist, had all the credentials for commissioned officer but, because of his race, rose only to the highest rank of a noncommissioned officer, sergeant major. For his bravery in action at the battle of New Market Heights, Congress awarded him the Medal of Honor. Yet, Fleetwood and the men of his unit had to forage and loot in order to support themselves and their families. The federal government offered support to white military families but not black military families.[67] Other sergeants played a crucial role in protest movements for equal pay. They and their men protested because they believed that somehow justice might be done. Sergeant Hiram Peterson wrote his father from Camp Casey, in Washington, D.C., on October 24, 1863, "[I] am willing to bee a soldier and serve my time faithful like a man but i think it is hard to bee poot off in sutch a dogesh maner as that." Sergeant Peterson added, "7 dolars a month and half rations is rather hard."[68] His father, indignant over the

unequal treatment, demanded a response from the secretary of war. Aaron
Peterson wrote:

> [N]ow what I wish to know is whether the sum of Seven dollars, per
> month is all that colored drafted men from this state are entitled to.
> my son supposed & so did I that he would receive the same pay, as
> white Soldiers He is a truly loyal Boy and says, he will serve his
> Country faithfully, but thinks there must be something wrong in rela-
> tion to his receiving only Seven dollars per month. pay . . . your reply
> will settle the matter and will be appreciated by a colored man who,
> is willing to sacrifice his son in the cause of Freedom & humanity.[69]

Some regiments refused any pay for a year, rather than be forced to
accept meager wages.[70] Northern African American communities that
raised volunteers from 70 percent of their recruitment-age men recoiled
at the news that the government deprived those same men of equal pay
and abused them. Thomas D. Freeman, of Boston, complained of no pay
for a year. He compared his service experience to slavery. He said that,
if a recruit claimed illness, he was "gaged, bucked and locked up" by the
army. As to promises of equality, Freeman stated baldly, "We were
deceived."[71] Most dramatically, Sergeant William Walker and men in
the Third South Carolina Volunteers laid down their arms until they
received equal pay. Charged with mutiny, Sergeant Walker pleaded in
his defense that his men had been deprived of their rightful pay and that
the officers of his regiment were "tyrannical in the extreme." He claimed
that it was this treatment that led to the strike. Walker was ordered
executed on February 29, 1864.[72] The disparity in pay weighed heavily
on families. Northern and Southern African American wives complained
that they suffered because their husbands and sons were not paid.[73]
Unequal pay and discriminatory treatment roiled black ranks until
June 15, 1864, when Congress legislated equal pay. Black volunteers, then,
successfully defended their rights for equal protection under the law. Equal
pay, however, remained slow to materialize. Family, community, and volunteer solidarity provided support for the protests. Patriotism exerted itself
in the protests, which touched a fundamental indignity and threat to
peaceful, lawful social coexistence.

Federal policy extending protection to the families of black enlistees
had not even the same limited success as the equal-pay issue. Enlistment
of husbands and family members placed heavy burdens on the family.
Enslaved families of recruits faced eviction or extra work to pick up the
slack of the missing male hand. Kidnappings, beatings, and death threats

followed in the wake of slave men's enlistment. An African American recruiter in Indiana wrote to the secretary of war decrying the kidnappings of contraband women and children. Former masters wrested them back into slavery in Kentucky.[74] Sergeant Whitson of a black company reported that "the wives of Simon Williamson and Richard Beasley has again been whipped by their Master most unmercifully."[75] Their master, John Crowder, beat them if they received any letters from their husbands. One woman reported that her master, R. L. Moore, threatened to kill "every woman that he knows that has got a husband in the army."[76] Wives directed their plight to husbands, who, in turn, complained to their noncommissioned black officers and up the chain of command. Slave wives of enlisted men endured intense abuse; yet, they held to freedom and freedom's cause. They, too, protested and hoped for protection.

Even more tragic for military families, impressment presented an oppressive circumstance, an irrational burden placed on those least able to bear it. Jane Wallis of York County, Virginia, wrote that her husband had been taken by federal forces unwillingly. She could not understand why the army would seize him, since he lived in such poor health. She pleaded that "if they keep him, they leave me, and 3 children, to get along, the best we can, and one of them is now verry sick." Those men who refused to enlist in order to support their families were threatened with musket fire, or they found impressment accompanied by punishment such as confinement "in the guard house [subsisting] on bread and water."[77]

Black soldiers agonized over the plight of their families while they served in the military, some involuntarily. The promise of equal pay and protection for the families of servicemen rarely materialized. Recruits found themselves helpless to defend and support their destitute families. However, they resisted ill-treatment of their families whenever they could. The sorest point of contention remained the contraband camps. Crowded, disease ridden, they presented a woeful problem for military families. When families fled slave conditions, they often did so with only the clothes on their backs. The contraband camps provided scarce amounts of clothing, no matter how generous charitable organizations were with donations. Federal troops evacuated islands of refuge, such as Edisto, and, therefore, disrupted seasonal plantings and left 2,000 people unemployed. As younger and healthier freed persons left the camps and drifted elsewhere, the aged and infirm remained isolated and largely uncared for, with a few relations who tended to them without many resources.[78] Probably the most damning evidence of federal neglect in the administration of the contraband camps came from Lucy Chase, an American Missionary Association volunteer in Portsmouth, Virginia, on

May 10, 1863. She attested that, on Crany Island, one of the most notorious of the camps, individuals died "by the thousands." In November 1863, Chase reported the overwhelming number of contrabands who entered Norfolk, Virginia. She said that 500 indigent blacks had recently arrived following on the heels of forces in search of guerilla fighters. Then, two weeks after that, 400 "Negros arrived at the invitation of Negro troops." Conditions for Southern refugees may be imagined, as a black soldier reported that no medical care existed in New Bern and that those who died of small pox were hastily buried without even a coffin. Rebel attacks and Union plundering kept contrabands on the move and destitute.[79]

Forty-five impressed soldiers who had not been paid, the most vulnerable of men, valiantly petitioned the Federal Commander of Virginia and North Carolina to relieve their families' distress and to protest lack of pay and protect their families. Their petition rings with the clarity of injustice:

> [W]e have not been paid for our work don at Roanoke, consequently our wives and family's are there suffering for clothes. Captn james has paid us for only two months work this year, the month's of February and January. No one knows the injustice practiced on the negro's at Roanoke, our garden's are plundere'd by the white soldiers. what we raise to suport ourselves with is stolen from us, and if we say anything about it we are sent to the guard house . . . its no uncommon thing to see weman and children crying for something to eat.[80]

Forty-five men gathered together to sign the petition. Their solidarity and consciousness of the rights of citizens infused their action with a sense of belonging to a command and government that would hear their appeal. Black soldiers affirmed their readiness to obey orders to put down the rebellion, but they despaired of relieving their suffering families. However, if petitions and lawful action failed, there were black recruits who took up arms against attempts to close the contraband camps, thereby depriving their families of shelter.[81] Such men despaired and lost confidence in government protection. As one recruit wrote, "[N]ever was we any more treated Like slaves then wee are now in our Lives."[82] At the end of the war, the federal army discharged black regiments last, since, ostensibly, they were the last recruited. Sent west to subdue remnants of resistance, men objected to separation from families. At least when close to their families, they had an opportunity to defend them. Later, discharge presented the problem of where to settle their families.

The nature of slaves' and repatriated slaves' identity and community is important in understanding transference of loyalty to the Union.

According to Michael Kammen, if an individual's identity is, indeed, fluid, then patriotism or loyalty is easier to assimilate.[83] Elizabeth Regosin and David Shaffer examined pension affidavits and noted the fluidity of black identity, since petitioners used aliases upon leaving slavery or chose different names upon enlistment in the army. Veterans' dependants explained their own name changes as the product of sale, individual choice after the war, illiteracy, or the incorrect recording of names, according to sound. Witnesses, depositions, and affidavits were needed to support petitioners' appeals to prove veteran identity or relation to the Civil War soldier. Identity was a matter of choice. However, while the name changes may have confused U.S. pension agents, they did not deter blacks from what Blassingame called "a core sense of belonging to one another."[84] Nonetheless, regardless of name changes and the assumption of new identities, in the case of the slave or freed person, race inhibited assimilation. Sarah Fitzpatrick, in 1938 looking back over a life lived in slavery and in freedom, admitted to fears of violence and racist retaliation in the United States. She explained, "See de 'Nigger' ain't got no law, no flag, no nothin. He lives under de white man's law, da's whut keeps him dis sad isfied, and nuverous all de time."[85] In the postwar years, the flag offered blacks only tenuous protection.

Migration and resettlement offered new challenges to the development of African American patriotism. Low wages or no wages and lack of transportation kept freed persons in Southern poverty.[86] Familiarity of place offered, at least, some sense of belonging. In the estimation of Ira Berlin, 90 percent of African Americans remained in the South after the Civil War and before World War I.[87] Thus, loyalty in black culture moved outward only gradually from the family and their proto-kin's place of origin to the riskier areas of employment and, later, settlement. That African Americans regarded their place of birth as a significant marker of identity can be seen in slave testimony. Liberated in boyhood, ex-slave "Uncle Ben" said of his Alabama home, "Den the war ended and here I is, where I was in de ole days." Jennie Hill remembered that, after emancipation, parents and children who had been separated by sale searched desperately for each other and nearly always failed. In the end, Jennie lamented, "[T]he children of slaves lost their identity when they were taken from the place of their birth into a new country."[88] John Jackson, who experienced many owners, among them Robert E. Lee, felt Missouri his true home. He returned there after serving as a private in the Union army. In Missouri, he raised pumpkins and married at age 100.[89] Horatio Eden preferred to remain in Tennessee, because he fared well as a professional bather, catering to the Southern white classes there.[90]

Bondsmen who fled to Canada found safety, but often at the sacrifice of their families. Lewis Richardson said, "I can truly say that I have only one thing to lament over, and that is my bereft wife, who is yet in bondage." His ill-usage by Henry Clay and his overseer prompted him to "flee from under the American eagle and take shelter under the British crown."[91] In 1844, Henry Bibb, who ran away several times from his masters, finally escaped to Detroit and Canada. Unable to retrieve his wife and child from slavery, he could only upbraid his former master for the lashing of his wife and beating of his child.[92] James Smith, who left his wife in Virginia, settled for some years in Ohio, but, with the passage of the Fugitive Slave Law, a warrant went out for his arrest. After that, Smith fled to Canada, where, after 17 years, he reunited with his wife.[93] Canada, a sure place of refuge, promised only tenuous bonds with family and, therefore, only a small prospect of a sense of belonging based on family ties.

Where African Americans felt they belonged became quite clear. Whether out of poverty, family loyalty, lack of transportation, Northern prejudice, or sheer choice, the majority of African Americans remained in the South. Thus, the extent to which Southern blacks could benefit from the national ideology remained limited, at best. Northern whites, including abolitionists, felt a certain reform fatigue, having vanquished the slave system. Reconstruction policy struggled to offer more beyond freedom from slavery. African Americans, therefore, looked to the federal government for protection of their rights as citizens with the passage of the Fourteenth Amendment. However, since "Forty Acres and a mule" proved a postwar myth, freedmen and freedwomen assumed ownership of a home meant a stake in citizenship. Henry Baker of Alabama said, "A 'nigger' is got tuh come round tuh de p'int wha he own his own home wherevah he lives." And, furthermore, he said plaintively, "I wanna be a citizen here es eny other citizen. I don't think hit is no harm for nobody tuh want tuh be a citizen uv de country wha he lives in."[94] Nonetheless, racial prejudice stymied radical efforts, leaving African Americans with an ambivalence toward the national government.

The national government itself held a contradictory opinion toward the newly freed black population. Northern opinion divided on the question of where to settle former slaves. The Superintendent of Negro Affairs in the First District of Virginia and North Carolina, Charles B. Wilder, provided families with tools and encouraged them to cultivate crops. Subsistence rations carried the families to harvest. The first district superintendent believed "that the paramount object of our labors, is the elevation of the colored race." As such, he outlined a plan of preaching, teaching, and living among the freedmen and freedwomen to bring knowledge and provide an example to an industrious people. Furthermore, he believed that experienced businessmen and farmers needed to work with ex-slaves and thus inspire them with the "true idea of liberty." Charles Wilder had no doubt that such a plan would "determine the status of the negro" and convince "an unbelieving world that the colored race are capable of self-support and elevation to citizenship with all its responsibilities."[95] Wilder's optimism contrasted with military oversight in the Fourth District of the Virginia Department of Negro Affairs. Lieutenant Colonel Frank J. White described conditions as he found them in February 1865: poverty, immorality, idleness. He, therefore, had no confidence in humanitarian or religious uplift.[96] As to where a million former slaves should settle, he had a decided answer:

> Not in New England. Her cities, fields and forests can only maintain men whose intellects are fitted for the learned professions or the enterprise of commerce, and sinewy sons of toil accustomed to unremitting labor and exposure. Not in the Middle States, where upon the return of our armies the labor markets will be supplied by men with whom the African could not compete: Nor in the free States of the West needed for our unceasing Emigration.[97]

Thus, black citizenship remained constrained and cosseted in the South immediately after the Civil War.

Postwar African American patriotism proved fragile and tenuous. Place held family and, wherever African Americans settled, families reconstituted and struggled to make a living. Those who remained in the South remained loyal to the black "nation" of the displaced and dispossessed and only gradually, sometimes through the work of former Union recruits, formed a broader national consciousness.[98] The South, the locus of family bonds, remained in the imagination, if not in the reality, of emigrants. Despite hardships suffered in the South, only a small number of ex-bondsmen and women migrated North. And few of the Southern black refugees who traveled North prospered, as Isaac H. Hunter did. He worked as a shoemaker in Raleigh, North Carolina. With the money he set aside from his earnings, and with contributions from Northern patrons, he bought his wife and children out of bondage. Hunter proved "an honest and industrious mechanic" in Brooklyn, New York. His family belonged to the Methodist Episcopal Church.[99] If prosperity meant attaining the goal of citizenship, then only a minority attained it. Massachusetts, which hosted leading centers of abolitionist radicalism, recognized black civil rights, boasted of nonsegregated public schools, and aided black refugees in finding housing and employment; yet, the state's support proved inadequate to sustain any but subsistence living. As a black "nation" displaced, ex-slaves dreamed of going home, back to the South. John Andrew Jackson, living in Rochester, New York, told his story to a reporter in 1893: "I came back to this country after the war. I'm getting old and feeble and I only want to live till I get the money for the Home, and then I will go down to Old Carliny and there is where I want to die, down in my old cabin home."[100] Charles C. Skinner, of Maine, sighed, "For a long time I have been thinking about going back to North Carolina to see if I could get any trace of my mother or my brothers, and as the years roll along the longing grows stronger. I'm 66 now, however and don't suppose I shall ever get back to the old plantation."[101] Displacement and widespread poverty made patriotism ambivalent, elusive.

Elizabeth Hafkin Pleck's study of postwar Boston traced the effect of poverty upon family and community. Chain migration from Virginia cities and, to a lesser extent, the countryside provided domestic and menial jobs to African American migrants. Whether free or ex-slaves, few blacks advanced economically. In addition, segregation, high mortality rates, sparse ownership of homes, and sparse capital accumulation for business proved obstacles to full citizenship. However, Pleck recognized the rich Southern culture that evolved in Boston around kin, community, and the Southern Baptist church. Despite such vibrancy, Pleck made clear the terrible toll poverty took on the African American family. Unemployment led to separation and divorce in one-third of black families. It was Northern-born upper-class professional black Yankees and the second generation of Southern black Bostonians who claimed their rights and defended their patriotism. The author quoted Elijah Smith, who argued, "What constitutes a native but birth on the soil? We were born and toiled here. The proud title of American is ours, therefore, by birth, by blood, and by toil." The lower class celebrated election day by public demonstrations and participation in Veterans Day parades.[102] Nonetheless, birth, blood, and toil did not confer full citizenship on displaced Southern blacks nor the black Yankee.

Worcester, Massachusetts, may be an exception to New England's limited response to black civil rights and ambivalent black patriotism. Historian Janette Thomas Greenwood, in her study of black migration to Worcester, traced the evolution of patriotism among the city's African Americans from the prewar period to the late 19th and early 20th centuries. Prior to the war, a few hundred mostly black Yankee and Southern-born African Americans joined abolitionist efforts to defend runaway slaves from the Fugitive Slave Law. Former slaves found Worcester congenial because Worcester County consistently voted antislavery and because of the highly organized black Yankee community that aided contrabands in finding homes and employment. Nonetheless, discrimination consigned blacks to domestic or unskilled labor jobs. Very few African Americans owned homes. After the war, the white community largely abandoned the black community. However, Southern horrors of lynching, Jim Crow, and disenfranchisement prompted a newly energized Worcester black community to demand civil rights. Organized in churches, veterans' posts, lodges and auxiliaries, and sororal and fraternal groups, African Americans celebrated West Indian and American emancipation days, and Memorial Day. Thus, African Americans insisted on the centrality of liberation and civil rights as the enduring legacy of the Civil War. Truly, Worcester African Americans evinced Alexis de Tocqueville's term, a "well considered" patriotism,[103] or the rational interest that led to participation in government. Central to Janette Thomas Greenwood's history of the African American Worcester community is the role of the black Yankees.[104]

William Brown's family is illustrative of the deep roots and humanitarian efforts of Worcester's black Yankees and their loyal generational quest for freedom and civil rights. John Moore, William Brown's grandfather, a free "negro," was born in New York in 1751, fought in the Battle of Lexington during the American Revolutionary War, and lived the life of a seaman. Moore sailed to Nova Scotia and then to Spain. He won the recommendation of a Mr. Wentworth of Halifax, who attested that Moore was a "sober, honest man and a useful servant." Upon leaving service, Moore owned a store near the Boston Harbor. At some point, however, Moore applied for Seaman's Relief and, in so doing, declared that he was a citizen of the United States, born in New York and now residing in Boston. He did not remain in poverty. By 1819, Moore had bought a piece of property from John Brown for $250. And, as a reliable and stable family member, toward the end of his life a court order appointed him the guardian of William Brown.[105]

William Brown, born in 1824 to Alice Bush Brown and John Brown, made his way as an upholsterer. He had early advice on how to run a business from the white firm of Kittridge and Blakes, Upholsterers and Importers, located in Boston. By the age of 25, William catered to many of Boston's elite white families and could boast of his prosperity.[106] His good fortune placed him in the category of much less than one percent of the tiny prewar black population of Worcester. Greenwood reports that black-owned businesses supplied jobs to contrabands.[107] Yet, William Brown may have been discriminating in his employment. He informed his partner, S. H. Bowman, that he would not take on his son in the

William Brown. (Courtesy of the American Antiquarian Society)

business. Nonetheless, he and other successful black Yankees found work and homes for ex-slaves. In addition, William Brown's family belonged to the Vigilance Committee and Freedom Club, which meant they were determined to protect the runaway slaves from the reach of the Fugitive Slave Law. Mrs. William Brown headed the Colored Freemen's Aid Society and contributed money and time to the support of Lunsford Lane's manual-labor school. At all times, the family joined in the political currents that promoted antislavery. Alice Bush attended a Free Soil Tea Party and a friend in Washington informed William Brown of the latest obstructions of the Democratic Party to the cause of freedom. And during the war, Brown received many letters from black soldiers who complained of their plight. They wrote to him as a family member or friend and as a man of influence.[108] Theirs was a patriotism in the service of liberation and humanitarianism that preserved Southern black culture and re-formed it into the basis of a new diversity within American society.

African American Civil War experience proved that patriots may have multiple identities[109] that evolve and clarify over time. These identities determine loyalties. The familial loyalty, sharpened by the grief of separation, propelled individuals to expand family and communal bonds, thereby reinforcing interdependence. Supported by their families, men coalesced in the rigor of military discipline and took on the larger cause of freedom and emancipation. Ultimately, family identity and universal cause clashed in the tragic issue of federal provision for military families. Men chose to protect their families and fight for freedom. Thus, their bonds of obligation reimagined patriotism as a fusion of identities. Theirs was not an either/or choice; both choices, moral and necessary, proved patriotism a virtue. If virtue is a value expressed, then blacks continued to practice patriotism as a virtue, to claim civil rights in the postwar period.

By the time of the Civil War, the proud boast of slave or freedman that his ancestor had fought for freedom in the American Revolution had shifted, and family and place mattered about as much as freedom. Loyalties overlapped; the moral consideration of freedom for individuals and a people could not be attained without the protection and elevation of families. Such patriotism could not have been expressed without the experience and struggle of a family institution adapted to freedom. Daniel's children saw visions, dreamed dreams, and headed into the whirl-wind of death, disease, starvation, only to survive and celebrate deliver-ance. Such conversion of spirit and body took time, since most ex-slaves remained in the place of birth out of sentiment and poverty. Enlisted men, taken out of their homeland, fought bravely for their freedom and the freedom of all their people. Nonetheless, their loyalty remained strong in fighting for their family's rights—rights that in time proved the struggle virtuous. Patriotism grew as blacks secured civil rights and enjoyed protec-tion of person and property. Liberation, enlistment, and the sacrifice of families evinced solidarity in the ranks and in families. Here was a patriot-ism that defied the separation of loyalties into greater and lesser, universal and particular.

5

❖❖❖

The Challenge of Moral Commitment in Three Civil War Families

He has sounded forth the trumpet that shall never call retreat.
—Julia Ward Howe[1]

My own, loved native home!
—Alexander Beaufort Meek[2]

Northern and Southern commitment to a long and bloody war tested the power of regional affiliation. Individuals, associations, and movements all sustained, with varied strength, the prewar buildup and massive undertaking of war North and South.[3] But none bore the duty, obligation, and sacrifice on the home front as consistently and intimately as the family. That is, the measure of moral commitment lay within the family structure and depended on its morale, moral discipline, and courage.

Commitment stabilizes, guides action, and is markedly characteristic of identity.[4] It may constitute virtue if it consistently adheres to what is true, fair, or equitable. Philosopher Alasdair MacIntyre argues even further that virtue, of adhering to a rational principle, cannot exist without a sense of vulnerability and a consciousness of the vulnerabilities or disabilities of others.[5] Commitment that recognizes vulnerability in oneself and others may begin in weakness, but aims to build strength and solidarity. The Civil War generation claimed commitment as a virtue in perfectionism, confederation, and union. Such claims needed to be tested against their ability to sustain a flourishing community.

Three families demonstrate the strengths and weaknesses of commitment in the years before and during the Civil War: the abolitionist Weston/Chapman family of Massachusetts, the slaveholding Devereux/Edmondston family of North Carolina, and the unstable Boston family of William Sever Lincoln. In all three families, the durability of family affiliation proved significant in sustaining commitment to a cause. Yet, commitment as a virtue often proved elusive in wartime as individuals and families shunned any display of weakness. Maria Weston Chapman and her family possessed a highly developed New England conscience that held to radical Garrisonian principles of abolition and nonresistance. Unarguably, Weston Chapman, with the support of her sisters, developed one of the most enduring abolitionist networks in the North.[6] Yet, she could countenance no opinion or strategy outside her own or her family's, causing consternation among her allies. Catherine Ann Edmondston, despite her father's Unionist sympathy, interpreted the Confederate cause in terms of freedom to own slaves but resisted government attempts to commandeer Edmondston slaves for that same cause. If the government could not protect family property, Edmondston could not support the government. Edmondston, devoted to her husband, wished to maintain their social status. When William Sever Lincoln, the son of Governor Levi Lincoln of Massachusetts, emigrated West, he nearly cut off ties with his parents and almost ruined his marriage. Later, he reconciled with his wife and family, returned home, and enlisted in the national cause. Affiliation proves strong in its power to direct moral energy, but also, as in the case of the Devereux/Edmondston family, affiliation can become an end in itself and serve an immoral purpose.

THE WESTON/CHAPMAN FAMILY

The full dimension of Maria Weston Chapman's commitment to reform cannot be understood unless we examine her family model. Weston Chapman acted as a centrifugal force that propelled family members into disparate reform associations. The Westons and Chapmans acted together but often also acted as individuals or as individual organizers of reform organizations. Activists often remarked on the presence of the Weston sisters at various reform events, especially at the antislavery fairs. It appears that, throughout their careers, Maria, one of six daughters and two sons, remained the motivator and leader of the clan. This upper-middle-class family lived on a farm in Weymouth; later, the parents, Warren and Nancy Bates Weston, established a residence in Boston. Anne Warren Weston, their daughter, would later recall, "There are no virtues that the house of Weston prizes in others beyond fidelity and constancy."[7] The youthful Maria, educated locally and in England, regarded her younger siblings with a certain patronizing attitude. From London, she wrote to her sisters: "I wish you would be here with me but as that is impossible. I can only wish that you may continue to improve yourselves as much as possible, to be good and affectionate daughters, kind to your brothers, obedient and industrious."[8]

Maria moved back home in 1828 to accept a position as the principal of Ebenezer Bailey's Young Ladies High School in Boston. Her sisters Deborah and Anne Weston followed Maria's example and headed their own elite school for girls. Later, sisters Caroline and Anne Weston taught school in Boston and Deborah taught for a period of time in New Bedford.[9]

Shortly after meeting Henry Chapman, Maria Weston resigned her principalship and married the wealthy businessman in 1830. Associated with the Boston Brahmins but set apart by reform leanings, the Chapmans steered their own social course. Henry had joined the temperance movement in his youth and, as a businessman, boycotted slave-produced goods. Maria cultivated international support for the antislavery cause. Deborah Weston dined with Maria one winter night and sat in wonder as her sister showed her the lock of hair and affectionate note that Harriet Martineau, the continental writer and reformer, had sent Maria. Among Maria's affiliations in Boston society included her Unitarian pastor William Ellery Channing, whom she later rejected as too conservative on the abolition issue, and her cousins Ann and Wendell Phillips who likely appealed to her more radical opinion.[10]

Between 1832 and 1835, Maria Weston Chapman and her sisters performed remarkable feats of organization. In 1834, Maria and her eldest sisters, Caroline, Anne, and Deborah, joined with eight other women to form the Boston Female Anti-Slavery Society (BFASS). The society weighed in as the counterpart to the all-male New England Anti-Slavery Society. The BFASS stepped outside the confines of polite, conservative opinion by espousing the Garrisonian cause of immediate emancipation. Maria maintained the BFASS through divisive internal tensions and, with the aid of her sisters and her extensive social and reform network, expanded its reach. In addition, in 1834, Maria organized the first annual antislavery fair designed to raise consciousness of the cause and funds for the continuance of antislavery endeavors. Many Bostonians donated goods for the cause. Even Thomas Gold Appleton, who might not have had much interest in joining an antislavery organization, sent a box of goods from Paris for sale at the fair. Maria's business acumen and social connections led her to accept executive positions in the Massachusetts Anti-Slavery Society and the American Anti-Slavery Society.[11] Her close association with William Lloyd Garrison meant that her family would carry some of the responsibility in hosting the controversial British charismatic antislavery speaker and activist George Thompson, a friend of Garrison's, to speak throughout Massachusetts.

Making arrangements for Thompson's appearance required great courage of the Westons and the Chapmans. One observer compared Thompson and his power of public speaking to George Whitefield's preaching. Whitefield, also English born, unleashed the Great Awakening, a religious crusade that generated social and political unrest. Thompson aroused forces and interests antithetical to the antislavery cause, even though, as Anne Warren Weston later observed, "he is of a timid nature."[12] Boston textile merchants, even if sympathetic to the plight of slaves, protected their interests in Southern cotton imports and textile exports by resisting the antislavery movement. Religious leaders, some fearful of losing communicants or distrustful of women's leadership, hesitated in supporting antislavery. And from the workingman to the gentleman, the notion of black equality raised the specter of white men's reduced social or economic status. For these reasons, Thompson's arrival stirred passions.

At first, his appearance caused no alarms and Maria entertained him, with her sisters and Anna Chapman, Henry's sister, in attendance, "paying her devotions" to the "great man." That evening, the gathering talked about "the sins of the church." Anne and Deborah Weston then resumed their usual activities attending a Temperance Convention and teaching school. However calm on the surface, Anne requested that her aunt Mary Weston keep Thompson in hiding. Henry and Anna would then pick up the eminent speaker in a cart or carriage to avoid the crowds and any difficulties. Thompson, meanwhile, met privately with interested and influential people. In the afternoon of September 28, 1835, Mary Parker, a BFASS member, called on Caroline Weston to tell her that an antislavery meeting at Abington had been mobbed. That same afternoon, the New England Anti-Slavery Society held its quarterly meeting, which Anne and Deborah Weston attended. Caroline stayed at home, out of fear. As soon as school was over, she hurried down the street and met an abolitionist who reported everything had gone peacefully at the quarterly meeting. Caroline then attended a prayer meeting and reported no mob action.[13]

On October 5, when Thompson spoke, a Mr. Gregg warned of the "throat-cut" intentions of the mob against antislavery adherents. Nonetheless, the BFASS met weekly in spite of threats against them. On October 17, the society invited the membership to its annual meeting at 46 Washington Street, the BFASS's office. Thompson was expected to give an address. The talk around Washington Street was of scourging Thompson because he was a foreigner and former slaveholder. Maria Weston Chapman would have none of it and compared Thompson's career to the lives of the disciples in the Acts of the Apostles. On October 21, the day of the BFASS meeting, Maria claimed a "massing" of men watched her house. Cries resounded on the street as Deborah Weston arrived. Men asked the selectman for Chapman's address, and he pointed it out saying, "Yes, Yes! She's there all the time!" Inside, Maria comforted her aunt Mary, distressed by the mob. Then, a slow ringing of the doorbell unnerved them both. But the doorbell ringing turned out to be that of Willie Garrison, William L. Garrison's son, sent to fetch Maria for an aunt who felt fearful. Maria remained "composed but very resolute," according to Deborah Weston. Henry Chapman, "wonderfully supportive" of his wife and concerned about her personal safely, insisted on accompanying his wife to the meeting.[14]

Maria and her sisters Anne and Caroline went to the BFASS meeting and heard Mary Parker's voice loud and clear as she gave the opening address. Almost instantly, a friend warned Thompson to get out before the lynch mob got to him. As pandemonium outside the meeting quarters increased, Mayor Theodore Lyman arrived at the scene and insisted the meeting disband. The women remained composed, despite the din. Maria protested to the mayor about the absence of police protection and said, resolutely, "If this is the last bulwark of freedom, we may as well die here as anywhere." Calmly, she organized an orderly withdrawal of the women, two by two as they walked through the mob. When the mob could not find Thompson at the meeting, they went for Garrison at his office. The mob seized Garrison and threatened his life with a rope around his neck. In the meantime, the sisters returned to the Chapman home. Some of the mob called out for the Chapmans. Anne felt overwhelmed by the events, while Maria said she "never had such a delightful time in her life." While they waited, they received word of Garrison's protection by a muscular Irish truckman, Arun Cooley, who lifted him out of the crowd, while he and others got Garrison to safety in a Boston jail.[15]

Reform, at base, is relational. As passionate as Maria Weston Chapman felt, and as much as she thrilled to the excitement of events, she acted in a context of family and organizational calm and determination. The mob riot of 1835 threatened not only the BFASS office but also the Chapman home. Opposition to antislavery took a decidedly personal turn and was met with the emotional resources of the Chapman and Weston families. Conscience bound both the reform families and the women of the BFASS, and the subsequent affiliation reinforced conscience. What is so striking about the 1835 mobbing of the BFASS is the contrast of the mob's fear and the reformers' calmness. The women had no vision of future victory but only a faith in the cause and their own identification with those who shared their faith.

Antislavery riots, as pervasive as they were throughout the 1830s, had one positive effect—namely, to raise the consciousness of ordinary Northern folk. The Weston sisters, through debate and organizational activities, began a network of antislavery affiliation throughout Massachusetts. Their views were decidedly Garrisonian: pacifist, perfectionist, anti-institutional, anticlerical. Anne Weston used every opportunity to engage opponents in debate on the subjects. On a crowded stagecoach going from Weymouth to New Bedford, Anne happened to call slaveholders "mansteaders," and that irritated "a haughty young man" who supposed that she did not think "anything at all of the Union." She told him, "[H]e was perfectly correct." No one else on the stagecoach dared enter the debate, according to Anne, "not Mrs. Kempton, [a fellow passenger] too much pinned to her minister's sleeve."[16] At another juncture, Anne had "a good time" arguing with a Mr. Ward about abolition, the woman question, and the (non-abolitionist) clergy.[17]

Abolitionists struggled with conservative religious support for their brand of reform. These clergymen criticized the role of women in the abolitionist movement and pronounced little moral urgency to the cause. Deborah Weston referred to the ineffectual response of religious preachers when she wrote in her diary that she went to the Free Church and "heard a very stupid preacher." She found a more amenable preacher in a Reverend Gannet, who spoke about duty "as if he had some sense of what it consisted in." However, she remained dubious about the preacher's dedication to the cause, as she continued, "I should much enjoy the prospects if I could see his *society* determined to go for ... abolition." Later, the Reverend Gannet termed abolitionists "the children of this world," as opposed to his "righteous" congregation, whom he characterized as "children of light."[18] And Henry B. Stanton, a leading abolitionist who eschewed women's leadership and sided with the clericalists, sent Anne Weston his

latest circular, which she praised, but she added: "You have made it difficult for us to support you. We firmly support Garrison." She wrote,

> But now those clerical Abolitionists who term the pro-slavery minis-
> try of Boston "our brethren" and the abolitionists our opponents we
> pray to be delivered. We begin to see the inconsistency of denounc-
> ing Southern ministers as "man-stealers" and at the same time
> upholding Northern ministers in the justification of . . . man stealing
> and social murder.[19]

The Westons believed in the abolitionist cause above state, church, and
any restricted role of women. That cost the movement solidarity;
abolitionist ruptures would only heal with the outbreak of the war.

From 1835 through the 1840s, Maria Weston Chapman's reform influence expanded as she held important concurrent positions. Her mind
worked "like a fulling mill,"[20] priming and pumping up the whole cloth
of antislavery reform in Boston. As corresponding secretary of the
BFASS, she became its chief propagandist, writing the annual reports
between 1836 and 1844, later published as *Right and Wrong in
Massachusetts*. The report detailed the "obstacles thrown in the way of
emancipation." In it, she catalogued the clericalists' criticism of antislavery
women acting as "free agents," clergy's fear of abolition causing division in
the church, and certain ministers' abhorrence of Garrison and his feminist
and pacifist principles.[21]

She praised Garrison for his defense of liberty in the *Liberator* and noted
that the principles associated with the call of liberty are "identical with
those of Christianity herself." In identifying Christianity as female,
Chapman emphasized that rights should be extended to all human beings,
including women. Along with Garrison, Chapman and the Westons supported a "come outer" policy of enticing church members away from anti-
reform churches. Moreover, Garrisonians adhered to nonresistance pacifist
principles that included abjuration of war and involvement in the politics
of voting.[22] Chapman defended Garrison's purity of intent and action in
upholding immediate abolition with no compromise on the principles of
equality and emancipation. For her, the cause contained an indivisible
truth—freedom, in which all moral questions existed inseparably. Thus,
she identified those who opposed immediate emancipation and nonresistance—the clericalists, the American Unionists, and conservative
women's groups—as those "whose moving spirit is the same—hatred of
the freedom that defies their control." Although professing support for
emancipation, such opponents hated "the free spirit" of the abolitionists.[23]

Maria Weston Chapman. (Collection of the Massachusetts Historical Society)

"The cause" was the freeing spirit that drove her and animated others through her. What she failed to understand was her need for control.

Her position as corresponding secretary in the BFASS enabled her to command considerable influence as a Garrisonian abolitionist. Conservative members also had to deal with the fact that she controlled the association's major policy by serving on the central committee of the BFASS. At the same time, she served on the business committee of the Massachusetts Anti-Slavery Committee and the executive board of the American Anti-Slavery Committee, thus ensuring radical abolitionism's place in those major committees.[24] Chapman, with her regional influence, had little regard for the New York Anti-Slavery Society, which remained neutral in Garrisonian contests with churchmen.[25]

She and her sisters, meanwhile, spread the reach of the Boston organizational hub. Maria and Anne organized the Weymouth Female

Anti-Slavery Society of about 30 members. Caroline "turned pedlar," going door to door soliciting funds for the Boston antislavery fair.[26] Debora Weston proudly reported that the New Bedford Female Anti-Slavery Society raised 100 dollars for the cause. She did not have her sister Maria's aggressive or fighting spirit, however, since she demurred accepting the vice-presidency of the organization because 11 blacks had applied for membership, causing a split among the women. She preferred not to engage in the fray. Nonetheless, in Salem and New Bedford, she tirelessly petitioned for congressional action on the abolition question.[27] Petitioning sometimes meant persuasion, along with a request to sign the petition. As one woman whom Debora interviewed said of slaves, "[N]o, I don't want 'em free ... let'em be where they will."[28] Gathering signatures on the petitions laid the groundwork for a Female Anti-Slavery Association in Salem. Anne Weston celebrated the success of the Westford Women's Anti-Slavery Association meeting that hosted Quaker activists Sarah and Angelina Grimke, since 300 women came out in the pouring rain to hear them. And, together, Anne and Maria traveled up and down Temple Street in Boston seeking signatures for their abolition petitions.[29]

In the 1830s and 1840s, Maria Weston Chapman also wrote for the cause. In Garrison's absences, she edited the *Liberator*. She also edited the *Non-Resistant*, a Garrisonian pacifist publication. She initially refused to accept editorship of the *National Anti-Slavery Standard*, because "duty keeps me here,"[30] she said. Her husband, Henry Chapman, died in 1842, leaving her to care for her four children. Yet, despite her family responsibilities, in 1844, she co-edited the New York-based *National Anti-Slavery Standard*. Her sister-in-law, Mary Gray Chapman, supported her efforts by contributing financially to the *Standard*.[31] Her other editing work included the popular annual gift book *Liberty Bell*. The anthology was published at various times until 1846 in conjunction with the antislavery fairs. The antislavery fairs had been organized by Maria and Anne Weston in 1834. A number of the contributors to the *Liberty Bell*—Lydia Maria Child, James Russell Lowell, and Wendell Phillips—were closely associated with Chapman. In 1848, she encouraged Jonathan Walker to publish his account of arrest, torture, and imprisonment for his aid to fugitive Florida slaves. She edited and wrote a preface to his manuscript detailing his ordeal. As an editor, she saw in Walker's account "the good, forgiving, self-denying spirit of the Christian, the indomitable determination of the Freedman and the severe devotedness of the Puritan."[32] In Walker's narrative, Chapman may have recognized the self-critical, self-denying, but determined qualities in herself.

As strong willed, imperious, and domineering as she was, Chapman never considered herself a "fanatical" abolitionist.[33] She engaged in self-reflection and dealt with her demons of self-worth and anger. Catherine Clinton notes how she struggled with her "shortcomings." Maria Weston Chapman berated herself, "How heretical, harsh, fanatical, moon-struck, unsexed am I. I hate much."[34] The indomitable courage she displayed at the Thompson affair in 1835 vanished in 1838. She gave a speech at Pennsylvania Hall while an angry mob gathered. The women feared for their lives and escaped before the mob burned down the hall. On the train back from Philadelphia, she had a breakdown and had to be hospitalized in Stonington, Connecticut. She recovered quickly but never gave another public address. When her husband died, she lamented that she had been "worn down to quietness."[35] It was grief that "wore down" her natural egoistic inclinations. And, influenced by Angelina and Sarah Grimke, Maria Weston Chapman asked, when proposing a course of action, "[H]ow does it feel to thee?"[36] Clearly, Chapman felt compelled, at times, to balance rationality with an emotional sense of things.

In 1846, she wrote a letter of consolation to James Russell Lowell, the poet, when Lowell lost his wife. At the same time, Maria Weston Chapman mourned the death of a close friend. She wrote:

> You know S. Hilbrick and his wife? Sober, plain, unimaginative people—it is of *her* I wish to speak now. I had never thought her a person of much thought, observation or depth of feeling. After the loss of which I speak, she stepped up to me in the crowded street with a look of sympathy, and said, "we have heard of thy sorrow. *How does it Feel to thee?* for there are *two* ways."
>
> It was a new thing to me—I did not know, and had never had a reason to think of the subject. But it was a touch of nature deeper than the voice that comes to us from tradition or theology. I answered from the same depths, "it feels as if her life had been poured out in to this summer air, to comfort me." And so it did and so death always comes to me. I thought and expected *before* that I should have gone mad. I felt *after*, as if my selfish bitterness of sorrow had been washed away by my natural tears . . . I cannot refer this to any opinions or faith, as the words are commonly understood. But the thing, whatever it is, that makes us forget ourselves in our fellow-creatures—that remains, when the personal presence of the other self is removed.
>
> The *Cause* has been the paraclete to me. May it be so to you my dear friend.[37]

Loss, at various times, of self-control, of self-regard, the death of her husband, and, finally, the crisis involved in the death of an intimate friend, broke open new ways of being for Maria Weston Chapman. She experienced, momentarily, an intellectual conversion—that is, a loss of self, beyond sense perception, into a "way of seeing as mystics see."[38] Maria's personal Pentecost slowly changed her conception of the cause. In 1848, she packed up her family and moved to Europe to educate her children. Caroline went with her. Her commitment to the cause developed out of a need for control but also an understanding of the human cost of slavery. Her removal from the antislavery scene just as the Mexican War heated up the abolition issue presumes a letting go, a new sense of self. As a widow, family obligations weighed heavily upon her, but she found a way, in Europe, to continue her work in a broader context. She recruited ideological and financial support for the American abolition cause overseas. And, most important to her and her sisters, monetary support for the antislavery fairs.

In 1848, sisters Anne, Deborah, and Emma helped organize a Boston antislavery convention and coordinated the antislavery bazaars. Throughout the early 1850s, Deborah and Anne ferried George Thompson to contentious meetings that debated the future of the Union. Garrisonians, who clearly guided Thompson, believed that, if the Constitution of the Union supported slavery, then Garrisonians supported disunion.[39] Deborah proudly reported to Maria in Paris, "I thought the roof would go off" as Thompson spoke at a meeting in Dorchester.[40] And in the uproar over the Fugitive Slave Act, the Chapman and Weston families joined in protests against Massachusetts returning fugitive slaves to owners. In the case of a Worcester fugitive slave, Deborah Weston, as a witness, reported Mary Chapman facing down the conservative "Amorys and Appletons" at the Federal Courthouse surrounded by demonstrators and armed guards.[41] And in the case of the fugitive slave Anthony Burns of Boston, again the Westons decried his return South under armed guard and joined Wendell Phillips in the highly volatile protests. During the demonstrations, Anne tried to talk reasonably in religious—even literary—terms to pro-slavery supporters, obviously, to no avail.[42]

Just prior to the Civil War and her return to Boston in 1858, Maria Weston Chapman changed strategy for the funding of the *National Anti-Slavery Standard*. She replaced the antislavery fairs with the Subscription Anniversary, a salon-like affair that included entertainment, refreshments, and conversations. The new arrangement raised funds, as well as hackles. Her allies were not consulted. Chapman's natural inclinations, the need for control, had not changed. But something had—namely, the antislavery movement's direction. The soirees raised more money than the fairs.

Nonetheless, as war loomed, Chapman began to withdraw gradually from activism.[43] In high spirits, she wrote, "Civil War, if we are to have it, ... is not so bad as slavery. Public opinion is so rapidly consolidating ... that I auger nothing but good."[44] When she reviewed her abolitionist career in light of her advocating the shutting down of the American Anti-Slavery Society, she said, "Garrison and I clapped our wings that the Society lasted so long."[45] With the Emancipation Proclamation, Chapman let go her anti-slavery management and retired, her perfectionism abandoned. She knew her limits and the limits of the cause. A friend remarked that, even in her declining years, "the eyes of this lady would outshine those of ball-room belles."[46]

Maria Weston Chapman and her family followed the path of Garrisonian "robust" virtue, sustained by a corporate family structure—the family business of abolition. Although inconsistent, because, as Garrisonian pacifists, they welcomed the war on slavery, the Westons and Chapmans were no less committed to the cause. Chapman and her sisters worked tirelessly for decades and risked mob violence. Maria Weston Chapman emerged as an independent-minded reformer who brooked no opposition to her organizational plans in the direction of the BFASS and in the promotion of the Subscription Anniversary. Her retirement in the event of the war and the Emancipation Proclamation made sense for a movement dedicated to the abolition of slavery. Nonetheless, the Westons and Chapmans learned a particular kind of dependence in that wealthy, educated family. The strength of commitment to each other propelled them beyond the family to a concern for the welfare of the enslaved. The virtue lay in the need to respond to others' vulnerabilities. They believed theirs was an initial task of liberation—not, however, the work of the political and economic integration of African Americans. Organizational ability such as the Westons and Chapmans possessed did not yet extend into a future vision of shared vulnerabilities, of mutual dependencies that political and social equality would later demand.[47] Yet, the Weston/Chapman clan succeeded both as a family and as an association; members shared family intimacy while managing the discipline of abolitionist organization.

THE DEVEREUX/EDMONDSTON FAMILY

In contrast to the associative organization of the Boston abolitionist Weston/Chapman family, the North Carolina Devereux/Edmondston family defined commitment to the Confederacy in terms of the family's economic production. The family plantation's productivity depended on a stable slave workforce. Hence, a dependent labor force remained crucial to Confederate loyalists. How Southern whites defined "family" and the issue of dependence determined the Southern family's fate. The most characteristic commitment of the Devereux/Edmondston family and Southern whites, generally, remained particular; family identified place, family defined morality, family delimited the social order. For Southern planters, land meant family ownership; loss of land meant disintegration of the family, or, equally important, loss of the family name.

Catherine Ann Devereux Edmondston's diary clearly expresses the heart of Southern family order. On July 20, 1860, Catherine Edmondston, mistress of Looking Glass plantation, situated on the Roanoke River in Halifax County, North Carolina, walked in her garden and gloried in her dahlias. Recording the moment, she wrote, "My Dahlias are magnificent! . . . My garden is beautiful—how I love it!" As if in the delivery of a portent, nine months later, a freshet flooded the fields of the plantation. Yet, Catherine Edmondston, gliding down the Roanoke River toward her land, described the scene as "beautiful & peaceful in the extreme, drifting along over the still, placid water through a wall of living green, for we went through the Swamp. The bright sunshine, the tender foliage, the graceful canoe—all made a picture which could we have banished the thought that the water covered our best land & that our corn was ten feet beneath its surface, we would have enjoyed exceedingly!"[48] The land, both loved and mourned, would, in the next few years, define both her and her family's commitment to the war effort.

For the Devereux and Edmondstons, the land had a family history. Thomas Pollock, a Scot who emigrated to North Carolina in 1683 and who was twice named governor, owned huge tracts of land on the "Chowan, Roanoke, Neuse, and Trent rivers" and real estate in Bath and New Bern. Governor Pollock could, therefore, claim over 20,000 acres as his property. Successive generations, naturally, benefitted from the patents down to the 19th century. Frances Pollock Devereux, Catherine Ann Devereux Edmondston's grandmother, wealthy in her own right, inherited the land of her brother George Pollock, one of the wealthiest landed men in the state. Fifteen hundred slaves toiled on George Pollock's plantations. Thomas Pollock Devereux, Catherine Ann's father, gave up his career as a lawyer, a U.S. district attorney, and a reporter for the state supreme court to manage the estate of his mother, Frances Pollock Devereux. Thomas and his second wife, Ann Mary Maitland, and their daughter, Susan, lived at Conneconara plantation in Halifax County. Catherine Ann and her husband, Patrick Muir Edmondston, lived on her father's adjoining plantation, Looking Glass, deeded to them in July of 1860.[49] The land joined the families as the families bonded to the land.

Thomas Devereux remained a Federalist and a supporter of the Union as storm clouds gathered. Though at times he wavered, he often criticized Confederate military behavior and, at the end of the war, petitioned the government for remuneration for lost cotton, claiming his faithful devotion to the Union.[50] Catherine Ann loved her father. As she declared to her husband, "[M]y love for him has been a sentiment with me all my life. The admiration, the pride, the earnest warm affection of my heart have all been concentrated on him since my childhood." But, as the shadow of the firing on Fort Sumter interrupted the quiet scene, she admitted, "This difference of opinion with father has been very sad to me for I think I can honestly say that it is the first time in my life that my judgment & feelings did not yield to him."[51] The other love of her life was Patrick. Patrick, in contrast, proved steadfast to the Southern cause and, therefore, her truest confidante. "Thank God," she said, "for the unity of spirit & feeling which exists between Patrick & myself. I do not believe I could live had I not him to lean on & confide in. He is the only person to whom I ever talk *out*, that is, unburden myself fully & fairly, feel perfectly at home, & say all I think."[52] Choosing principle meant choosing among family hierarchies in this Southern patriarchy. Commitments proved complex.

The Edmondstons' domestic circle included mostly relatives who had varied opinions on the Southern cause. In one of Catherine's entries for April 13, 1861, for example, she dined at her father's house with the husband of her step-mother's sister, where they discussed Sumter. The Sumter event evoked conflicted familial anxieties. Major Anderson, the commander of Sumter, was married to Eliza Clinch Anderson, Catherine's cousin. One topic of conversation at the dinner must have been the fact that Eliza had dressed her little son in a U.S. major's uniform and sent the picture both to Catherine and to Catherine's friend, Ellen Mordecai. Ellen Mordecai, as a friend, was no stranger to the family either. She was the aunt of Margaret Mordecai Devereux, married to Catherine's brother, John Devereux.[53] Interlocked, interwoven family members inhabited a primary circle of Southern life and rarely identified with those outside it.[54] Yet, within the family structure, hairline cracks appeared.

Members of the household and outside it were the servants, the slaves, who lived and worked in intimate association with the Edmondstons. Catherine Edmondston exercised both care and possessiveness with regard to her domestic slaves. She tended to Franky, her old servant, until Franky died. Then, Catherine lamented, "Poor Franky . . . she has been a great sufferer & and has borne it with great patience poor old thing! I hope I did all I could for her. She seemed so grateful for my reading & praying with her that I felt reproached that I had not commenced sooner!" Duty and concern mixed in Catherine's emotions. Duty sometimes had its limits. Duty replaced her natural inclination to benevolence. When she considered her job of religious instruction, she struggled to strike a balance. She noted, "This teaching of negroes is a sore problem to me. . . . They learn nothing from me but the mere rudiments of Christianity. . . . My difficulties I am convinced beset many a well intentioned mistress who like me because she cannot do what she feels she *ought* does *nothing*. One duty I am sure of—I am put here to be Patrick's companion & help meet, & I cannot spend all Sunday preaching, teaching & 'missionizing' without an evident neglect of that plain duty." But, then, she told herself she might give "*part* of the day."[55] In the end, however, the "right" of possession trumped the slaves' personal consideration. When Fanny, a slave, gave birth, it was Catherine who named him "Sumter."[56] She felt committed to her servants, although, at times, she faltered. Nonetheless, she acted within a power relationship; her charges had no choice in their circumstances.

It may be argued that all individual identity is relational.[57] If so, antebellum Southern identity developed intimacies and relationships to a high degree of complexity, thus complicating ethical boundaries and straining the meaning of commitment. Slaves contributed their labor, their lives, and their families to a unique community constrained by discipline and forced to remain bound to one place and one white family. When thieves attempted to rob the Edmondston's storage shed, the Pork House, Patrick, as master, demanded the men on the plantation yield up the perpetrators. When they did not, Patrick had them draw straws and arbitrarily punished the two who drew the unlucky lots. "This plan seemed hard," said Patrick, but necessary "to prevent thieves being as rampant here as they are at Conneconara."[58] Deeply embedded in Southern patriarchal culture is the notion of family as ethical arbiter. Catherine sometimes wondered that her marital partnership with Patrick was "not more than should be there—whether my prayers may not turn to sin because there is an idol there!"[59] She counted herself happiest in her marriage, since she believed "it is because I yield myself up more to Patrick's guidance & regulation than I did."[60] Such dependence on family authority weakened understanding of wider, critical, and thus moral commitment.[61]

In this Southern community enclosure, commitment moved along familial lines but sometimes snapped when individual family members challenged slavery, thus questioning loyalty to family and allegiance to the Confederate cause. Shortly before the war, Catherine Ann Edmondston helped her sister, Frances Devereux Miller, tend to Frances's sick child. Then, the pair visited the Edmondstons' summer home in

Hascosea. All seemed pleasant until Frances voiced strong Union sentiments. She said, "This glorious Union broken up for the sake of a few
negroes! Rather let them go than destroy the Union." Catherine Ann
recorded her thoughts in reply. "This is to me treason against Liberty.
In the first place, it is not a 'few negroes.' It is the country, for I should like
to know who could live here were they freed?—& then the principle
involved! I *yield nothing*—no compromise—where my *liberty*, my *honor*,
dearer than life is concerned." For Catherine Ann, liberty conflated
personal and political freedom. The former defined an inviolable space
and the latter delimited personal freedom by law.[62] Her idea of freedom
curtailed the rights of African Americans because the community defined
"rights" to land, liberty, and honor. Frances betrayed those principles
because, as Catherine reasoned, she managed her slaves badly and
undermined family authority. Catherine noted, rather irritatingly,
"She [Frances] knows ... no more about the proper management of
negroes than a child."[63]

Frances's source of honor and dignity, her identity, lay elsewhere than
in a Confederacy as mistress of slaves. Thus, she demonstrated a different
kind of control, over herself, rather than family or community belonging.[64]
Nonetheless, as the war progressed, Frances changed her mind and supported the Confederacy. The course of events, the invasion and killing,
exerted its own internal logic and control even over the strong minded.
Fluidity of identity did not characterize the white Southern wartime personality. The threat of invasion shifted an entire set of symbolic meanings
toward family and land.[65] Catherine Ann Edmondston's identity in the
land and her "property" moved her to denounce the U.S. flag as a "rag."
She claimed that the principles the flag represented had vanished.
Therefore, she could abrogate any moral commitment to the Union.
She argued, "How can it be upheld when the spirit—nay, even the
body—that gave it value is lost?"[66]

At the beginning of the war, Catherine Edmondston confidently
believed she knew herself and her slaves. As mistress of land and slaves,
she observed black children who measured their worth by their sale price.
Dolly, a faithful servant, consoled her mistress, who appeared saddened by
her husband's departure for military service, and said, "Never mind. Master
will not be gone long, for them folks will not have the impudence to stand
up now that Master himself is gone out again 'em." When, in 1862, the
Edmondstons heard that the militia in their neighboring town of
Clarksville had been called up, Catherine made preparations to move to
their summer home, Hascosea. The servants, she wrote, were "much
affected and ... in much fright. ... They entreated me not to leave them

Catherine Ann Devereux Edmondston. (Courtesy of the State Archives of North Carolina)

& I have promised to remain at home & take what care I can of them."[67] Her responsibility, her duty to the land and slaves, carried with it a singular identity that attached itself to the emerging Confederate nation. Her vulnerability in such a precarious position would naturally make her feel the necessity of national protection. The meaning of her peaceful life had shifted and, with it, a reinterpretation of her collective sense of well-being.[68]

At first, the terrible challenge of war elicited only the most noble thoughts and actions. Catherine Ann Edmondston worked with neighboring women on sewing uniforms and during the session a Mr. Benton read poetry to the ladies. Although she dismissed such sentimental poetry, Edmondston wrote in a romantic mode, "I feel as tho' I could *live* poetry, poetry of the sternest and most heroic cast."[69] In the summer of 1861, white women worked enthusiastically supplying uniforms and volunteering in hospital work. Edmondston served the Confederate cause by setting the women slaves to work on uniforms. The Confederate Congress commended Southern women for their contributions. Well they might, Edmondston thought, since women had even donated their precious copper kettles to the cause. Patrick Edmondston volunteered for military service but was disappointed repeatedly in his efforts.[70] When the block-ade dried up the supply of salt, Thomas Devereux, who had saved up a quantity, began to sell it in the neighborhood at rates well below those of speculators. In some cases, he exchanged the salt for yarn or socks; he then donated the goods to the government. Catherine and Patrick sent hospital stores to Richmond for the wounded. Even though the Edmondstons and Catherine's father supported the war effort, she retained a sense of guilt about the killing.[71]

Even a conscience alert to the real meaning of war, and a heart full of sacrifice and generosity, tended to divide the world into two. With such a perception, commitment hardened. According to Catherine Ann Edmondston, Southerners remained gentlemen in the midst of battle, and Northerners were "riff-raff." She cited "English papers" that the Southern government evinced intelligence and integrity, while the Northern government lied about victories.[72] Southerners aligned with the rest of the world and thought about posterity, while Yankees alone lived "on the future," and Edmondston presumed "it has not had a very ennobling effect on them."[73] Yankees could not be called Christian. In contrast, General T. J. "Stonewall" Jackson "died a Christian and a patriot."[74] According to Edmondston, the Union meant conquest and confiscation, a tyranny that, with its blockades and invasion, warred upon the sick and vulnerable. The South fought for freedom, she believed. After Gettysburg and the continued invasion by Northern troops, fear generated vengeful thinking. Edmondston supported the guerilla fighter William Quantrell, whose attacks in 1863 leveled Lawrence, Kansas, and whose depredations spread havoc in Missouri.[75] Quantrell killed General James Gilpatrick Blunt's command because Blunt, she reported, had destroyed more than two counties in Missouri, forcing women and children to flee.[76]

In the midst of a war, where atrocities occurred on both sides, objectiv-ity remained a scarce commodity. Since an impartial view necessitates some detachment of self, war-torn populations rarely possess it. For most populations, but especially Civil War Southern cultures, detachment from primary family and community group values proved difficult. Rational self-criticism or a religious humility needs a disciplined mind alert to the imperfection and limitations of commonly held opinions, including one's own. Catherine Ann Edmondston admitted: "My religious life does not cost me the struggles, the pangs, the unhappiness, it used. Is it that my con-science is less tender?" She realized that, although in the past she had criti-cized herself for impatience and laziness, she rarely did so now. Religious and moral issues entered automatically into her mind. "The machinery that they [issues of conscience] result from does not cost me a thought," she wrote. Nonetheless, she considered herself "a happier woman now." The reason for such self-satisfaction lay in her yielding more "to Patrick's guidance & regulation."[77] Without a critical sense of self, Catherine Edmondston had only her role as mistress to act upon.

Ownership of land and slaves constituted the limits of Southern moral commitment. As Catherine Ann asserted, "We want simply to be left alone & allowed to manage our own domestic institutions in our own way."[78] House servant Dolly remained faithful to the Edmondstons throughout their lives; however, the white family relegated the field slaves to the role of miscreants/strangers. The slaves who transgressed the boundaries of ownership by robbing the Pork House met severe punishment for their "felonious" acts. Thus, planters assumed control without familial compassion. At best, slaves might be regarded with affectionate condescension. Edmondston assumed she knew slaves' docility and ineptitude. She jeered at Northern recruitment of black soldiers and observed that the African American soldiers assigned to guard Port Royal prisoners of war allowed them to escape.[79] And as the war progressed, rumors spread of Northern expeditions designed to promote slave insurrections. Nevertheless, despite her fears, Catherine Ann believed she could still manage her slaves. Edmondston professed to love her slaves and they her: "Ah! Cuffee! Cuffee! you are no manager, & yet I love you. Faults & all I accept you and prefer your carelessness & affection to the best groom that England ever sent forth!"[80] The myth of African American ignorance and servility proved useful in retaining particular commitment to the land and the institution of slavery.

The fact that the faltering Confederacy needed slave labor to build defenses added tension to the Edmondston family commitment. Catherine Ann Edmondston questioned why the impressment of slaves took place in her area for the defense of Petersburg. "There are negroes enough on the James River whom their owners would be glad to employ & keep from the domination of the Yankees—negroes whom they fear will go over to them," she opined. With survival at stake, Edmondston reasoned, "To remove forty hands now from Father's and Mr E's crops is to destroy it."[81] When personal interest collided with sectional interest, only the threat of coercion moved the Edmondstons to comply with government demand.[82] By December 1864, when General Lee advised the conscription, emancipation, and arming of 200,000 slaves, Edmondston raised the personal matter of control to one of principle. She wrote:

We give up a principle when we offer emancipation as a boon or reward, for we have hitherto contended that Slavery was Cuffee's normal condition, the very best position he could occupy, the one of all others in which he was the happiest, & to take him from that & give him what we think misery in the place of it, is to put ourselves in the wrong essentially. No! freedom for whites, slavery for negroes, God has so ordained it![83]

Notice of the conscription process panicked Edmondstons' neighbor's slaves, and that began a general abandonment of his plantation. When the order for a list of eligible men on the plantation came to the Edmondstons, Catherine Ann advised Patrick to take no notice of it. Patrick, however, complied. The Edmondstons' slaves evidenced none of the neighborhood panic. Catherine Ann explained, "Probably the extreme isolation in which we keep them has prevented their being affected by it."[84] Edmondston decried the recruitment process, promising freedom and a "home amongst their own people." She reiterated her resolve, "They will get none of ours. I consider it a point of patriotism to keep them at home."[85] Patriotic sentiments did not move the Edmondstons to give up their slaves to conscription. There were limits to patriotism—namely, freedom for blacks. Freedom meant what Catherine Ann said, "freedom for whites." The land and slaves constituted a major source of memory and experience. To give up the past for an uncertain and dangerous future threatened the very survival of Southern culture. In this regard, commitment indicated planters' self-interest.

By 1864, the planters' dangerous future became apparent as slaves upended white domination. The Edmondstons heard of slaves who, in a reversal of fortune, believed the planters owed them. In addition, former slaves resisted any form of docility and claimed equality with whites. Mrs. T. D. Jones, Catherine Ann Edmondston's niece, wrote to her aunt and reported that Yankees and "armed negroes" came looking for her son, Joshua, a ranger. He escaped into the woods but was later captured and surrendered. As soon as Joshua was out of the house, "Sister Mary's ex-nurse," who dressed "finely," demanded bedclothes and ripped them off a bed. She and the cohort carried off other bed linens and furniture. Then, Mrs. Jones claimed the worst indignity, being cursed "& *calling* us by our *names*."[86] One by one, the slaves ran away; then, most of the men and a few women from Thomas Devereux's plantation escaped. The Edmondstons' slaves remained.[87] And then, "the nation surrendered," wrote Catherine.

The defeat of Confederacy for Catherine Ann Edmondston meant a loss of belonging, of status, of one's place in the land. Thus, what Catherine owned was "faith in the *country*" and "faith in the *cause*."[88] Embedded in family and community, the Edmondstons did not oppose and rarely criticized the cause that protected their fortunes.[89] Southern commitment to the cause fortified itself as a kind of justice—that which an individual owes to her or his country—but it was always of a specific kind, tied to family, community, region, and experience. Southern white commitment to the Confederacy held to a specificity of white family loyalty and tradition and thereby traduced the rights of slaves. Solidarity based on a hierarchy of white power that eliminated the rights of slaves meant the distortion of commitment as a virtue.

Virtue comes in many degrees. Maria Weston Chapman, the abolitionist, and Catherine Ann Edmondston, the dedicated slaveholder, demonstrated radical commitment to their respective causes. The difference, of course, was slavery, by any measure an immoral institution, which Edmondston defended and Chapman challenged. Devoid of self-criticism, Edmondston could not envision a life beyond the family members and its slave population. Chapman developed a both/and strategy for her family/association. She lived in Europe for the sake of her children's education, but she continued her efforts on behalf of the abolition movement. In short, commitment becomes a virtue when an individual responds to her or his own vulnerabilities, and vulnerabilities, in turn, engender greater mutual dependencies, greater aspiration to a more common good.[90] William Sever Lincoln learned about commitment through his weaknesses and practiced heroism in spite of great disabilities.

WILLIAM SEVER LINCOLN AND FAMILY

As a scion of a distinguished family of the early Commonwealth of Massachusetts, William Sever Lincoln was taught its Puritan heritage of politics and probity, which ranged through the Republican and Whig popular ideology of the Early Republic. William was born in 1811, a few years after his grandfather was elected governor of Massachusetts, in 1808. Earlier, Levi Lincoln Sr. had been a minute man and a distinguished state and congressional Republican and had served as Jefferson's attorney general and acting secretary of state. William's father, Levi Lincoln Jr., was elected governor in 1825, served in Congress from 1834 to 1841, and returned to serve in the Massachusetts Senate in 1844. He was elected mayor of Worcester in 1848. Levi Jr. took delight in celebrating the virtues of the Pilgrim Fathers with the New England Society of the City of New York.[91] William, his second son, learned Puritan discipline and adherence to a calling that rewarded hard work with "the gift" of material success.

But moderation in all things, order and balance in one's life, marked the character of a righteous elite. Levi Jr.'s Puritan/Whiggish principles by the mid-19th century meant that he balanced his profits from business investments with his simple life as a farmer. Levi Jr. often expressed deep disappointment with newer, more partisan members of Congress who were profligate with government expenditures. He felt the new congressmen lacked virtue.[92] Republican and Whiggish virtues enshrined "justice, benevolence and the social virtues."[93] At the end of his federal career, in 1841, Levi Lincoln waited in vain to see if the old democratic principles and its Republican virtues would be practiced in the Tyler era.[94]

William Sever Lincoln proved to be a child of promise. At the Old Centre School House, in Worcester, he belonged to the "brightest and merriest" of the boys. But very early in his life, military pageantry seduced him. One morning, while a number of students attended "writing school," a "fife and drum were heard in the street" that immediately distracted William so much so that the teacher asked him what he might choose to do, "tend to his lessons or follow the soldiers?" "I would rather follow them," he replied. Consequently, the teacher dismissed the entire class. He attained the rank of captain as a very young man, and the rank of lieutenant colonel in the Worcester Light Infantry by the age of 22. The local militia included the most distinguished men of the town, including William's father, Levi Lincoln Jr., William's uncle John Lincoln earned a captain's rank and, later, William's brother Waldo commanded the unit. Also, two of William's sons would command the local troops.[95] The Worcester Light Infantry was a Lincoln family affair.

William entered Bowdoin College, in Brunswick, Maine, at age 14, and graduated ahead of his class at age 17. After graduation, he returned to Worcester and apprenticed at the law office of his uncle Enoch Lincoln. Not yet 21 years old, William was admitted to the bar and began practice in Millbury, Massachusetts. In 1835, he married Elizabeth Trumbull, the daughter of a wealthy businessman and realtor in Worcester.[96]

Shortly after their marriage, William caught Western fever. He wrote to his wife about his thinking. He noted gloomily that his law clients increased slowly and that only "stir and strife and excitement and turmoil" attached to some new purpose interested him. William acted like a peacetime soldier when he admitted to his wife, "I am more fitted for a turbulent life." He even toyed with the idea of giving up his profession.[97] The plan was to go West without Elizabeth, set up housekeeping, and then send for her. Elizabeth did join her husband in Alton, Illinois, in the spring of 1838, and settled into a decidedly rural life. She reports her chief concern was a litter of diseased pigs.[98] Distressed, Elizabeth's sister, Lucy, reported to their mother that, although they moved to a more comfortable home, Elizabeth lived "entirely among strangers" in preparing for her confinement. She observed that only the work of Mrs. Lincoln, Elizabeth's mother-in-law, and her sisters-in-law aided Elizabeth in the birth of a son, Willie. Meanwhile, William opened a law practice in Alton, and it expanded.[99] However, his clients did not pay and forced him into debt. Perhaps the straitened circumstances and Elizabeth's reference to their home as "*that hole*"[100] prompted Elizabeth to return to her parents in Massachusetts. In any case, she left William to his own devices in 1841. Prone to depression and physically ill, he suffered greatly by the separation, which exacerbated his conditions. At one point, Sarah Trumbull, Elizabeth's cousin, offered to underwrite a long treatment for William, but he refused.[101] He wrote to Elizabeth, "I go on willing to bear as cheerfully as I may in the life of unhappiness I am destined to." Defensive, he protested, "I have done the best that could, under the circumstances, be done." And yet, apologetically, he said:

> I have been looking back on our married life ... I feel that I have much to be forgiven for ... cross words and cross looks should not have been given you. ... But Lisy dearest when we meet again a new life shall be opened to you. You knew my health was anything but good. You cannot dream how much my own affairs and the business of others have embarrassed me the last year. I have been in situations where I hope never to be again placed.[102]

Elizabeth soothed her husband's anxiety by reminding him that she had gone East to see her parents before they died. Mollified, William contented himself with the feeling of his unselfishness in letting Elizabeth take the trip. Yet, when she encouraged him to return to the East, he argued he could not leave his business. Ambivalent, he worried how his father would take his coming home, a failure in his profession. He cautioned Elizabeth, "In his first moments of disappointment he will express himself bitterly. I doubt not, yet I feel that he asks too much when he asks me to sacrifice health and all the best years of my life in a profession in pursuit of which has always avoided my grasp." He preferred the life of a farmer.[103] Still, he soldiered on alone in Alton, attempting to run a household without a housekeeper, tend to business with deadbeat clients, and make additions to his farm. More and more, he relied upon financial help from his father and his uncle William. His health deteriorated to the point where he took quinine and arsenic to quell the head pain. In his fevered condition, he sent an irate letter to his father. Evidently, his father, Levi Jr., accused

William of fraud. William vehemently denied the charge, and contended he used his father's loan money for nothing other than what his father intended. When he realized that he acted hastily, he felt "like a fool," but he blamed it on his "disappointed hopes." He remembered how he had been raised—praised for his "unflinching" habit of truth-telling. But, he lamented the "underlying duplicity of his profession" that had somewhat destroyed his honesty. He admitted he had a drinking problem and said he had given up drinking.[104]

Elizabeth and their son Willie eventually rejoined William, and for a few years, they made a life in Alton. William remained in Alton for 10 years. During that time, he corresponded with his father, and Levi Jr. took an interest in his grandson Willie.[105] Yet, the joy with rehabilitation of one son could not compensate for the death of another. The Lincoln family experienced a tragedy when Brevet Captain George Lincoln, one of William's brothers, was killed in the Mexican War, at the battle of Buena Vista. When Junius Hall, a family friend, wrote to William to express his sympathy about George's death, he noted, "[H]is life has had a purpose."[106] Purpose had perhaps eluded William, as his practice in Alton grew but he and his wife wanted to return to a more settled life near family in Worcester. As a friend remarked, "the love of home is so pronounced a trait in the whole Lincoln family."[107] The tumultuous years in Alton taught William that commitment required defeating self-delusion and accepting a hard and complicated reality. In 1855, William inherited Quinsigamond farm, in Worcester, from his uncle John. William sold it for $20,000 and eventually bought Willow Farm. He did not abandon his practice of law, but he found contentment on Willow farm, and thereafter contributed much to the development of agriculture in Worcester County.[108] Such peace remained fragile as the politics of war threatened to disrupt the family stability.

William and Elizabeth had three sons by now—William, Levi, and Winslow. All but William worked on the farm. It was a close-knit farm family that labored together from about 1848 until the eve of the Civil War. Winslow, Levi, and their cousin George tended the herd of cows. The farm had a dairy and produced an abundance of apples and vegetables. Nonetheless, hired farmhands and William's occasional ill health cost the family in time and trouble. Elizabeth refused household help, and therefore, worked almost endlessly.[109] When William ("Willie"), the eldest son, left home, for the first time, to attend law school at Harvard, Elizabeth wrote, "Your father misses you." William Sr. wrote to his son, when he accompanied him to Cambridge, "I hated to leave you." And then he added, "There isn't anything I wouldn't do for you if it is in my power."[110] The tie between father and son soon led to a commitment beyond their familial roles, as the political tides moved in and engulfed the safety of domestic shores.

Levi first noticed the number of cadets, 65 in all, who attended a neighboring school run by a Mr. Metcalf. It was the first stirring of a more martial character in the area. And, among family and friends, discussions about politics, local and national, waxed ever more divisive. In writing to grandson Willie in law school, Governor Levi Lincoln held up Abraham Lincoln, the Republican candidate for president, as an exemplar. Lincoln, he said, "is a striking example of what a man may accomplish for himself . . . there are no obstacles which talent and labor may not overcome."[111] Elizabeth held no such opinion of Lincoln. She insisted to Willie that she did not believe "a man of his ability can manage the affairs of a nation. I think the President of the United States should be a Statesman and a scholar which I am sure he is not." Furthermore, Elizabeth described her own Trumbull family as "insane crazy," for Thayer, a local conservative candidate, and the rest of her family, she said, were "abolitionists," for her a pejorative term.[112] Elizabeth's mother lamented, "our honor is divided."[113] Willie found unconscionable the preachings of Wendell Phillips and others who branded Southerners "cowards and Tyrants." He excoriated the New Englanders who applauded "such men." He hoped his grandfather could ease such partisan political tensions.[114] And William Sr., a former Whig and an avowed independent, reported that, at the regular meeting of the agricultural club, at which the subject of politics was strictly forbidden, he could not help needling Martin Bremmer, a staunch Republican.[115] The torchlight parades, however, excited the family. Levi went down to Boston for the night-time processions and was at once pressured by the Boston Light Infantry to join its ranks. His father did not encourage that.[116]

However, as war broke out, the Lincoln men joined the fight for the Union. Willie Lincoln enlisted as a private in Captain H. W. Pratt's Company G, Sixth Regiment of the Massachusetts Volunteers. The volunteers served for three months, since the government expected the fight would be short. The regiment enlisted men on April 16, the day after President Lincoln called for volunteers, and ended their service on August 2, 1861.[117] In the meantime, William Sr., 50 years old, applied repeatedly for a commission, citing his experience as a lieutenant colonel in the Massachusetts militia. He preferred, he said, to command or be placed as second in command "among friends and neighbors."[118] He did not mention family. On June 3, 1862, William Sr. received appointment as Lieutenant Colonel of the 34th Massachusetts Infantry Regiment.

Lincoln recruited many of its members. William's son Levi, having served as captain in the Worcester Light Infantry, then volunteered and was appointed lieutenant in his father's regiment.[119]

With "hearty hurrahs" from men and the waving of handkerchiefs from women, the 34th Massachusetts Infantry Regiment headed south through Baltimore and Washington, all the while witnessing increasing desolation. William S. Lincoln, who wrote the history of the regiment, described the scene in Baltimore as "a city of the dead."[120] It offered no welcome but silence. Although the city remained tense, residents did not attack the volunteers, as they did in 1861. Moving into the territory around Arlington, recently occupied by Confederate forces, Lincoln observed houses in ruins and "acres upon acres of forest trees with their bare limbs and brown trunks."[121] The Northern force that marched through this wilderness presented itself to its commanders as a raw, untamed, and undisciplined body. When encamped near Alexandria, some men missed reveille; therefore, a lieutenant was detailed to patrol the city and find the stragglers. When one of the missing men refused to halt when spotted, the lieutenant fired a shot, which grazed the retreating man. The sight of the wounded man returning under guard roused the whole camp into defiance. Men armed themselves and shouted threats to the commanders. Fortunately, discipline returned when the order was given to "fall in." Thereafter, Lt. Col. Lincoln himself patrolled the streets of Alexandria and closed all the bars. Nonetheless, unending drills, parades, and skirmish practices ultimately formed the 34th, according to its second in command, into the envy of the army in the Shenandoah Valley.[122]

Illness attacked the regiment long before Southern forces did. A good number of the men endured typhoid, measles, diarrhea, small pox, scurvy, scarlet fever, and brain fever. Exposure to the elements, including snow and hurricane-like rain, contributed to colds and flu. Lt. Levi Lincoln was plagued by "aphonia," or laryngitis.[123] Faced with the death and disease of his men, Lt. Col. Lincoln complained: "Finally winter is upon us, but we are illy prepared to meet it. Desirous of flooring our tents, we make a requisition for lumber, which is returned, *refused*, 'because the 34th is not in garrison.' Another one for straw is refused, 'because the 34th is not on the march;' and so red tape bids fair to kill both soldiers and horses."[124]

Finally, in February 1863, during a severe snow storm, the post quartermaster in Alexandria approved a requisition for wood. The desperate commander ordered Lt. Levi Lincoln to return to camp with the 13 railway cars loaded with wood that were awaiting the regiment in Washington. When the conductor refused to stop at the camp and steamed ahead toward

Alexandria, Lt. Levi Lincoln had his men apply the brakes. The lieutenant would not allow the train to move until the conductor promised to deliver the wood at the camp's railroad crossing. Furious, the conductor threatened to report Lt. Lincoln to headquarters for "obstructing a 'rain'. Report, and be d___d; I have obeyed my orders," said the lieutenant. The wood arrived at the camp and Lt. Lincoln won admiration for his "trophies."[125] His father, Lt. Col. Lincoln, also weighed his responsibilities and thereby demonstrated his ability to command. He failed to comply with the orders of General Wheaton to hold 75 men ready to march at a moment's notice. When dressed down by General Wheaton, Lt. Col. Lincoln explained that the excessive details ordered by superior headquarters had exhausted the ability of his men to fulfill yet another request for manpower. As General Wheaton inspected the regiment's morning reports of work details, he immediately concurred with Lincoln that the oppressive work load was "shameful!"[126]

Movements and counter-movements brought the regiment to encamp between Charlestown and Martinsburg, where the company met its first engagement in mid-September 1863, at the "Battle of Ripon." Artillery reports were heard in the direction of Charlestown, and Lt. Col. Lincoln ordered the regiment ready to march. Upon the intelligence that a Major Cole had engaged the Confederate commander, John D. Imboden, and forced his retreat, the 34th hastened toward Charlestown to support the major. Two companies of skirmishers split off from the 34th as the regiment marched along a pike. Soon, the skirmishers were engaged and shell flew over the heads of the marchers. The country, with its rolling hills, made it difficult for the flanks to advance, as rebels simply occupied the strategic position atop one knoll after another. Heavy Confederate artillery fire kept up, while the main body of the regiment continued down the pike. Suddenly, as the regiment halted and formed, a body of cavalry disguised as Union men attacked the line. The contest continued "sharp," but the 34th held its ground and ultimately pushed Imboden to retreat. After the battle, the regiment marched with its wounded men 36 miles back to camp. It took 15 hours and the men marched without food.[127]

Fatiguing marches back and forth from Harper's Ferry to Winchester characterized the 34th Massachusetts Valley Campaign. Occasionally, bushwackers and rebel parties harassed the force through the cold winter and warm spring between 1863 and 1864. The fateful march from Strasburg to New Market began in May 1864. The 34th arrived in Strasburg from Winchester on May 10, already exhausted from an "illy conducted" march. Men fell of sunstroke and succumbed to diarrhea; nonetheless, the regiment stripped down to bare essentials in preparation for another march. Ordered to assist Col. Moore, the commanding officer, Col. George Wells hastened to comply. The line formed in early morning marched out with a grim-faced commander who pushed forward, on and on—"Still on;—beyond support; past hope of help, if help should be needed."[128] With no sign of Col. Moore, the regiment marched on until Col. Boyd appeared and conveyed the intelligence that his army had been attacked and the rear of his New York Cavalry blocked his retreat. Regardless of the information, the 34th pressed onward recklessly, it seemed to Lt. Col. Lincoln, to find Col. Moore. Advancing, the 34th encountered shots and artillery fire, a sign that the regiment had found Col. Moore. The New York Cavalry and the 18th Connecticut held their ground, while the 34th assisted those forces and, in addition, the First Virginia and the 54th Pennsylvania at New Market. General John C. Breckenridge charged the Northern army's front as Imboden bore down on the army's left flank and opened intense artillery fire. The 34th retreated until Captain Bacon ordered a halt and the 34th turned and faced the enemy only to endure withering fire, which felled the captain of the Color Company and Lt. Col. Lincoln. Wounded and unable to join in the retreat, Lt. Col. Lincoln was left "in the hands of the enemy."[129]

On May 15, 1864, the Confederates captured Lincoln and members of his regiment and marched them 21 miles in seven hours, with only a 10-minute break. Meanwhile, the torrential rain dogged the prisoners' movements. Captain Bacon of the Color Company died on the way. The next day, the men were escorted to a hospital, where they were treated and then they "looked after themselves." Afterward, they lodged in a hotel until a wagon took them to Harrisonburg. Tragically, guards hastened Lt. Malcolm Ammidon, a member of the captive party, past Harrisonburg and on to Andersonville, where he died. In Harrisonburg, Lincoln and Lt. Albert C. Walker found themselves in a hospital, a former academy, with about 50 other men. No supplies, and a bare floor on which to sleep, made life uncomfortable. Mrs. Lewis, a loyal Confederate, nonetheless, tended to the needs of the sick and wounded, as did Unionists Col. Asa S. Gray and his daughter, Orra Gray. Dr. George Gilmer administered medical care until the arrival of Dr. Allen, assistant surgeon of the 34th regiment, arrived.[130]

Suspicions that recovery would mean removal to Andersonville arose among the men. Wagons arrived to escort Lincoln, Walker, and others south. Dr. Allen interceded with the acting post quartermaster to countermand the orders to move the patients. After some time, a Union force under Hunter entered Harrisonburg, visited the hospital, and promised evacuation shortly. Before his departure, Hunter left supplies for the wounded captives. Nonetheless, shortly thereafter, a Confederate captain named Jourdon entered the building and confiscated all the hospital supplies, including food, clothing, and medicine. This incident, and the loss of hope that Hunter would return to liberate them, drove some of the men to die of despair. Continued pressure on Dr. Allen forced him to decide the number of patients to move south. Dr. Allen rejected sending Lincoln on such a treacherous journey, since he believed him not well enough. The commander, Major Meem, himself then inspected Lincoln's wounds and, exasperated, said to the sick man, "Why the hell don't you get well, Colonel?" With supplies gone and a second call for Lincoln's removal looming, Lincoln and Walker discussed an escape.[131]

Walker, on crutches and unable to venture out, believed Lincoln also not fit to endure an escape, but Lincoln insisted. Lincoln cast about for anyone to join him, and Doherty and Snow agreed. The Union soldiers relied upon the African-American washerwoman "Old Auntie" to smuggle them sets of clothing. "Old Auntie" provided clothes for Doherty and Snow but not Lincoln, and Lincoln was forced to make his escape in Union blue. Dr. Gilmer, advised of Lincoln's escape plan, provided information on local roads and possible routes. Lincoln believed his greatest support would be the slave network in the vicinity.

A fellow conspirator diverted the guards' attention, while Lincoln, Doherty, and Snow escaped. However, because of an accidental gunshot that frightened them, Lincoln and Doherty were immediately separated from Snow. Snow had intelligence of the slaves' way stations. Although Lincoln and Doherty looked for their designated place of refuge at the "little cabin inhabited by a negro family, with a wheelwright's shop, by the banks of a little creek," they never found it and, instead, hid in the underbrush for fear of the searchers. Hungry, thirsty, and with Lincoln's painful wounds, they staggered on until they found grain in a field and stagnant water to drink. They looked for contrabands who might also be on the run and aid them. Instead, desperate for food and directions, they had to rely on white farm families, a risky bet, at best.[132]

At first, they struck out for Hawley Springs and decided to take a southerly direction parallel to that route. Somehow, they missed the road and took a northerly direction. Then, the road simply ended. Lost, they decided to ask an elderly farm couple for food. Claiming they were conscripts anxious to join their Confederate division, the couple gave them bread, but the farmer accosted them and questioned them closely. Satisfied, he directed them to Moorfield, occupied by McNeil's forces. Realizing they were on a dangerous path, they, nonetheless, decided to push on. The road they took led onward, up a steep mountain, until, finally, they found themselves on its summit, in the opposite direction of where they wanted to go. Retracing their steps, they met the next farm couple, who questioned them but gave them bread and directed them to Winchester and Imboden's forces. They retreated to the mountains after being chased from one farm and moved to another, where an old couple informed them that McNeil had moved to Romney. They then knew that they had to pass McNeil's forces to get to the Union lines, and they set out for Romney. After another bewildering turn, they were lost again.[133]

The pair endured rain, heat, hunger, thirst, and exhaustion in the 11 days they spent lost and taking shelter in the mountain brush. Lincoln's feet swelled and blistered badly, and his arm wound deeply pained him. In this condition, they headed straight for McNeil's territory. They discussed the possibility of re-imprisonment, but they felt being taken by McNeil was preferable to being captured by the bushwackers. They traveled until halted by a sentinel who demanded that they identify themselves. "Refugees," said Doherty. When the guard hesitated and said, "Well! I suppose it's all right, isn't it?" Lincoln used bravado and replied "Yes you d___d fool, do you suppose we should be here, with McNeil just in front, if it was'nt?" They passed by the sentinel and went down the highway until they came to a mansion hosting a large ball. Music played inside, while groups of rebel soldiers camped outside. Lincoln and Doherty hid in a ditch until they heard the voice they recognized as McNeil's order the men to depart. Thirteen days out and anxious to get to Union lines, they waited until McNeil's forces, ordered to battle, fell back from Oldtown, Maryland, driving cattle and horses before them. When the Confederate force left the area, the two men continued on their course, crossing the Potomac on a destroyed suspension bridge, Lincoln using one arm.[134]

Crossing into Oldtown, the men found only a short respite, since the townspeople hesitated to believe Doherty and Lincoln's story of escape. Besides, since McNeil stole their cattle, the woman tavern keeper had not even milk to give them. A Union officer advised them to continue on to Cumberland, 19 miles away. With no transportation available, the exhausted pair had no choice. Lincoln wrote, "Nobody can imagine how we suffered." After seven miles of walking, they came to Patterson's Creek, the current of which was dangerously swift. They forded the stream, despite the warning shouts of a group of workers on the other side. When they reached the other side, they were greeted by Dr. Everett, a Unionist and relative of Edward Everett of Massachusetts. Dr. Everett fed and hosted the men until he placed them on a train bound for Cumberland and safety. Lincoln endured 17 days of privation and agonizing pain in his harrowing escape.[135] He rejoined his regiment five months later, in

William Sever Lincoln. (Courtesy of the American Antiquarian Society)

November 1864, when he was designated colonel in charge of the brigade. He mustered out as acting brigadier general. He returned home and lived on his farm with his wife and sons Levi and Winslow. Willie died in the war.[136]

William Sever Lincoln's vulnerable humanity served his commitment well because, early on, he learned to separate himself from his unrealizable ambitions and live soberly. His was not the rational, Puritan set of rules that his father had set for him, but, rather, he had learned through experience that, if he calculated his weaknesses, he could build up his strengths. The admission of vulnerability aided in reconstituting his family, building up his raw, untamed regiment, and surviving his ordeal for the sake of the Union cause.

Commitment is not a virtue without an understanding of the vulnerability that creates a need for solidarity. Maria Weston Chapman grasped the overwhelming necessity of a network of abolition organizations, because she knew the human toll of slavery. She and her family worked for the most vulnerable in the population in order to obtain their freedom. Her dedication to the plight of slaves was not predicated upon a sense of her own vulnerability. Chapman's wealth, status, and temperament precluded such searing identification. Nonetheless, her sense of loss intimated her human limits as she let go of the movement and her Garrisonian absolutism in the wake of the war. Catherine Ann Edmondston believed she had a duty toward her slaves, an obligation, a commitment. She tried her best to be dutiful. Nonetheless, her approach and Patrick Edmondston's only widened the gap between the vulnerable slave and themselves as the all-powerful owners. And, because Catherine abrogated all decision-making and power to Patrick, she was left with a role that ended in the Civil War. The desire for slave ownership, not counterbalanced by an objective point of view, one separate from her own self-interest, negated any higher commitment, including patriotic military necessity. William Sever Lincoln's vulnerable humanity served his commitment well. He demonstrated that acknowledgment of dependence, accompanied by a self-critical attitude, is the key to both independence and solidarity. The virtue of commitment may be more than an adherence to a person or an idea, since it is a process undertaken with all of one's resources and liabilities in order to sustain others. The Civil War family demonstrates the values and problems inherent in maintaining a national solidarity.

Conclusion

In his Independence Hall speech of February 22, 1861, Abraham Lincoln spelled out in unmistakable terms his unqualified dedication to the principles and values included in the Declaration of Independence. Whatever the strains between the North and the South, the Union based on these principles ought to be preserved, even, if necessary, by war. And if war did come, the preservation of the Union would require of the citizenry an equally firm dedication to these values. Nonetheless, as this book shows, the prospect of war and its eventual outbreak brought to light strong divisions even within individual families. The virtues of war that Lincoln called for did not find easy acceptance. Families interpreted Lincoln's principled plea in terms of their own moral development and consequent habitual practices. Habits of righteousness, self-sacrifice, empathy, and determination learned in the family moved individuals to act rightly according to their own measure. Furthermore, the *practical wisdom* gained and in habitual experience aimed toward a greater good proved crucial to judge wisely about the case for or against war. And families, like communities, evolved their moral culture in stages over time.

Family relations are clearly related to the issues of war and are as significant as economic and political considerations in wartime. What is apparent in both national and familial patterns of habit is that virtues cannot exist without an understanding of dependence on others. Civil War families discovered the need for others in order to sustain the rigors and sacrifices of war. This need exposed the raw nerve of vulnerability and dependence. Only a healthy self-knowledge and detachment from their own wants and desires preserved the common good, the Union. Slave-owning families did not demonstrate detachment from self-interest; rather they denied the slaves' human rights and, therefore, obscured the notion of the common good. Lincoln's Emancipation Proclamation offered a stronger case for a flourishing community by insisting that all members of a community are *created equal.*

The litany of the Civil War is often told in terms of the overwhelming list of causalities, of brutal and bloody encounters in battle, loss of property, of displacement and disease, and funerals, unending funerals. And this is so. Yet the Civil War also preserved the Union and prompted emancipation. Thus, families sustained both the bitterness and the triumph of that war. How they endured is the quiet story, the lesser denomination or name, of patriotism, honor, justice, and commitment. In the ever-complicated tangle of family relationships, family members sorted out their loyalties, evaluated their vulnerabilities, and held to their cause. What this study shows is that to grasp well a war and its meaning, attention has to be paid to how it is lived out in the moral lives of families.

Abraham Lincoln, who faced death, defeat, and depression, somehow exhibited life-giving virtue—in his history, in the history of his country. Lincoln's honor would not allow secession while his patriotism held him firmly to the principles of the Declaration of Independence. Lincoln's sense of justice ultimately proclaimed emancipation, and lastly, his commitment was such that he was assassinated because he upheld the principles of the Declaration of Independence. In *mystic chords of memory* he bound his fragmented life into an instrument for national unity. What these lives show is that a virtue blind to vulnerability and need cannot support a solidarity of family or nation. The structure of family is neither the cause nor the cure of war, and yet because families endure, they augment the chance that associations and communities endure and states flourish.

Notes

INTRODUCTION

1. Recall Thomas Hobbes's declaration that "force and fraud are in war the two cardinal virtues." Thomas Hobbes, "The Leviathan," in Steven M. Cahn, ed., *Classics of Modern Political Theory: Machiavelli to Mill* (New York: Oxford University Press, 1997), p. 120.

2. An argument based on Alasdair MacIntyre's *Dependent Rational Animals: Why Human Beings Need the Virtues* (Chicago: Open Court, 1999).

3. For a discussion of virtue and the suspicions of virtue, see Jennifer A. Herdt, *Putting on Virtue: The Legacy of the Splendid Vices* (Chicago: University of Chicago Press, 2008), pp. 2–5, 47, 51, 66–68; Abraham Joshua Heschel, *God in Search of Man: A Philosophy of Judaism* (New York: Farrar, Straus and Giroux, 1955), pp. 389, 393, 402.

CHAPTER 1

1. Phillip Van Doren Stern, ed., *The Life and Writings of Abraham Lincoln* (New York: The Modern Library, 1940), p. 644.

2. *The New York Times*, February 12, 1861.

3. *The New York Times*, February 16, 1861.

4. Stern, *The Life and Writings of Abraham Lincoln*, pp. 644–645.

5. Ibid., p. 645.

6. See Paul Ricoeur, "Notes on the Wish and Endeavor for Unity," in *History and Truth* (Evanston: Northwestern University Press, 1965), pp. 192–186.

7. Ronald C. White, *A. Lincoln* (New York: Random House, 2010), pp. 9–10, 16, 143; Abraham Lincoln, "Autobiography," in Roy P. Basler, ed., *The Collected Works of Abraham Lincoln* (New Brunswick: Rutgers University Press, 1954), IV, pp. 60–61.

8. David Herbert Donald, *Lincoln* (New York: Simon and Schuster, 1995), p. 24.

9. Basler, *Collected Works*, II, p. 362.

10. Dennis F. Hanks's interview with William H. Herndon, in Douglas L. Wilson and Rodney O. Davis, eds., *Herndon's Informants* (Urbana: University of Illinois Press, 1998), p. 39.

11. Harden County History Museum, "The Knob Creek Home."

12. White, *A. Lincoln*, p. 26.

13. Dennis F. Hankss interview, June 13, 1865, Chicago, Ill., "Sanitary Fair," *Herndon's Informants*, p. 40.

14. Basler, *Collected Works*, I, p. 367; IV, p. 63.

15. Basler, IV, p. 62; Dennis Hanks's interview, *Herndon's Informants*, p. 41.

16. Harriet A. Chapman's interview with WHH, November 21 and December 10, 1866, *Herndon's Informants*, pp. 407, 512.

17. See Michael J. Sandel, *Justice: What's the Right Thing to Do?* (New York: Farrar, Strauss and Giroux, 2009), p. 186.

18. Basler, *Collected Works*, IV, p. 61; III, p. 511.

19. (1797) Early American Imprint Series, Series 1, no. 50002, pp. 4, 9, 14, 111.

20. Digitized by Cardinalis Etext, C. E. K., 1942 edition, p. 36.

21. Parson Mason Weems, *A History of the Life and Death, Virtue and Exploits of George Washington*, (1800) Early American Imprints, Series 1, no. 39063, pp. 4, 27, no. 3659, p. 61.

22. Matilda Johnson Moore's interview with WHH, September 8, 1865, *Herndon's Informants*, p. 109.

23. Daniel Defoe, *Robinson Crusoe* (London: London Electronic Books, 2001), pp. 12–14, 27, 47, 56, 102, 184, 211–219, 221.

24. Dennis Hanks's interview, June 13, 1865, p. 41; John Hanks's interview, June 13, 1865, *Herndon's Informants*, p. 41; David Herbert Donald, *Lincoln* (New York: Simon and Schuster, 1995), pp. 30–31.

25. See Harry L. Coles, *The War of 1812* (Chicago: University of Chicago Press, 1965); Dumas Malone, *Jefferson the President: First Term, 1801–1805* (Boston; Little, Brown and Company, 1970); Donald R. Hickey, *The War of 1812: The Forgotten Conflict* (Urbana: University of Illinois Press, 1989).

26. Donald, *Lincoln*, p. 34.

27. White, *A. Lincoln*, p. 38; Donald, *Lincoln*, p. 39; John Hanks's interview, June 13, 1865, *Herndon's Informants*, p. 44. For a discussion of "reason, or the mind, is the proper subject of virtue," see Thomas Aquinas, "The Summa Theologica," in Anton C. Pegis, ed., *The Basic Writings of Saint Thomas Aquinas* (New York: Random House, 1945), p. 418.

28. See White, *A. Lincoln*, pp. 54–55.

29. For Lincoln's voting record in the election of 1831, see Benjamin F. Thomas, *Lincoln's New Salem* (Springfield, IL: The Abraham Lincoln Association, 1934), p. 42.

30. See Orville Vernon Burton, *The Age of Lincoln* (New York: Hill and Wang, 2007), pp. 5, 107, 127. As historian Orville Vernon Burton explains, Southern honor determined respect for one's place in the community. A Southern yeoman would have defined honor as equality of opportunity and adherence to the law that protected such opportunity. Burton noted Lincoln continued his "wrestling match" with the honor of the Union at stake.

31. See Sandel, *Justice*, p. 197.

32. J. Rowan Herndon's interview with WHH, May 28, 1865; William G. Green's interview with WHH, May 30, 1865, *Herndon's Informants*, pp. 6, 18–19; Douglas L. Wilson, *Honor's Voice: The Transformation of Abraham Lincoln* (New York: Alfred A. Knopf, 1998), p. 48.

33. Hardin Bale's interview with WHH, May 29, 1865; see also Lynn McNulty Greene's interview with WHH, July 30, 1865; George U. Miles's interview with WHH, March 23, 1866; Robert B. Rutledge's interview with WHH, October 29, 1866, *Herndon's Informants*, pp. 13, 80, 236, 383. White, *A. Lincoln*, p. 100.

34. Mark E. Neely Jr., *The Last Best Hope of Earth: Abraham Lincoln and the Promise of America* (Cambridge: Harvard University Press, 1995), p. 9.

35. Burton, *The Age of Lincoln*, p. 127.

36. Justin G. Turner and Linda Levitt Turner, *Mary Todd Lincoln: Her Life and Letters* (New York: Alfred A Knopf, 1972), p. 21.

37. Catherine Clinton, *Mrs. Lincoln: A Life* (New York: Harper Perennial, 2010), pp. 9–13; Jean H. Baker, *Mary Todd Lincoln: A Biography* (New York: W. W. Norton and Company, 1987), pp. 34, 54; Turner and Turner, *Mary Todd Lincoln.* p. 3.

38. Ninian Edwards's interview with WHH, September 22, 1865, *Herndon's Informants*, p. 133; Joshua Speed's interview with WHH, November 30, 1866, p. 430; Wilson, *Honor's Voice*, p. 194. Lincoln believed he was honor bound to marry Mary Owens, an earlier romantic entanglement. She turned him down. See also Lincoln's conflict between love and honor, pp. 223–226, 261.

39. Clinton, *Mrs. Lincoln*, p. 52.

40. Abraham Lincoln to Mary Speed, September 27, 1841, in Basler, ed., *Collected Works*, I, p. 261.

41. White, *A. Lincoln*, pp. 113–117; Wilson, *Honor's Voice*, p. 283.

42. Joshua Speed's interview with WHH, November 30, 1866, *Herndon's Informants*, p. 431.

43. Don E. Fehrenbacher, ed., *Abraham Lincoln: Speeches and Writings, 1832–1858* (New York: The Library of America, 1989), p. 158.

44. Basler, *Collected Works*, I, p. 440.

45. Edward L. Pierce's statement for WHH, 1887 (?), *Herndon's Informants*, p. 697.

46. Ibid., p. 689.

47. Charles Sumner to Frances Longfellow, May 1848, in Beverly Wilson Palmer, ed., *Selected Letters of Charles Sumner* (Boston: Northeastern University Press, 1990), p. 229.

48. Abraham Lincoln to Mary Speed, September 27, 1841, in Basler, *Collected Works*, I, p. 260.

49. "Eulogy on Henry Clay," July 6, 1852, in Basler, *Collected Works*, II, p. 126.

50. Ibid., p. 131.

51. Donald, *Lincoln*, p. 139.

52. "Fragments on Slavery," July 1, 1854 (?), in Basler, *Collected Works*, II, pp. 222–223.

53. Stern, *The Life and Writings of Abraham Lincoln*, p. 436.

54. Cardinalis Etext, C. E. K., 1942, p. 36.

55. Basler, *Collected Works*, III, p. 247.

56. Ibid., pp. 4–5, 13, 36.

57. Ibid., p. 51.

58. Ibid., pp. 18–19, 23, 276, 394.

59. Ibid., p. 105.

60. Ibid.

61. Donald, *Lincoln*, p. 221.

62. Basler, *Collected Works*, II, p. 255.

63. Doris Kearns Goodwin, *Team of Rivals: The Political Genius of Abraham Lincoln* (New York: Simon & Schuster, 2005), p. 208.

64. Basler, *Collected Works*, II, p. 461.

65. See Abraham Lincoln to James N. Brown, October 18, 1858, Basler, *Collected Works*, III, p. 327.

66. Philip Van Doren Stern, *The Life and Writings of Abraham Lincoln* (New York: The Modern Library, 1940), pp. 569–591.

67. "Personal Recollections of Abraham Lincoln," *The New York Times*, February 11, 1917.

68. Goodwin, *Team of Rivals*, pp. 13, 26, 113, 146, 190–191; White, *Lincoln*, p. 328.

69. Elizabeth Trumbull to Willy Lincoln, November 7, 1860, Lincoln Family Papers, American Antiquarian Society, Worcester, Mass.

70. Basler, *Collected Works*, IV, p. 192.

71. Basler, *Collected Works*, IV, p. 240, February 22, 1861.

72. Emory M. Thomas, *The Dogs of War, 1861* (New York: Oxford University Press, 2011), p. 43. See also David Potter, *Lincoln and His Party in the Secession Crisis* (New Haven: Yale University Press, 1965), pp. 70–71, 114–116, 242, 247, 317–318, 320–323, 375.

73. Basler, *Collected Works*, II, p. 362.

74. See Stephen Berry's discussion of Lincoln's appeal to the national family in *House of Abraham: Lincoln and the Todds, a Family Divided by War* (Boston: Houghton Mifflin Harcourt, 2008), pp. 174–177; Basler, *Collected Works*, IV, p. 271.

75. Stern, *The Life and Writings of Abraham Lincoln*, "First Inaugural Address," pp. 651–657.

76. Francis P. Blair to Abraham Lincoln, January 14, 1861, The Abraham Lincoln Papers, "American Memory," Library of Congress, Washington, D.C.

77. Goodwin, *Team of Rivals*, pp. 318–319.

78. Basler, *Collected Works*, IV, p. 316.

79. Goodwin, *Team of Rivals*, p. 337.

80. Catherine Ann Devereux Edmondston, *Journal of a Sesesh Lady: The Diary of Catherine Ann Devereux Edmondston, 1860–1866* (Raleigh: Department of Cultural Resources, 1979), p. 39.

81. Maria Weston Chapman to Debra Weston, February 26, 1861; Debra Weston to Maria Weston Chapman and Anne Chapman, March 17, 1861, Weston Sisters Collection, Boston Public Library.

82. Basler, *Collected Works*, IV, pp. 341–342; see also Burton, *Age of Lincoln*, p. 128.

83. James M. McPherson, *Tried by War: Abraham Lincoln as Commander-in-Chief* (New York: Penguin Books, 2009), p. 46.

84. See Margaret Leech, *Reveille in Washington, 1860–1865* (New York: New York Review Book, 1941), pp. 11, 14, 291–293, 298, 302–304, 307; Basler, *Collected Works*, VI, p. 178; VII, pp. 138, 164–165.

85. Clinton, *Mrs. Lincoln*, pp. 181–182; Baker, *Mary Todd Lincoln*, p. 217.

86. November 3, 1862, Abraham Lincoln Papers, "American Memory," Library of Congress, Washington, D.C.

87. Basler, *Collected Works*, II, p. 385.

88. Ibid., p. 320.

89. Basler, *Collected Works*, VI, p. 48.

90. Berry, *House of Abraham*, pp. 83–89, 167–169.

91. Basler, *Collected Works*, VI, p. 517, October 15, 1863. For a discussion of the relationship between Emily and Mary Todd, see Clinton, *Mrs. Lincoln*, p. 214.

92. Abraham Lincoln to Major General Stephen G. Burbridge, August 8, 1864, in Fehrenbacher, ed., *Abraham Lincoln: Speeches and Writings, 1859–1865* (New York: Library of America, 1989), p. 616.

93. See Catherine Clinton, *Mrs. Lincoln*, p. 223.

94. Basler, *Collected Works*, V, pp. 170–171, 369.

95. Ibid., p. 170.

96. Ibid., p. 261.

97. Basler, *Collected Works*, VI, pp. 70–71.

98. Basler, *Collected Works*, IV, pp. 506–507.

99. Sandel, *Justice*, p. 194.

100. Basler, *Collected Works*, V, p. 145.

101. Ibid., p. 192.

102. Ibid., pp. 222–223.

103. Charles Sumner to John Jay, August 11, 1861, p. 76; Charles Sumner to Harriet Martineau, October, 29, 1861, p. 82; Charles Sumner to Orestes Brownson, May 25, 1862, pp. 113–114; Charles Sumner to Abraham Lincoln,

August 29, 1862, p. 123; Charles Sumner to Benjamin Perley Poore, September 23, 1862, p. 126, in Beverly Wilson Palmer, ed., *The Selected Letters of Charles Sumner* (Boston: Northeastern University Press, 1990), II.

104. Basler, *Collected Works*, V, p. 278.

105. Ibid., p. 279.

106. Ibid., p. 329.

107. Ibid., pp. 278, 317–319, 336–338; Goodwin, *Team of Rivals*, pp. 464–468.

108. Basler, *Collected Works*, V, p. 338.

109. Ibid., p. 388, August 22, 1862.

110. Ibid., pp. 356–357, August 4, 1862, pp. 419–420.

111. Ibid., pp. 370–371.

112. Ibid., pp. 433–436, September 22, 1862.

113. Ibid., pp. 438–439.

114. Maria Weston Chapman to Anne Greene Chapman, November 22, 1862, Weston Sisters Collection. BPL.

115. Basler, *Collected Works*, V, p. 444.

116. Ibid., pp. 529–537.

117. Basler, *Collected Works*, VI, pp. 28–31; Stern, *The Life and Writings of Abraham Lincoln*, pp. 746–748.

118. Joshua Speed's interview with WHH, February 1866, *Herndon's Informants*, p. 197.

119. Henry Wilson's interview with WHH, May 30, 1867, *Herndon's Informants*, pp. 561–562.

120. Ibid., p. 562.

121. Palmer, ed., *Selected Letters of Charles Sumner*, Charles Sumner to Abraham Lincoln, 7 August 1863, p. 186.

122. Basler, *Collected Works*, VI, p. 291.

123. Ibid., p. 358.

124. Ibid., p. 388.

125. Basler, *Collected Works*, VII, p. 226.

126. See also Abraham Lincoln to John A. J. Creswell, March 17, 1864, Basler, *Collected Works*, VII, p. 251.

127. Abraham Lincoln to Albert G. Hodges, April 4, 1864, Basler, *Collected Works*, VII, pp. 281–283.

128. Maria Weston Chapman to Lizzie, February 16 and 23, 1864. Weston Sisters Collections. BPL.

129. McPherson, *Tried by War*, pp. 203, 213–216; John Keegan, *The American Civil War* (New York: Vintage Civil War Library, 2009), pp. 236–237.

130. Basler, *Collected Works*, VII, p. 380.

131. Abraham Lincoln to Ulysses S. Grant, August 17, 1864, Basler, *Collected Works*, VII, p. 499.

132. Interview with Alexander W. Randall and Joseph T. Mills, August 19, 1864, Basler, *Collected Works*, VII, pp. 506–507.

133. Goodwin, *Team of Rivals*, pp. 686–690; White, *A Lincoln*, pp. 653–654.

CHAPTER 2

1. Bertram Wyatt-Brown, *The Shaping of Southern Culture: Honor, Grace, and War, 1760s–1880s* (Chapel Hill: University of North Carolina Press, 2001), pp. xii, xiv, 85, 104, 133, 214; Wyatt-Brown, *Southern Honor: Ethics and Behavior in the Old South* (New York: Oxford University Press, 1982), pp. xv, 26–27, 114; Wyatt-Brown, *Honor and Violence in the Old South* (New York: Oxford University Press, 1986), pp. viii, 4, 14, 22, 39.

2. Edward Tivnan uses the term "moral imagination" as an attempt to debate moral convictions in a confusing contemporary moral environment where no consensus exists on what is right or wrong. See *The Moral Imagination: Confronting the Ethical Issues of Our Day* (New York: Simon & Schuster, 1995). My view of moral imagination implies the capacity of individuals to confront or challenge a moral consensus, such as the code of honor during the Civil War.

3. James Q. Wilson, *The Moral Sense* (New York: Free Press, 1993), p. 144.

4. Charles Taylor, *Sources of the Self: The Making of the Modern Identity* (Cambridge, MA: Harvard University Press, 1989), p. x.

5. For the argument that "personal history determines partisan course," see Jean H. Baker, *Affairs of Party: The Political Culture of Democrats in the Mid-Nineteenth Century* (Ithaca, NY: Cornell University Press, 1983), p. 66. For other works that analyze the role of family upon morality and politics, see Kimberly K. Smith, *The Dominion of Voice: Riot, Reason, and Romance in Antebellum Politics* (Lawrence: University Press of Kansas, 1999); Daniel J. Elazar, *Building Toward Civil War: Generational Rhythms in American Politics* (New York: Madison Books, 1992); George C. Rable, *The Confederate Republic: A Revolution Against Politics* (Chapel Hill: University of North Carolina Press, 1994); Emory M. Thomas, *The Confederate Nation: 1861–1865* (New York: Harper & Row, 1979), pp. 19–28; and John C. Inscoe and Gordon B. McKinney, "Highland Households Divided: Family Deceptions, Diversions, and Divisions in Southern Appalachia's Inner Civil War," in John C. Inscoe and Robert C. Kenser, eds. *Enemies of the Country: New Perspectives on Unionists in the Civil War South* (Athens: University of Georgia Press, 2001), pp. 54–72. For arguments on the interactions of gender and moral issues, see Stephen W. Berry, *All That Makes a Man: Love and Ambition in the Civil War South* (New York: Oxford University Press, 2003); Stephanie McCurry, "The Politics of Yeoman Households in South Carolina," in Catherine Clinton and Nina Silber, eds., *Divided Houses: Gender and the Civil War* (New York: Oxford University Press, 1992), pp. 22–42; Reid Mitchell, "Soldiering, Manhood, and Coming of Age: A Northern Volunteer," ibid., pp. 43–54; and Drew Gilpin Faust, "Altars of Sacrifice: Confederate Women and the Narratives of War," ibid., pp. 171–199. Although scholars might agree that varied cultural factors weighed upon the attitudes toward war, they disagree on how moral conflict within the family led to the support or nonsupport of war.

6. Wyatt-Brown, *Southern Honor*, pp. 33, 55, 57, 93, 95, 166–167, 328, 330–331, 349–361, 365, 406; Stephen M. Stowe, *Intimacy and Power in the Old*

South: Ritual in the Lives of the Planters (Baltimore: Johns Hopkins University Press, 1987), pp. 1–4, 24–49.

7. Taylor, *Sources of the Self*, pp. x, 14, 27–35, 47.

8. For a history of the Mordecai family and their educational experiments, see Jean E. Friedman, *Ways of Wisdom: Moral Education in the Early National Republic* (Athens: University of Georgia Press, 2001). See also Emily Bingham, *Mordecai: An Early American Family* (New York: Hill and Wang, 2003); Edgar E. MacDonald, ed., *The Education of the Heart: The Correspondence of Rachel Mordecai Lazarus and Maria Edgeworth* (Chapel Hill: University of North Carolina Press, 1977); and Myron Berman, *Richmond's Jewry, 1769–1976: Shabbat in Shockoe* (Charlottesville: University of Virginia Press, 1979).

9. Richard Lovell Edgeworth and Maria Edgeworth, *Practical Education*, 2 vols., 2nd ed. (Boston: T. B. Wait & Sons, 1815).

10. Friedman, *Ways of Wisdom*, pp. 11–22; MacDonald, *Education of the Heart*, pp. 107, 124, 251.

11. Edgeworth and Edgeworth, *Practical Education*, 1, p. 4.

12. Friedman, *Ways of Wisdom*, pp. 22–26, 84–88; Taylor, *Sources of the Self*, pp. 268–270.

13. Bingham, *Mordecai*, p. 5.

14. Ellen Mordecai to Solomon Mordecai, July 31, 1817, Jacob Mordecai Papers, Duke University, Durham (hereinafter DU).

15. Alfred Mordecai to Solomon Mordecai, February 24, 1819, Mordecai Family Papers, Southern Historical Collection, University of North Carolina, Chapel Hill (hereinafter MFP SHC UNC).

16. Alfred Mordecai, "Memoirs," in Jacob Radar Marcus, ed., *Memoirs of American Jews, 1775–1865*, 3 vols. (Philadelphia: Jewish Publication Society of America, 1955–1956), pp. 219–221; Stanley L. Falk, "Major Alfred Mordecai: First Ordnance Officer to Apply Scientific Methods to Armament," *Nearprint* (November–December 1959), p. 396.

17. James R. Endler, *Other Leaders, Other Heroes: West Point's Legacy to America and Beyond the Field of Battle* (Westport, CT: Praeger, 1998), p. 6.

18. Taylor, *Sources of the Self*, p. x.

19. Stephen E. Ambrose, *Duty, Honor, Country: A History of West Point* (Baltimore: Johns Hopkins University Press, 1966), pp. 62–68, 73–74, 87–90, 104; George S. Pappas, *To the Point: The United States Military Academy, 1802–1902* (Westport, CT: Praeger, 1993), p. 114.

20. Falk, "Major Alfred Mordecai," pp. 395–397.

21. Ellen Mordecai to Solomon Mordecai, July 12, 1821, MFP SHC UNC.

22. Rachel Mordecai Lazarus to Ellen Mordecai, December 6, 1821, ibid. Orlando is a reference to the older brother of Rosamond in Maria Edgeworth's collection of popular children's stories, *Early Lessons*. He is the very model of an enlightened, scientifically minded young man who leads his sister toward moral reasoning. See "Rosamond," *Early Lessons* (London: George Routledge & Sons, 1856), pp. 42–61.

23. Rebecca Mordecai to Jacob Mordecai, September 6, 1825, MFP SHC UNC.

24. MacDonald, *Education of the Heart*, pp. 28n, 289, 332.

25. Bingham, *Mordecai*, pp. 236–237. Prophets and psalmists regarded an upright man as one who loves justice, practices beneficence and humility, and thus "is not afraid of evil tidings; his heart is firm, he trusts in the Lord." See Micah 6 and Psalm 112 for an expression and definition of the righteous man. Adele Berlin and Marc Zvi Brettler, eds., *The Jewish Study Bible* (New York: Oxford University Press, 2004), pp. 1215, 1409–1410.

26. Alfred Mordecai to Little Ellen Mordecai, c/o George Mordecai, July 21, 1836, MFP SHC UNC.

27. Emma Mordecai to Ellen Mordecai, March 15, 1846.

28. Alfred Mordecai to Samuel Mordecai, December 7, 1859, Jacob Mordecai Papers, DU; Alfred Mordecai to George Mordecai, August 29, 1860, George Mordecai Papers, MFP SHC UNC.

29. Alfred Mordecai to George Mordecai, January 6, 1861, George Mordecai Papers, ibid.

30. Alfred Mordecai to George Mordecai, August 29, 1860; January 9, 1861, ibid.; Alfred Mordecai to Samuel Mordecai, December 10, 1860, ibid.

31. Alfred Mordecai to Little Ellen Mordecai, c/o George Mordecai, July 21, 1836, ibid. Alfred applied the derisive term "white nigger" to abolitionist sympathizers and, by extension, to white Northerners. See Eugene D. Genovese, *Roll, Jordan, Roll: The World the Slaves Made* (New York: Vintage Books, 1976), p. 438; and Eric Foner, *Free Soil, Free Labor, Free Men: The Ideology of the Republican Party Before the Civil War* (New York: Oxford University Press, 1970), pp. 263–264.

32. Alfred Mordecai to George Mordecai, January 20, 1861, George Mordecai Papers, MFP SHC UNC.

33. Samuel Mordecai to George Mordecai, March 26, 1861, ibid.

34. Samuel Mordecai to George Mordecai, April 23, 1861, ibid.

35. Alfred Mordecai to George Mordecai, January 20, 1861, ibid.

36. Samuel Mordecai to George Mordecai, April 22 and June 9, 1861, ibid.

37. Rebecca Mordecai to Alfred Mordecai, August 25, 1861, ibid.

38. *Troy (N.Y.) Daily Times*, May 8, 1861.

39. *Daily Whig*, May 9, 1861.

40. *Troy (N.Y.) Daily Times*, May 10, 1861.

41. Wyatt-Brown, *Southern Honor*, pp. 33.

42. Obituary, "Major Alfred Mordecai," *The Jewish Exponent*, November 25, 1887.

43. Ibid.

44. E. Brooks Holifield, *The Gentlemen Theologians: American Theology in Southern Culture, 1795–1860* (Durham, NC: Duke University Press, 1978), p. ix. Holifield notes the English and Scottish enlightened influences upon American Christian "rational orthodoxy," but the same might apply to Jewish Orthodoxy as shaped by Moses Mendelssohn and the German Enlightenment.

45. William G. Shade, *Democratizing the Old Dominion: Virginia and the Second Party System, 1824–1861* (Charlottesville: University Press of Virginia, 1996), p. 10; Christine Leigh Heyrman, *Southern Cross: The Beginnings of the Bible Belt* (Chapel Hill: University of North Carolina Press, 1997), p. 8; Steven Elliott Tripp, *Yankee Town, Southern City: Race and Class Relations in Civil War Lynchburg* (New York: New York University Press, 1997), pp. 8–9, 34–35; F. N. Boney, *John Letcher of Virginia: The Story of Virginia's Civil War Governor* (Tuscaloosa: University of Alabama Press, 1966).

46. La Salle Corbell Pickett, *Literary Hearthstones of Dixie* (Philadelphia: J. B. Lippincott, 1912), p. 230.

47. For a discussion of Romantic sensibility, see Lawrence S. Lockridge, *The Ethics of Romanticism* (New York: Cambridge University Press, 1989), p. 51; Alex Comfort, "The Ideology of Romanticism," in Robert F. Gleckner and Gerald E. Enscoe, eds. *Romanticism: Points of View* (Englewood Cliffs, NJ: Prentice Hall, 1970), pp. 165–180; Morse Peckman, *Romanticism and Behavior: Collected Essays II* (Columbia: University of South Carolina Press, 1976), p. 21.

48. George W. Bagby, *The Old Virginia Gentleman and Other Sketches*, Ellen M. Bagby, ed. (Richmond, VA: The Dietz Press, 1943), pp. xviii–xix.

49. George Bagby to Ellen Matthews, December 22, 1853, George William Bagby Papers, Virginia Historical Society, Richmond (hereinafter GWBP VHS). For a discussion of the effect of paternal aggression upon sons' moral development, see Wilson, *Moral Sense*, p. 105; and Justin Aronfreed, *Conscience and Conduct* (New York: Academic Press, 1968), pp. 308–309.

50. George Bagby to George William Bagby, November 21, 1835, GWBP VHS.

51. George Bagby to George William Bagby, September 11, 1834, ibid.

52. George Bagby to George William Bagby, May 3, 1842, ibid.

53. George Bagby to George William Bagby, January 10, 1843, ibid.

54. "Private Bagby Book," ibid.

55. Edgehill School Report Card, April 30, 1841, ibid.; George Bagby to George William Bagby, January 10, 1843, March 18, 1844, ibid.

56. For Wilson's argument that lack of attachment hinders moral development, see *Moral Sense*, p. 105.

57. George William Bagby to Ellen Bagby, December 8, 1846, and Thomas Jellis Kirkpatrick to George William Bagby, August 13, 1850, GWBP VHS.

58. George Bagby to George William Bagby, December 28, 1848, ibid.

59. Pickett, *Literary Hearthstones*, 236–238; Bagby, *Old Virginia Gentleman*, pp. xix, 173, 176.

60. Kirkpatrick to George William Bagby, August 22, 1850, GWBP VHS.

61. Ibid.

62. Kirkpatrick to George William Bagby, November 16, 1851, ibid.

63. Kirkpatrick to George William Bagby, February 10, 1852, ibid.

64. Kirkpatrick to George William Bagby, April 29, 1859, ibid.

65. Shade, *Democratizing the Old Dominion*, pp. 10, 14, 25–40; George S. Morris and Susan L. Foutz, *Lynchburg in the Civil War: The City—the People—the Battle*, 2nd ed. (Lynchburg, VA: H. E. Howard, 1984), pp. 1–7.

66. George Bagby to George William Bagby, February 4, 29, and 27, 1856; January 5, May 27, and September 3, 1857, GWBP VHS.

67. George Bagby to George William Bagby, January 28, 1859, ibid.

68. George Bagby to George William Bagby, February 9, 1859, ibid.

69. Allen Johnson, ed., *Dictionary of American Biography* (New York: Charles Scribner's Sons, 1928), p. 492; Bagby, *Old Virginia Gentleman*, p. xxi.

70. Shade, *Democratizing the Old Dominion*, pp. 14, 16.

71. John Hampton Chamberlayne to George William Bagby, December 18, 1860, GWBP VHS.

72. Stephen Davenport Yancy to George William Bagby, January 27, 1861, ibid.

73. George William Bagby to John Esten Cooke, January 29, 1861, ibid.

74. William C. Davis, *Rhett: The Turbulent Life and Times of a Fire-Eater* (Columbia: University of South Carolina Press, 2001), p. 391.

75. *Charleston Mercury*, November 30, 1861.

76. Ibid., December 6, 1862.

77. Robert Barnwell Rhett to George William Bagby, January 12, 1861, GWBP VHS.

78. Robert Barnwell Rhett to George William Bagby, April 2, 1861, ibid.

79. Robert Barnwell Rhett to George William Bagby, November 25, 1861, ibid.

80. Robert Barnwell Rhett to George William Bagby, April 9, 1862, ibid.

81. *Charleston Mercury*, October 28 and 30 and December 11, 1862; *Mobile Register*, January 10, 1863; January 6, 1864.

82. W. G. Clark to George William Bagby, February 15, 1864, and W. W. Cary to Col. Joseph Forsyth, February 13, 1864, GWBP VHS.

83. Bagby, *Old Virginia Gentleman*, p. xxii.

84. Lucy Parke Chamberlayne to George William Bagby, October 8, 1862, GWBP VHS. See also Bagby, *Old Virginia Gentleman*, p. xxii.

85. George William Bagby to Lucy Parke Chamberlayne Bagby, May 20, 1865, GWBP VHS.

86. George William Bagby to Lucy Parke Chamberlayne Bagby, May 21, 1865, ibid.

87. George William Bagby to Lucy Parke Chamberlayne Bagby, May 26, 1865, ibid.

88. George William Bagby to Lucy Parke Chamberlayne Bagby, July 25 and December 23, 1865, ibid.

CHAPTER 3

1. For a definition of Northern principles of justice, see Lincoln's *First Inaugural Address* and *Second Inaugural Address*, the *Emancipation Proclamation*, and the *Gettysburg Address*.

2. Harry S. Stout, *Upon the Altar of the Nation: A Moral History of the Civil War* (New York: Penguin Books, 2006).

3. James M. McPherson, *What They Fought For, 1861–1865* (New York: Anchor Books, 1994).

4. Melvin J. Lerner, "Pursuing the Justice Motive," in Michael Ross and Dale Mille, eds., *The Justice Motive in Everyday Life* (Cambridge: Cambridge University Press, 2002), p. 12.

5. For a classical discussion of justice as a process of human development, see Aristotle, *Nicomachean Ethics*, in Michael L. Morgan, ed., *Classics of Moral and Political Theory* (Indianapolis/Cambridge: Hackett Publishing Company, 1992), pp. 250–251. Thomas Aquinas's "Summa Theologia," in Anton C. Pegis, ed., *Basic Writings of Saint Thomas Aquinas* (New York: Random House, 1945), I, pp. 42–49, 786–791, 938–941, presents the theological perspective. John Locke, "Second Treatise on Government," in Morgan, ed., *Classics of Moral and Political Theory*, pp. 754, 768. David A. Welch, *Justice and the Genesis of War* (Cambridge: Cambridge University Press, 1993), pp. xiv, 8; and Joseph H. Carens, *Culture, Citizenship and Community: A Contextual Exploration of Justice as Evenhandedness* (New York: Oxford University Press, 2000), pp. 3–4; discuss the legal, moral, and political contexts of justice.

6. Paul Ricoeur, in David Pellauer, trans., *The Just* (Chicago: University of Chicago, 2000), p. xv, argues that justice begins with a desire, rooted in an examined life. Those who sought justice would ask, "How would I like to lead my life?" For a psychological notion of the desire for justice, see also Melvin J. Lerner, "Pursuing the Justice Motive," pp. 10–37, and Daniel Batson, "Justice Motivation and Moral Motivation," *The Justice Motive in Everyday Life*, pp. 91–106.

7. Stuart Hampshire, *Justice Is Conflict* (Princeton University Press, 2000), pp. 11–12.

8. Paul Ricoeur, *The Just*, p. xv, offers a discussion of justice as "an integral part of the desire to live well." See also Michael Sandel, *Justice: What's the Right Thing to Do?* (New York: Farrar, Straus and Giroux, 2009), p. 9.

9. Nathan Appleton, *Memoir of Samuel Appleton and His Descendants*, n.d., vol. 21, Appleton Family Papers, Massachusetts Historical Society, Boston (hereinafter AFP MHS).

10. John Hannibal Sheppard, *Sketch of Hon. Nathan Appleton*, pp. 1–3, pamphlet, Lehigh University Rare Book Room, Bethlehem, Pennsylvania.

11. Ibid., p. 4.

12. Nathan Appleton, "Labor, Its Relations in Europe and the United States Compared" (Boston: Eastburn's Press, 1844), p. 3. (From *Hunt's Merchant's Magazine*) State Historical Society of Wisconsin. Microform.

13. Ibid., p. 8. See also Nathan A. Appleton, "What Revenue Standard?" (Pamphlet) (Boston: Eastburn's Press, 1846), pp. 11, 16. State Historical Society of Wisconsin. Microform. The pamphlet argues that the tariff of 1842 took the United States out of economic depression and that, since the tariff, the wages of Lowell workers rose.

14. Robert C. Winthrop, ed., Nathan Appleton, *Memoir of the Hon. Nathan Appleton, LL.D.* (New York: Greenwood Press, 1969), pp. 59–60 [1861].

15. Nathan Appleton, "Memoir of Samuel Appleton and His Descendants," n.d., vol. 21, AFP MHS; Nathan Appleton, *Journal*, April 12, 1802, MHS; Nathan Appleton, "Introduction of the Power Loom and the Origin of Lowell" (Lowell: B. H. Penhollow, 1861), pp. 7, 9, 15, 17, 29; Winthrop, ed., *Memoir of the Hon. Nathan Appleton,* pp. 3, 16, 28, 32; Robert F. Dalzell Jr., *Enterprising Elite: The Boston Associates and the World They Made* (Cambridge: Harvard University Press, 1987), pp. 6, 22, 33, 39; Frances W. Gregory, *Nathan Appleton: Merchant and Entrepreneur, 1779–1861* (Charlottesville: University of Virginia Press, 1975), pp. 25–28.

16. *Congressional Record, Debates in Congress*, part III, vol. VIII [1831–1832], p. 3189.

17. Ibid., pp. 3190–3192.

18. *Congressional Record, Debates in Congress*, part II, vol. VIII [1831–1832], p. 1601.

19. Barrington Moore Jr., "The American Civil War: The Last Capitalist Revolution," in Irwin Unger, ed., *Essays on the Civil War and Reconstruction* (New York: Holt, Rinehart and Winston, Inc., 1970), pp. 45, 54.

20. Ibid., part III, vol. VIII [1831–1832], pp. 3193, 3196–3198, 3204–3206, 3209. For a discussion of the Panic of 1837, see Jean E. Friedman, *The Revolt of the Conservative Democrats: An Essay on American Political Culture and Political Development, 1837–1844* (Ann Arbor: UMI Research Press, 1979).

21. *Congressional Record, Debates in Congress*, part III, vol. VIII [1831–1832], p. 3209.

22. Nathan Appleton, *Journal*, December 21 and 22, 1804; January 18, 1805; February 4, 8, and 11, 1805, AFP MHS.

23. Ibid., January 8, 1805.

24. Nathan Appleton, "Considerations on Slavery in a Letter to a Friend," AFP MHS.

25. Ibid.

26. Nathan Appleton, "Abolition," n.d., Notes and Articles on Slavery, AFP MHS.

27. For a discussion of distributive justice, see Sandel, *Justice: What's the Right Thing to Do?* pp. 187–192; Walter J. Burghardt, *Justice: A Global Adventure* (Maryknoll, New York: Orbis Books, 2004), p. 5. See David G. Pugh, *Sons of Liberty: The Masculine Mind in Nineteenth-Century America* (Westport, CT: Greenwood Press, 1983), p. 34, for a discussion of capitalists' pursuit of profit because of "happiness in the process itself."

28. "Correspondence between Nathan Appleton and John G. Palfrey" (Boston: Eastburn's Press, 1846), p. 5, MHS.

29. Edward Everett to Nathan Appleton, February 4, 1850, AFP MHS.

30. Nathan Appleton, "Notes and Articles on Slavery," Scrapbook, p. 66, AFP MHS.

31. Nathan Appleton to Rev. M. M. Dillon, August 23, 1854, AFP MHS.

32. David Welch, *Justice and the Genesis of War* (Cambridge: Cambridge University Press, 1993), pp. 197, 202; Paul Tillich, *Love, Power and Justice* (New York: Oxford University Press, 1984), pp. 10–11; Sandel, *Justice: What's the Right Thing to Do?* pp. 187, 193.

33. Nathan Appleton to William Pringle, December 15, 1860, AFP MHS.

34. Ibid.

35. Ibid., January 7, 1861, AFP MHS.

36. William Edward Heygate and Nathan Appleton, *The Doctrines of Original Sin and the Trinity: Discussed in a Correspondence between a Clergyman of the Episcopal Church of England and a Layman of Boston* (Boston: J. H. Eastburn's Press, 1859), p. 23.

37. Ibid., p. 7.

38. Ibid., p. 28.

39. Ibid., p. 32.

40. Ibid., p. 33.

41. George M. Fredrickson, *The Inner Civil War: Northern Intellectuals and the Crisis of the Union* (New York: Harper & Row, 1965), pp. 12–13.

42. David Robinson, *William Ellery Channing: Selected Writings* (New York: Paulist Press, 1985), p. 226.

43. Andrew Delbanco, *William Ellery Channing: An Essay on the Liberal Spirit in America* (Cambridge: Harvard University Press, 1981), pp. 12, 23, 30, 56, 61, 103, 126–129.

44. Delbanco, *William Ellery Channing*, p. 12.

45. Edward Wegenknecht, *Mrs. Longfellow: Selected Letters and Journals of Fanny Appleton Longfellow, 1817–1861* (New York: Longmans Green and Co., 1956), pp. 2–4, 6, 11, 14–15.

46. Ibid., p. 21.

47. Ibid., p. 35.

48. Henry Wadsworth Longfellow, *Hyperion: A Romance* (Boston: Houghton, Mifflin and Co., 1893), p. 29.

49. Ibid., pp. 219–223, 284.

50. Charles C. Calhoun, *Longfellow: A Rediscovered Life* (Boston: Beacon Press, 2004), p. 196. Henry Wadsworth Longfellow to Thomas Gold Appleton, January 23, 1837, Thomas Gold Appleton Correspondence, Houghton Library, Harvard University, Cambridge.

51. Andrew Hillen, ed., *The Letters of Henry Wadsworth Longfellow*, vol. II (Cambridge: Belknap Press, 1972), p. 93.

52. Ibid., p. 243.

53. Ibid., pp. 236, 256, 281; David Donald, *Charles Sumner and the Coming of the Civil War* (New York: Knopf, 1967), p. 94.

54. Ibid., pp. 335, 340.

55. Donald, *Charles Sumner*, pp. 71, 74.

56. Wagenknecht, *Mrs. Longfellow*, pp. 67, 79–82; see also Rollo May, *Love and Will* (New York: Dell Publishing Company, 1969), p. 101.

57. Calhoun, *Longfellow*, p. 166.

58. Ibid., II, p. 257.

59. David Donald, *Charles Sumner and the Coming of the Civil War* (New York: Knopf, 1967), pp. 104–105, 133; Hillen, *The Letters of Henry Wadsworth Longfellow*, p. 538.

60. Arthur Reed Hogue, ed., *Charles Sumner: An Essay by Carl Shurtz* (Westport, CT: Greenwood Press, 1972), p. 24.

61. David Donald, *Charles Sumner and the Coming of the Civil War* (New York: Knopf, 1967), p. 119.

62. Hillen, *The Letters of Henry Wadsworth Longfellow*, III, p. 204.

63. See David Donald, ed., "Toward a Reconsideration of Abolitionists," *Lincoln Reconsidered* (New York: Vintage Books, [1947] 2001), pp. 39–40, for a discussion of the disdain abolitionist and antislavery elements had for labor's cause.

64. Hillen, *The Letters of Henry Wadsworth Longfellow*, III, pp. 105, 106, 169.

65. Ibid., p. 107.

66. Ibid., pp. 89–91.

67. Ibid., p. 108.

68. Ibid., p. 123.

69. Ibid., III, pp. 236–237; Wegknecht, *Mrs. Longfellow*, p. 158.

70. Donald, *Charles Sumner*, pp. 170–175.

71. Ibid., p. 203.

72. Wegknecht, *Mrs. Longfellow*, p. 179.

73. Hillen, *The Letters of Henry Wadsworth Longfellow*, III, pp. 240, 254–255, 288.

74. Ibid., III, p. 314.

75. Wegknecht, *Mrs. Longfellow*, p. 168.

76. Ibid., III, p. 351.

77. Donald, *Charles Sumner and the Coming of the Civil War*, pp. 224, 228–232; Hillen, *The Letters of Henry Wadsworth Longfellow*, III, p. 354. For a discussion of the chivalric ideals that bound even enemies, see Gerald F. Linderman, *Embattled Courage: The Experience of Combat in the American Civil War* (New York: The Free Press, 1987), p. 16.

78. Wegknecht, *Mrs. Longfellow*, p. 198.

79. Ibid., p. 198; Donald, *Charles Sumner and the Coming of the Civil War*, p. 269.

80. James M. McPherson, *Ordeal by Fire: The Civil War and Reconstruction* (New York: Alfred A. Knopf, 1982), pp. 79–80.

81. Carl Schurz, in Arthur Reed Hogue, ed., *Charles Sumner, An Essay* (Urbana: The University of Illinois Press, 1951). p. 59; Donald, *Charles Sumner and the Coming of the Civil War*, pp. 281, 288.

82. Hillen, *The Letters of Henry Wadsworth Longfellow*, III, p. 540.

83. Ibid., III, p. 542.

84. Henry Ward Beecher of Plymouth Church, Brooklyn's Second Congregational Church, was the brother of Harriet Beecher Stowe, who wrote *Uncle Tom's Cabin*, and the son of Lyman Beecher, a noted antislavery preacher.

85. Wegknecht, *Mrs. Longfellow*, pp. 218–219.

86. Ibid., p. 226.

87. Ibid., p. 229.

88. Ibid., p. 236.

89. Ibid.

90. Ibid., p. 237.

91. Ibid.

92. Ibid.

93. Ibid., pp. 238–240.

94. Ibid., p. 240.

95. Hillen, *The Letters of Henry Wadsworth Longfellow*, IV, p. 240.

96. Ricoeur, *The Just*, pp. 65–66.

97. Donald, "Toward a Reconsideration of Abolitionists," *Lincoln Reconsidered*, pp. 31–43.

98. Charles Sumner to the Duchess of Argyll, November 18, 1861, in Beverly Wilson Palmer, ed., *The Selected Letters of Charles Sumner* (Boston: Northeastern University Press, 1990), p. 84.

99. Nathan Appleton Jr., *Journal of Memoirs*, 1871, vol. 30, AFP MHS.

100. Nathan Appleton Jr., *Diary*, February 21–26, 1850, March 4 and 19–20, 1850, AFP MHS.

101. Ibid., April 3, 1850.

102. Ibid., March 10, 1851. See E. Anthony Rotundo, "Boy Culture: Middle-Class Boyhood in Nineteenth-Century America," in Mark C. Carnes and Clyde Griffen, eds., *Meanings for Manhood: Constructions of Masculinity in Victorian America* (Chicago: University of Chicago, 1996), pp. 9–15, 18, for a discussion of freedom and excitement in boyhood. Nate Appleton, however, displays more upper-class reticence in his young life.

103. *Diary*, May 24, 1856; May 27, 1857, AFP MHS.

104. Ibid., January 10 and 20–21, 1858, AFP MHS.

105. Ibid., January 28–29, 1858, AFP MHS.

106. Ibid., March 1, 1858, AFP MHS.

107. Rotundo, "Boy Culture," pp. 22, 26.

108. *Diary*, April 11, 1858; May 22, 1858; June 24, 1858, AFP MHS.

109. Ibid., September 12, 1858, AFP MHS.

110. Ibid., August 10, 1859, AFP MHS.

111. [illeg.] Brown to Nathan Appleton, August 11, 1859, AFP MHS.

112. Caroline Le Roy Appleton to Nathan Appleton Jr., August 16, 1859; Nathan Appleton Jr. to Nathan Appleton, 1859; Nathan Appleton Jr., *Diary*, January 1, 2, 4, 1860, AFP MHS.

113. Nathan Appleton, *Diary*, January 10, 1860, AFP MHS; *An Authentic History of the Lawrence Calamity* (Boston: John J. Dyer and Company, 1860), pp. 6–11, 64–67, 72, 77.

114. Newspaper clipping from Nathan Appleton Jr., *Diary*, January 13, 1860, AFP MHS.

115. Nathan Appleton Jr., *Diary*, January 15, 1860, AFP MHS.

116. Ibid., February 24, 1860, AFP MHS.

117. Ibid., February 17, 1860; March 29, 1860; Robert Winthrop to Nathan Appleton Jr., August 10, 1859, AFP MHS.

118. February 4, 1860, AFP MHS.

119. Nathan Appleton, *Diary*, May 5, 10, 11, and 17, 1860; June 1 and 18, 1860; July 19, 21, 22–26, 1860, AFP MHS.

120. Harriot Appleton to Nathan Appleton Jr., September 4, 1860, AFP MHS.

121. Nathan Appleton Jr. to Harriot Sumner Appleton, September 1860, AFP MHS.

122. Rotundo, "Boy Culture," pp. 15, 28–29.

123. Harriot Sumner Appleton to Nathan Appleton Jr., September 1860, AFP MHS.

124. Nathan Appleton, *Diary*, May 14, 1860; July 22, 1860, AFP MHS.

125. Nathan Appleton Jr. to Tom Appleton, January 1861, AFP MHS; Nathan Appleton Jr., *Harvard College During the War*, reproduced from the *New England Magazine*, March 1890, p. 12, AFP MHS.

126. E. H. Kidder to Nathan Appleton Jr., February 15, 1861, AFP MHS.

127. E. H. Kidder to Nathan Appleton Jr., April 29, 1861, AFP MHS.

128. Charles Emerson to Nathan Appleton Jr., May 5 and 30, 1861; Ned to Nate Appleton, January 13, 1862; Nathan Appleton Jr., to Harriot Appleton, January 31, 1862; February 3, 1862, Nathan Appleton Jr., *Journal (Memoirs)*, vol. 30, 1871; Nathan Appleton Jr., *Harvard College During the War*, reproduced from the *New England Magazine* (March 1890), pp. 3, 6, 11, AFP MHS. For a discussion of male ritual, see Mark C. Carnes, "Middle-Class Men and the Solace of Fraternal Ritual," *Meanings for Manhood*, pp. 43, 50.

129. Nathan Appleton Jr., *Memoirs* [1871], AFP MHS.

130. Nathan Appleton Jr. to Harriot Sumner Appleton, November 15, 1863, AFP MHS. See also Reid Mitchell, *The Vacant Chair* (New York: Oxford, 1988), pp. 4, 7, 11.

131. Nathan Appleton Jr. to Family, September 1, 1863; Nathan Appleton Jr. to Hattie Appleton, October 23, 1863; Nathan Appleton Jr. to Harriot Sumner Appleton, October 19, 1863, AFP MHS. See also Mitchell, *The Vacant Chair*, p. 10.

132. Nathan Appleton Jr. to Harriot Sumner Appleton, November 20, 1863, AFP MHS.

133. Nathan Appleton Jr. to Harriet Sumner Appleton, November 20, 1863, AFP MHS.

134. Nathan Appleton Jr. to Hattie Appleton Curtis, December 11, 1863, AFP MHS. See also E. B. Long with Barbara Long, *The Civil War Day by Day: An Almanac, 1861–1865* (New York: Doubleday & Company, Inc., 1971), p. 444.

135. Appleton Jr., *Harvard College During the War*, p. 22, AFP MHS.

136. Nathan Appleton, *Journal*, vol. 30 [Memoirs], 1871, AFP MHS.

137. Nathan Appleton to Hattie Appleton Curtis, February 4, 1864, AFP MHS.

138. Reid Mitchell, *Civil War Soldiers* (New York: Viking Penguin, Inc., 1988), p. 57.

139. Nathan Appleton Jr., *Journal*, vol. 30 [Memoirs]; Nathan Appleton Jr. to Family, "Head and Hind Quarters in the Saddle Near Spotsylvania C. H.," May 9, 1864, "Fifth Day of the Fight"; Nathan Appleton Jr. to Hattie Appleton Curtis, August 26, 1864, AFP MHS.

140. Nathan Appleton Jr. to Hattie Appleton Curtis, August 26, 1864; March 19, 1865; Nate to Mawther, December 22, 1864; Harriot Sumner Appleton to Nathan Appleton Jr., December 26, 1864; January 3, 1865, AFP MHS.

141. Nathan Appleton Jr., *Journal* [Memoirs], 1871; Nathan Appleton Jr. to Harriot Sumner Appleton, April 3 and 10, 1865, AFP MHS. See also Long, *The Civil War Day by Day*, p. 666.

142. Gerald F. Linderman, *Embattled Courage: The Experience of Combat in the American Civil War* (New York: The Free Press, 1987), p. 84.

143. Nathan Appleton, "Notes and Articles on Slavery," Scrapbook #13.7, p. 66, AFP MHS.

144. Welch, *Justice and the Genesis of War*, pp. 18–21; Steven L. Blader and Tom R. Tyler, "Justice and Empathy: What Motivates People to Help Others?," *The Justice Motive in Everyday Life*, pp. 229–233; and Sandel, *Justice: What's the Right Thing to Do?*, pp. 193–194.

CHAPTER 4

1. Speech before the American Anti-Slavery Society, May 4, 1847, as quoted in Walter Berns, *Making Patriots* (Chicago: University of Chicago, 2001), p. 104.

2. John W. Blassingame, ed., *Slave Testimony: Two Centuries of Letters, Speeches, Interviews, and Autobiographies* (Baton Rouge: Louisiana State University Press, 1977), p. 501.

3. George P. Fletcher, *Loyalty: An Essay on the Morality of Relationships* (New York: Oxford University Press, 1993), pp. 5, 33–40, notes that others have argued loyalty may initiate political life when cooperation with others becomes the most important way of solving problems. Also loyalty may be any attempt to right an injustice. Fletcher emphasizes the tragedy when loyalties, such as that of family and nation conflict, as sometimes they must when an individual member of a group exercises independent moral judgment.

4. As quoted in Gary B. Nash, *The Forgotten Fifth: African Americans in the Age of Revolution* (Cambridge: Harvard University Press, 2006), p. 6.

5. Elizabeth D. Samet, *Willing Obedience: Citizens, Soldiers, and the Progress of Consent in America, 1776–1898* (Stanford: Stanford University Press, 2004), p. 146.

6. James M. McPherson, *For Cause and Comrades* (New York: Oxford University Press, 1997), p. 128.

7. Pvt. Spotswood Rice to my children, Benton Barracks Hospital, St. Louis, Missouri, September 3, 1864, in Ira Berlin and Leslie S. Rowland, eds., *Families and Freedom: A Documentary History of African-American Kinship in the Civil War* (New York: The New Press, 1997), pp. 195–196.

8. Alasdair MacIntyre, "Is Patriotism a Virtue?" in Michael Rosen and Jonathan Wolff, eds., *Political Thought* (New York: Oxford University Press, 1999), p. 280. See also Fletcher, *Loyalty*, 35; Merle Curti, in *The Roots of American Loyalty* (New York: Atheneum, 1968), p. 170, warns that loyalty may be a sentiment rather than a virtue. For a discussion of patriotism as self-interest, see Margaret Levi, *Consent, Dissent and Patriotism* (Cambridge: Cambridge University Press, 1997); and Jennifer A. Herdt, *Putting on Virtue: The Legacy of the Splendid Vices* (Chicago: University of Chicago Press, 2008), pp. 2–4, 11, 74–76. Stephen Nathanson, *Patriotism, Morality and Peace* (Lanham, Maryland: Rowman & Littlefield Publishers, Inc., 1993), pp. 3, 107, states that he believes in the necessity of patriotic social cohesion but eschews uncritical loyalty. Steven Johnson, *The Truth about Patriotism* (Durham: Duke University Press, 2007), p. 5, quotes Frederick Douglass as asserting, "Patriotism requires serious criticism." John H. Schaar, *Legitimacy in the Modern State* (New Brunswick: Transaction Books, 1981), p. 291, argues for a moderate patriotism but concedes the tension inherent in patriotism.

9. Melinda Lawson, *Patriot Fires: Forging a New American Nationalism in the Civil War North* (Lawrence, Kansas: University of Kansas Press, 2002), p. 11.

10. For a discussion of the stability of black families in slavery, see John Hope Franklin, "African American Families: A Historical Note," in Donna L. Franklin, ed., *Ensuring Inequality: The Structural Transformation of the African-American Family* (New York: Oxford University Press, 1997), pp. 3–6. See also Donna L. Franklin's discussion of black consanguine networks, pp. 14–15, 37–42; and Niara Sudarkasa, "Interpreting the African Heritage in African American Family Organization," in Harriette Pipes McAdoo, ed., *Black Families* (Thousand Oaks, California: Sage Publications, 2007), pp. 29–47.

11. As quoted in Howard Zinn, *The Other Civil War: Slavery and Struggle in Civil War America* (New York: Harper Perennial, 2011), p. 12.

12. Herbert G. Gutman, *The Black Family in Slavery and Freedom, 1750–1925* (New York: Pantheon Books, 1976).

13. Berlin and Rowland, *Families and Freedom*, p. 130.

14. Eugene D. Genovese, *Roll, Jordan, Roll: The World the Slaves Made* (New York: Vintage Books, 1972), p. 452.

15. Michael P. Johnson, "Looking for Lost Kin: Efforts to Reunite Freed Families after Emancipation," pp. 15–34; Michelle A Krowl, "For Better or for Worse; Black Families and 'the State' in Civil War Virginia," pp. 35–58; and Donald B. Shaffer, "In the Shadow of the Old Constitution: Black Civil War Veterans and the Persistence of Slave Marriage Customs," pp. 59–76, in Catherine Clinton, éd., *Southern Families at War: Loyalty and Conflict in the Civil War South* (New York: Oxford University Press, 2000).

16. Albert J. Raboteau, *Slave Religion: The "Invisible Institution" in the Antebellum South* (New York: Oxford University Press, 1978), pp. 13, 35, 59, 61, 69, 98, 146, 178, 218; Christine Leigh Heyrman, *Southern Cross: The Beginnings of the Bible Belt* (New York: Alfred A. Knopf, Inc., 1997), pp. 6, 49–52.

17. Clifton H. Johnson, ed., "I Ain't Got to Die No More," *God Struck Me Dead*, Social Science Documents, Amistad Research Center and Race Relations Department, Dillard University, New Orleans, Louisiana, p. 55.

18. Johnson, ed., "Slavery Was Hell without Fires," ibid., p. 209.

19. Jean E. Friedman, "The Movement of the Spirit in Historical and Literary Experience: An Essay on Alice Walker's *Meridian*," in Charles Reagan Wilson, ed., *Southern Perspectives on the American South Religion*, 5th edition (New York: Gordon and Breach, 1991), pp. 155–168.

20. Ira Berlin, Mary Favreau, and Steven F. Miller, *Remembering Slavery: African Americans Talk about Their Personal Experiences of Slavery and Freedom* (New York: The New Press, 1998), p. 213.

21. Johnson, ed., "The Loveliest Singing in the World," *God Struck Me Dead*, pp. 14–15.

22. Johnson, "I Came Down from Heaven and Now Return," *God Struck Me Dead*, Social Science Source Documents #2, Social Science Institute, Fisk University, Nashville, Tennessee, pp. 23–24.

23. Heyrman, *Southern Cross*, pp. 68, 257; Raboteau, *Slave Religion*, pp. 171, 177–182.

24. Johnson, ed., "Time Brought You to This World," *God Struck Me Dead*, p. 102.

25. Johnson. ed., "Hewn from the Mountains of Eternity," ibid., p. 101.

26. Traditional African American Folk Song.

27. John W. Blassingame, ed., *Slave Testimony: Two Centuries of Letters, Speeches, Interviews, and Autobiographies* (Baton Rouge: Louisiana State University Press, 1977), pp. 151–153.

28. Ibid., p. 250.

29. Lawrence W. Levine, *Black Culture and Black Consciousness: Afro-American Folk Thought from Slavery to Freedom* (New York: Oxford University Press, 1979), pp. 91–99, 108–110, 120–125; Charles Joyner, *Down by the Riverside: A South Carolina Slave Community* (Urbana: University of Illinois Press, 1984), pp. 164–165, 172–174.

30. Blassingame, *Slave Testimony*, pp. 359–360.

31. Fletcher, *Loyalty*, p. 6.

32. October 8, 1841, Telfair Family Papers; see also A. N. Urquhart to Mary Telfair, November 4, 1839, Telfair Family Papers, Georgia Historical Society, Savannah.

33. Blassingame, *Slave Testimony*, p. 590.

34. Ibid., p. 592.

35. George P. Rawick, ed., *The American Slave: A Composite Autobiography*, vol. 3, series I (Westport, CT: Greenwood Press, 1972), p. 25; Blassingame, *Slave Testimony*, pp. 23, 418.

36. Rawick, ed., *The American Slave*, vol. 3, series I, p. 28; vol. 12, series II, pp. 156, 168; Johnson, ed., "Sixty-Four Years, a Washer and Ironer," *God Struck Me Dead*, p. 185.

37. Elizabeth A. Regosin and Donald R. Shaffer, eds., *Voices of Emancipation: Understanding Slavery, the Civil War and Reconstruction through the United States Pension Bureau Files*(New York: New York University Press, 2008), p. 116.

38. Rawick, ed., *The American Slave*, vol. 6, series I, pp. 91–94.

39. Ibid., vol. 18, p. 39.

40. Ibid., vol. 3, series III, p. 249.

41. Ibid., vol. 12, series II, p. 149.

42. Ibid., vol. 6, series I, p. 201.

43. See Joel Rosenthal's address, "Patriotism and Cosmopolitanism," in *Policy Innovations* (Carnegie Council, July 29, 2009), online magazine. In his address, Rosenthal cites Martha Nussbaum's description of her notion of cosmopolitanism, which extends beyond nationalism to humanity.

44. Ann S. Masten and Anne Schaffer, "How Families Matter in Child Development: Reflections from Research on Risk and Resilience"; Michael Rutter, "The Promotion of Resilience in the Face of Adversity"; W. Andrew Collins and Glenn L. Roisman, "The Influence of Family and Peer Relationships in the Development of Competence during Adolescence"; in Alison Clark-Stewart and Judy Dunn, eds., *Family Counts: Effects on Child and Adolescent Development* (Cambridge: Cambridge University Press, 2006), pp. 11, 15, 26–30, 89; Douglas and Barbara Schave, *Early Adolescence and the Search for Self: A Developmental Perspective* (New York: Praeger, 1989), pp. 2–6.

45. Rawick, *The American Slave*, vol. 15, p. 66.

46. Ira Berlin, Steven F. Miller, Joseph P. Reidy, and Leslie S. Rowland, eds., *The Wartime Genesis of Labor: The Upper South in Freedom; A Documentary History of Emancipation, 1861–1867* (Cambridge: Cambridge University Press, 1993), vol. I, p. 133.

47. Blassingame, *Slave Testimony*, p. 13.

48. Donald Shaffer, "In the Shadow of the Old Constitution," in Catherine Clinton, ed., *Southern Families at War: Loyalty and Conflict in the Civil War* (New York: Oxford University Press, 2000), p. 67.

49. Elizabeth A. Regosin and Donald R. Shaffer, eds., *Voices of Emancipation*, pp. 180, 183.

50. Ibid., pp. 166–167.

51. Ibid., p. 22.

52. Blassingame, *Slave Testimony*, p. 608.

53. Ibid., pp. 359–360.

54. James M. McPherson, *The Negro's Civil War: How American Negroes Felt and Acted during the War for the Union* (Urbana: University of Illinois Press, 1982), p. 21.

55. Blassingame, *Slave Testimony*, pp. 373, 378.

56. Melvin Claxton and Mark Puls, *Uncommon Valor: A Story of Race, Patriotism, and Glory in the Final Battles of the Civil War* (Hoboken, New Jersey: John Wiley Press, 2006), pp. 18–19, 38.

57. As quoted in McPherson, *For Cause & Comrades*, p. 128.

58. John Keegan, *The American Civil War*, pp. 292–298.

59. Blassingame, *Slave Testimony*, p. 545.

60. Ibid., p. 546.

61. Ibid., pp. 546–547.

62. Ibid., pp. 394–395.

63. Ibid., pp. 371–373.

64. Ira Berlin and Leslie S. Rowland, *Families and Freedom: A Documentary History of African-American Kinship in the Civil War Era* (New York: The New Press, 1997), pp. 39, 48.

65. Lucy Chase to Miss Lowell, November 29, 1863, Chase Family Papers, American Antiquarian Society, Worcester, Massachusetts.

66. See the earlier reference to Benjamin Quarles in Nash, *The Forgotten Fifth*, p. 6.

67. Melvin Claxton and Mark Puls, *Uncommon Valor*, pp. 11, 15–18, 112–113.

68. Berlin and Rowland, eds., *Families and Freedom*, p. 85.

69. Ibid., p. 84. See also the recruitment poster reproduced from the National Archives that promises "colored soldiers" equal pay, p. 83.

70. Ibid., p. 86.

71. Thomas D. Freeman to William Brown, March 26, 1864, Brown Family Papers, AAS.

72. Ira Berlin, Joseph P. Reidy, and Leslie S. Rowland, eds., *The Black Military Experience*, series II, in *Freedom: A Documentary History of Emancipation, 1861–1867* (Cambridge: Cambridge University Press, 1983), pp. 21, 393, 394.

73. Ibid., pp. 402, 657.

74. Ibid., p. 696.

75. Ibid., p. 687.

76. Ibid., p. 697. For further evidence of such treatment, see pp. 402, 657–659, 587–588, 691, 694, 696–697, 699–700; and Berlin and Rowland, *Families and Freedom*, pp. 35, 26–27, 64, 71, 100–101, 131–132, 223.

77. Berlin and Rowland, *Families and Freedom*, pp. 69–70. For more testimony on impressment, see Berlin, Miller, Reidy, and Rowland, eds., series I, vol. II, *The Wartime Genesis of Free Labor*, p. 202.

78. Ira Berlin, Thavolia Glymph, Steven F. Miller, Joseph Reidy, Leslie S. Rowland, and Julie Saville, eds., *Freedom: A Documentary History of Emancipation, 1861–1867*, vol. 3, series I, *The Wartime Genesis of Free Labor: The Lower South* (Cambridge: Cambridge University Press, 1990), pp. 203, 209, 362–363, 367–368.

79. Berlin et al., vol. 2, series I, *Genesis of Labor*, pp. 152, 182–183, 200–202; Lucy Chase to Miss Lowell, November 29, 1863, Chase Family Papers, AAS.

80. Berlin and Rowland, *Families and Freedom*, p. 72.

81. Ibid., pp. 76, 89.

82. Ibid., p. 130.

83. Michael Kammen, *Mystic Chords of Memory: The Transformation of Tradition in American Culture* (New York: Alfred A Knopf, 1991), pp. 50–52.

84. Regosin and Shaffer, *Voices of Emancipation*, pp. 10, 11, 14, 18, 25, 27, 31–32.

85. Blassingame, *Slave Testimony*, pp. 639, 653.

86. William Cohen, *At Freedom's Edge: Black Mobility and the Southern White Quest for Racial Control, 1861–1915* (Baton Rouge: Louisiana State Press, 1991), pp. 16, 52–54, 109. Carole Patemen, *The Problem of Political Obligation: A Critical Analysis of Liberal Theory* (New York: John Wiley & Sons, 1979), p. 74, points out that David Hume argued a populace might remain in a country not out of consent to be governed but, rather, out of sheer poverty.

87. Ira Berlin, *The Making of African America: The Four Great Migrations* (New York: Viking, 2010), p. 132.

88. Blassingame, *Slave Testimony*, pp. 513, 593.

89. Ibid., pp. 551–555.

90. Ibid., pp. 631–633.

91. Ibid., pp. 164–165.

92. Ibid., p. 49.

93. Ibid., pp. 276, 283.

94. Ibid., p. 671.

95. Berlin et al., vol. 2, *Genesis of Labor*, pp. 212–219.

96. Ibid., pp. 222–224.

97. Ibid., p. 225.

98. Herbert C. Kelman, "Nationalism, Patriotism, and National Identity: Social-Psychological Dimensions," p. 170, and Janusz Reykowski, "Patriotism and the Collective System of Meanings," p. 110, in Daniel Bar-Tal and Ervin Staub, eds., *Patriotism: The Lives of Individuals and Nations* (Chicago: Nelson-Hall Publishers, 1996); Berlin, *The Making of African America*, p. 131.

99. Blassingame, *Slave Testimony*, pp. 47–48.

100. Ibid., p. 513.

101. Ibid., p. 551.

102. Elizabeth Hafkin Pleck, *Black Migration and Poverty: Boston, 1865–1900* (New York: Academic Press, 1979), p. 110. See also William D. Piersen, *Black Yankees: The Development of an Afro-American Subculture in Eighteenth-Century*

New England (Amherst: University of Massachusetts Press, 1988); James Oliver and Lois E. Horton, *Black Bostonians: Family Life and Community Struggle in the Antebellum North* (New York: Holmes and Meier, 1999).

103. Adrian Oldfield, *Citizenship and Community: Civic Republicanism and the Modern World* (New York: Routledge, 1990), p. 130. For a discussion of the importance of loyalty as social cohesion in relation to justice, see Fletcher, *Loyalty*, p. 21.

104. Janette Thomas Greenwood, *The First Fruits of Freedom: The Migration of Former Slaves and Their Search for Equality in Worcester, Massachusetts, 1862–1900* (Chapel Hill: University of North Carolina Press, 2009). For an analysis of the politics of Worcester County, see John L. Brooke, *The Heart of the Commonwealth: Society and Political Culture in Worcester County, Massachusetts, 1713–1861* (Cambridge: Harvard University Press, 1989).

105. Obituary, John Moore (1751–1836); Bond Louis Stock and John More for 100 (pounds), March 11, 1786; Mr Wentworth, Halifax, Nova Scotia, 1789; Application for Seaman's Relief, March 10 (no year). Land Grant to John Brown for $250, Plymouth, Massachusetts, September 10, 1819; court order appointing John Moore guardian of William Brown, August 16, 1831. Brown Family Papers (hereinafter BFP), AAS.

106. "Vital Statistics of Family," Alice (Brown) Bush to sons, January 28, 1849; Kittridge and Blakes to William Brown, February 8, 1849. BFP, AAS.

107. Greenwood, *First Fruits of Freedom*, pp. 50–51.

108. S. H. Bowman to William Brown, March 11, 1853; Alice Bush to William Brown, March 19 (no year), unknown to William Brown, June 2, 185?, BFP, AAS; Greenwood, *First Fruits of Freedom*, pp. 51, 65.

109. For a discussion of Amartya Sen's proposal that each of us holds multiple identities and that we do not belong to a single group and how that holds implications for patriotism, see Joel Rosenthal's, "Patriotism and Cosmopolitanism," in *Policy Innovations* (Carnegie Council, July 29, 2009), online magazine, pp. 4–8.

CHAPTER 5

1. "The Battle Hymn of the Republic," in Oscar Williams, ed., *Immortal Poems of the English Language* (New York: Washington Square Press, 1960), p. 428.

2. "Land of the South," a poem in Leonidas Warren Payne Jr., ed., *Southern Literary Readings* (New York: Rand McNally & Company, 1913), p. 115.

3. For a discussion of the associational links in the Northern war effort, see Melinda Lawson, *Patriot Fires: Forging a New American Nationalism in the Civil War North* (Lawrence: University of Kansas, 2002).

4. For further discussion, see Marcel Liberman, *Commitment, Value and Moral Realism* (Cambridge: Cambridge University Press, 1998).

5. *Dependent Rational Animals: Why Human Beings Need the Virtues* (Chicago: Open Court, 1999), pp. 8–9.

6. For a discussion of Maria Weston Chapman as a forceful, determined reformer, see "The Boston Bluestocking: Maria Weston Chapman," in Jane H. Pease and William H. Pease, eds., *Bound with Them in Chains: A Biographical History of the Antislavery Movement* (Westport, CT: Greenwood Press, Inc., 1972), pp. 28–59.

7. Anne Warren Weston to Wendell and Ann Phillips, July 25, 1852, Anne Warren Weston Letters in the Crawford Blagden Collection of the Papers of Wendell Phillips, Houghton Library (hereinafter HL), Harvard University (hereinafter HU), Cambridge, Massachusetts.

8. Maria Weston Chapman to Annie and Deborah Weston, London, n.d. Weston Collection (hereinafter WC), Boston Public Library (hereinafter BPL).

9. Catherine Clinton, "Maria Weston Chapman (1806–1885)," in G. J. Barker-Benfield and Catherine Clinton, eds., *Portraits of American Women: From Settlement to the Civil War* (New York: St. Martin's Press, 1991), I, pp. 147, 149; Deborah Weston to Mother, n.d. Weston Collection, BPL. Joan Goodwin, "Maria Weston Chapman and the Weston Sisters," in Barry Andrews, et al., eds., *Dictionary of Unitarian Universalist Biography*.

10. Deborah Weston to Mary Weston, February 23, 1835, WC BPL. Pease and Pease, "The Boston Bluestocking," p. 32.

11. Clinton, "Maria Weston Chapman (1806–1889)," p. 151; Thomas Gold Appleton to Maria Weston Chapman, November 16, 1843, Appleton Papers, BPL.

12. Anne Warren Weston to Wendell Phillips, January 8, 1851, Anne Warren Weston Letters in the Crawford Blagden Collection of the Papers of Wendell Phillips, HL HU. See also Archibald H. Grimke's reminiscences of William Lloyd Garrison in *The Seattle Republican*, November 17, 1905, Library of Congress.

13. Caroline Weston Diary, September 19, 21, 23–24, and 28, 1835; Anne Warren Weston to Deborah Weston, September 1835, WC BPL.

14. Maria Weston Chapman to Bella (Deborah Weston), October 1835; Deborah Weston to Aunt Mary Weston, October 22, 1835, WC BPL.

15. Deborah Weston to Aunt Mary Weston, October 22, 1835, WC BPL; Clinton, "Maria Weston Chapman (1806–1885)," p. 152; Pease and Pease, "The Boston Bluestocking," p. 32.

16. Anne Warren Weston to mother, Nancy Ann Bates Weston, May 30, 1836, WC BPL.

17. Anne Warren Weston to Deborah Weston, 1836, Weston Sisters Papers BPL.

18. Deborah Weston Diary, September 13, 1835; September 28, 1835; January 22, 1837, WC BPL.

19. Anne Warren Weston to Henry B. Stanton, October 11, 1837, WSP BPL.

20. In Anne Warren Weston's letter to Wendell Phillips, April 13, 1851, she describes this as her mother's favorite expression. As a family phrase, it is a good description of Maria Weston's mind. Crawford Blagden Collection, HL HU.

21. Maria Weston Chapman, *Right and Wrong in Massachusetts* (Boston: Dow & Jackson's Anti-Slavery Press, 1839), pp. 12–13, 16, 20, 33, 53. (The 1837 annual report adapted by Maria Weston Chapman for *Right and Wrong in Massachusetts* demonstrated the intensity of feminist abolitionism, as it carried the polemical title *Right and Wrong in Boston: Annual Report of the Boston Female Anti-Slavery Society, with a Sketch of the Obstacles Thrown in the Way of Emancipation by Certain Clerical Abolitionists and Advocates for the Subjection of Women in 1837.*)

22. For a chronology of Chapman's writings, see Joan Goodwin, "Maria Weston Chapman and the Weston Sisters," in *Dictionary of Unitarian Universalist Biography*. See also *Right and Wrong in Massachusetts*, pp. 5–6, 26, 34.

23. *Right and Wrong in Massachusetts*, pp. 154, 158.

24. Clinton, "Maria Weston Chapman (1806–1885)," p. 151.

25. Pease and Pease, "The Boston Blustocking," p. 42.

26. Caroline Weston Diary, September 28, 1835; Caroline Weston to Maria Weston Chapman, 1836, WSP BPL.

27. Deborah Weston to Anne Warren Weston, January 15, 1836; Deborah Weston to Anne Bates Weston, June 5, 1836; Deborah Weston to Caroline Weston, October 15 and 17, 1836, WSP BPL.

28. Deborah Weston to Aunt Mary, November 6, 1836, WSP BPL.

29. Deborah Weston to Caroline Weston, October 15, 1836; Anne Warren Weston to Lucia Weston, August 12, 1837; Anne Warren Weston to Deborah Weston, September 3, 1837, WSP BPL.

30. [illeg.] Maria Weston Chapman to S, February 12, 1843, WSP BPL.

31. Mary Gray Chapman to Wendell Phillips, n.d. Boston, Mary Gray Chapman Letters in the Crawford Bragden Collection of the Papers of Wendell Phillips, HL HU.

32. Jonathan Walker, "Trial and Imprisonment of Jonathan Walker, at Pensacola, Florida: For Aiding Slaves to Escape from Bondage" (Boston: Published at the Anti-Slavery Office, 1848), p. vi. New York Public Library, Legacy Reprint Series.

33. Ibid., p. iv.

34. Clinton, "Maria Weston Chapman (1806–1885)," p. 150.

35. Maria Weston Chapman to Wendell and Ann Phillips, October 5, 1842, the Crawford Blagden Collection of the Papers of Wendell Phillips, HL HU.

36. Maria Weston Chapman to Louisa Loring, May 23, 1840, WSP BPL.

37. Circa 1846. Maria Weston Chapman Letters, HL HU. For further discussion, see Jean E. Friedman, "Antebellum Religious Identities of Northern and Southern Women," *Review & Expositor: The Journal of the Faculty of the Southern Baptist Theological Seminary*, vol. 92 (Summer 1995), pp. 319–335.

38. Bernard Lonergan, "A Second Collection," in William F. J. Ruan, eds., *Collected Works of Bernard Lonergan*, vol. 13 (Toronto: University of Toronto Press, 1996), p. 79.

39. Maria Weston Chapman to Deborah Weston, January 1845; Maria Weston Chapman to Caroline Weston, May 1846; Emma Weston to Samuel May Jr.,

July 1848 Anti-Slavery Sewing Circle to Anne Warren Weston, December 15, 1850; M. R. Hatch to Anne Warren Weston, December 18, 1850; November 18 and 20, 1852, WSP BPL; Anne Warren Weston to Wendell Phillips, January 8, 1851, Crawford Blagden Collection, HL HU.

40. February 6, 1851, WSP BPL.

41. Deborah Weston to Anne Weston, April 7, 9, and 15, 1851, WSP BPL.

42. Anne Warren Weston to "Dear Folks," May 30, 1854; Deborah Weston to Anne Warren Weston, June 2, 1854, WSP BPL.

43. Pease and Pease, "The Boston Bluestocking," pp. 45, 53.

44. Maria Weston Chapman to W. Michell, January 1861, WSP BPL.

45. Maria Weston Chapman to Anne Greene Chapman, June 24, 1862, WSP BPL.

46. Annie Adams Fields Diary, March 2, 1867, HL HU.

47. For a discussion of the necessity of dependence in the consideration of virtue, see MacIntyre, *Dependent Rational Animals*, pp. 2–3, 73–75.

48. *Journal of a Secesh Lady: The Diary of Catherine Ann Devereux Edmondston, 1860–1866*, Beth G. Crabtree and James W. Patton, eds. (Raleigh: Division of Archives and History, Department of Cultural Resources, 1979), pp. xxxvi, 7, 54.

49. Ibid., pp. xv, xviii–xxiii.

50. Ibid., p. xxii.

51. Ibid., p. 54.

52. Ibid., p. 44.

53. Ibid., p. 47n.

54. See Martha Nussbaum's description of the limits of compassion and understanding outside the primary circle of relationships in Joshua Cole, ed., *For Love of Country: Debating the Limits of Patriotism* (Boston: Beacon Press, 1996), pp. ix–xiv.

55. Edmonston, *The Diary*, pp. 21–22.

56. Ibid., p. 34.

57. Paul Ricoeur, *The Just*, David Pellauer, trans. (Chicago: University of Chicago Press, 2000), p. 61; Fletcher, *Loyalty*, p. 16.

58. Ibid., p. 220.

59. Ibid., p. 5.

60. Ibid., p. 344.

61. For a discussion of the moral danger of primary loyalties in relation to patriotism, see MacIntyre, "Is Patriotism a Virtue," p. 271. See also Fletcher, *Loyalty*, p. 6.

62. Isaiah Berlin, "Two Concepts of Liberty," in Michael Rosen and Jonathan Wolff, eds., *Political Thought* (New York: Oxford University Press, 1999), p. 124.

63. Edmondston, *The Diary*, pp. 36–37.

64. Herbert C. Kelman, "Nationalism, Patriotism, and National Identity: Social-Psychological Dimension," in Daniel Bar-Tal and Ervin Staub, eds., *Patriotism in the Lives of Individuals and Nations* (Chicago: Nelson-Hall Publishers, 1997), p. 167.

65. Janusz Reylowski, "Patriotism and the Collective System of Meanings," *Patriotism*, pp. 108–109.

66. Edmonston, *The Diary*, p. 38.

67. Ibid., pp. 45, 74, 115.

68. For a discussion of the transition of individual to national loyalty, see Reylowski, "Patriotism and the Collective System of Meanings," *Patriotism*, pp. 108–111.

69. Edmondston, *The Diary*, p. 58.

70. Patrick Edmondston attempted to muster a battalion, but Confederate officials refused to recognize one of his regiments as part of his battalion. Officials then gave command to another, and Patrick resigned his commission in order to achieve a better position. That essentially finished his military career, although he remained active in home defense and building nearby defenses until an illness disabled him. See Edmondston, *The Diary*, pp. 238n, 247–249, 293, 436–437, 442, 446, 672, 679.

71. Ibid., pp. 57–58, 100, 154–155, 205–210.

72. Ibid., pp. 72, 84, 153–154.

73. Ibid., p. 144.

74. Ibid., pp. 390–392.

75. James M. McPherson, *Ordeal by Fire: The Civil War and Reconstruction* (New York; Alfred A. Knopf, 1982), p. 158, and *Drawn with the Sword: Reflections on the American Civil War* (New York: Oxford University Press, 1996), p. 95.

76. Edmondston, *The Diary*, pp. 317, 507.

77. Ibid., p. 344.

78. Ibid., p. 342.

79. Ibid., p. 226.

80. Ibid., p. 287.

81. Ibid., p. 233.

82. Ibid., p. 236.

83. Ibid., p. 651.

84. Ibid., p. 669.

85. Ibid., p. 686.

86. Ibid., p. 520.

87. Ibid., p. 670.

88. Ibid., p. 696.

89. For a discussion of blind loyalty, see Ervin Staub, "Blind and Constructive Patriotism: Moving from Embeddedness in the Group to Critical Loyalty and Action," *Patriotism*, p. 213.

90. For a discussion of the necessity of vulnerability in any consideration of virtue among independent rational agents, see MacIntyre, *Dependent Rational Animals*, pp. 1–9, 68–83.

91. James G. Carter to Levi Lincoln, February 20, 1826, Lincoln Family Papers (hereinafter LFP), American Antiquarian Society.

92. Caleb Arnold Wall, *Reminiscences of Worcester* (Worcester, Mass: Tyler and Seagraves, 1877), pp. 345–346; Marvin J. Petroelje, "Levi Lincoln, Sr.,

Jeffersonian Republican of Massachusetts," in Dndrew R. Dodge, Betty K. Koed, et al., eds, *Biographical Directory of the United States Congress* (Washington, DC: United States Government Printing Office, 2005); Bernard Bailyn, *The Origin of American Politics* (New York: Vintage Books, 1968), pp. 39, 57; Perry Miller, *The New England Mind: From Colony to Province* (Boston, Beacon Press, 1961), p. 22; Levi Lincoln to AAS Dearborn, January 3, 1818; Levi Lincoln to David Waldo, March 23, 1831; Levi Lincoln to Matthew Carey, June 27, 1834, LFP, AAS.

93. Gordon S. Wood, *The Creation of the American Republic, 1776–1787* (New York: W.W. Norton & Company, Inc., 1969), p. 69.

94. Levi Lincoln to Col. Pliny Merrick, January 21, 1841, LFP, AAS.

95. "A Memorial of William Sever Lincoln, Col. 34th Massachusetts Infantry and Brevet Brigadier General U.S. Volunteers, 1811–1889" (Library of Congress, Open Library), pp. 6–9.

96. "A Memorial of William Sever Lincoln," pp. 6–7; Caroline Lincoln to George C. Trumbull, n.d, LFP, AAS.

97. William Sever Lincoln to Elizabeth Trumbull Lincoln, July 6, 1836, LFP, AAS.

98. William Sever Lincoln to Elizabeth Trumbull Lincoln, March 1, 1838; Elizabeth Trumbull Lincoln to mother, March 24, 1838; April 1, 1838, LFP, AAS.

99. Lucy Clap to mother, March 6, 1839, LFP, AAS.

100. William Sever Lincoln, November 7, 1841, LFP, AAS.

101. Sarah Trumbull to Elizabeth Trumbull Lincoln, n.d., LFP, AAS.

102. William Sever Lincoln to Elizabeth Trumbull Lincoln, October 10, 1841, LFP, AAS.

103. William Sever Lincoln to Elizabeth Trumbull Lincoln, October 31, 1841, LFP, AAS.

104. William Sever Lincoln to Elizabeth Trumbull Lincoln, November 7, 21, and 28; December 2, 5, 12, and 15, 1841, LFP, AAS.

105. William Sever Lincoln to Elizabeth Trumbull Lincoln, December 15 and 25, 1841; Levi Lincoln to William Lincoln Jr., October 13, 1844, LFP AAS.

106. April 5, 1847, LFP, AAS. William Lincoln, *History of Worcester* (Worcester, Mass: Charles Hersey, 1862), p. 385, AAS.

107. "A Memorial of William Sever Lincoln," p. 7.

108. Ibid., pp. 7–8.

109. George Lincoln to William Lincoln, September 9, 1860; Levi Lincoln to William Lincoln, September 9 and 20, 1860; William Sever Lincoln to William Lincoln, September 23, 1860; Elizabeth Lincoln to William Lincoln, October 28, 1860; December 18, 1860; Susan Trumbull to William Lincoln, October 28, 1860; November 7, 1860, LFP, AAS.

110. September 2, 1860, LFP, AAS.

111. September 3, 1860, LFP, AAS.

112. Elizabeth Lincoln to William Lincoln, October 28, 1860; Elizabeth Lincoln to William Lincoln, on the eve of Abraham Lincoln's election, LFP, AAS.

113. Elizabeth Trumbull to William Lincoln, November 7, 1860, LFP, AAS.

114. Willie Lincoln to Grandfather, 1860, LFP, AAS.

115. William Sever Lincoln to William Lincoln, December 25, 1860, LFP, AAS.

116. William Sever Lincoln to William Lincoln, October 14, 1860; Elizabeth Lincoln to William Lincoln, n.d., LFP, AAS.

117. William Lincoln, Discharge Papers, September 14, 1861, LFP, AAS.

118. William Sever Lincoln to J. W. Wetherell, November 13, 1861; November 10, 1861, LFP, AAS.

119. "A Memorial of William Sever Lincoln," p. 8; William S. Lincoln, *Life with the Thirty-Fourth Massachusetts Infantry in the War of Rebellion* (Worcester: Press of Noyes, Snow and Company, 1879), p. 80; "The Seaver Family," *New England Historical and Genealogical Register and Antiquarian Journal*, vol. 26, 1872, p. 315.

120. Lincoln, *Life with the Thirty-Fourth*, p. 25.

121. Ibid., p. 27.

122. Ibid., pp. 29, 39, 230.

123. Ibid., pp. 50, 53, 65, 70, 78, 83, 135, 159–160, 163, 217, 220.

124. Ibid., p. 53.

125. Ibid., pp. 85–86.

126. Ibid., pp. 214–215.

127. Ibid., pp. 141–147.

128. Ibid., p. 277.

129. Ibid., p. 283.

130. Ibid., "Imprisonment and Escape of Lieut. Col. Lincoln," Appendix, pp. 1–2.

131. Ibid., pp. 3–5.

132. Ibid., pp. 5–7.

133. Ibid., pp. 7–12.

134. Ibid., pp. 13–16.

135. Ibid., pp. 16–18.

136. "A Memorial of William Sever Lincoln," pp. 9–11.

Bibliography

Ambrose, Stephen E. *Duty, Honor, Country: A History of West Point.* Baltimore: Johns Hopkins University Press, 1966.

Appleton, Nathan. *Memoir of Nathan Appleton.* New York: Greenwood Press, 1969.

Bagby, George W. *The Old Virginia Gentleman and Other Sketches.* Edited by Ellen M. Bagby. Richmond, VA: Dietz Press, 1943.

Bailyn, Bernard. *The Origin of American Politics.* New York: Vintage Books, 1968.

Baker, Jean H. *Affairs of Party: The Political Culture of the Northern Democrats in the Mid-Nineteenth Century.* Ithaca, NY: Cornell University Press, 1983.

Baker, Jean H. *Mary Todd Lincoln: A Biography.* New York: W. W. Norton and Company, 1987.

Barker-Benfield, G. J., and Catherine Clinton, eds. *Portraits of American Women: From Settlement to the Civil War.* New York: St. Martin's Press, 1991.

Bar-Tal, Daniel, and Ervin Staub, eds. *Patriotism: The Lives of Individuals and Nations.* Chicago: Nelson-Hall Publishers, 1996.

Basler, Roy P., ed. *The Collected Works of Abraham Lincoln.* 8 vols. and *Supplement.* New Brunswick, NJ: Rutgers University Press, 1954.

Berlin, Adele, and Marc Zvi Brettler, eds. *The Jewish Study Bible.* New York: Oxford University Press, 2004.

Berlin, Ira. *The Making of African America: The Four Great Migrations.* New York: Viking, 2010.

Berlin, Ira, Marc Favreau, and Steven F. Miller, eds. *Remembering Slavery: African Americans Talk about Their Personal Experiences of Slavery and Freedom.* New York: New Press, 1998.

Berlin, Ira, and Leslie S. Rowland, eds. *Families and Freedom: A Documentary History of African-American Kinship in the Civil War.* New York: New Press, 1997.

Berlin, Ira et al., eds. *Freedom: A Documentary History of Emancipation, 1861–1867.* Cambridge: Cambridge University Press, 1983–1990.

Berman, Myron. *Richmond's Jewry, 1769–1976: Shabbat in Shockoe.* Charlottesville: University Press of Virginia, 1979.

Berns, Walter. *Making Patriots.* Chicago: University of Chicago Press, 2001.

Berry, Stephen. *All That Makes a Man: Love and Ambition in the Civil War South.* New York: Oxford University Press, 2003.

Berry, Stephen. *House of Abraham: Lincoln and the Todds, a Family Divided by War.* Boston: Mariner Books, 2008.

Bingham, Emily. *Mordecai: An Early American Family.* New York: Hill and Wang, 2003.

Blassingame, John W., ed. *Slave Testimony: Two Centuries of Letters, Speeches, Interviews, and Autobiographies.* Baton Rouge: Louisiana State University Press, 1977.

Boney, F. N. *John Letcher of Virginia: The Story of Virginia's Civil War Governor.* Tuscaloosa: University of Alabama Press, 1966.

Brooke, John L. *The Heart of the Commonwealth: Society and Political Culture in Worcester County, Massachusetts, 1713–1861.* Cambridge: Harvard University Press, 1989.

Burghardt, Walter J. *Justice; A Global Adventure.* Maryknoll, NY: Orbis Books, 2004.

Burton, Orville Vernon. *The Age of Lincoln.* New York: Hill and Wang, 2007.

Calhoun, Charles C. *Longfellow: A Rediscovered Life.* Boston: Beacon Press, 2004.

Carens, Joseph H. *Culture, Citizenship and Community: A Contextual Exploration of Justice as Evenhandedness.* New York: Oxford University Press, 2000.

Carnes, Mark C., and Clyde Griffen, eds. *Meanings for Manhood: Constructions of Masculinity in Victorian America.* Chicago: University of Chicago Press, 1996.

Chapman, Maria W. *Right and Wrong in Massachusetts*. Boston: Dow & Jackson's Anti-Slavery Press, 1839.

Clark-Stewart, Alison, and Judy Dunn, eds. *Family Counts: Effects on Child and Adolescent Development*. Cambridge: Cambridge University Press, 2006.

Claxton, Melvin, and Mark Puls. *Uncommon Valor: A Story of Race, Patriotism, and Glory in the Final Battles of the Civil War*. Hoboken, NJ: John Wiley Press, 2006.

Clinton, Catherine. *Mrs. Lincoln: A Life*. New York: Harper Perennial, 2010.

Clinton, Catherine, ed. *Southern Families at War: Loyalty and Conflict in the Civil War South*. New York: Oxford University Press, 2000.

Clinton, Catherine, and Nina Silber, eds. *Divided Houses: Gender and the Civil War*. New York: Oxford University Press, 1992.

Cohen, William. *At Freedom's Edge: Black Mobility and the Southern White Quest for Racial Control, 1861–1915*. Baton Rouge: Louisiana State University Press, 1991.

Coles, Harry L. *The War of 1812*. Chicago: University of Chicago Press, 1965.

Curti, Merle. *The Roots of American Loyalty*. New York: Atheneum, 1968.

Dalzell, Robert F. *Enterprising Elite: The Boston Associates and the World They Made*. Cambridge: Harvard University Press, 1987.

Davis, William C. *Rhett: The Turbulent Life and Times of a Fire-Eater*. Columbia: University of South Carolina Press, 2001.

Defoe, Daniel. *Robinson Crusoe*. London: London Electronic Books, 2001.

Delbanco, Andrew. *William Ellery Channing: An Essay on the Liberal Spirit in America*. Cambridge, MA: Harvard University Press, 1981.

Donald, David H. *Charles Sumner and the Coming of the Civil War*. New York: Knopf, 1967.

Donald, David H. *Lincoln*. New York: Simon and Schuster, 1995.

Donald, David H. *Lincoln Reconsidered*. New York: Vintage Books, 2001.

Edgeworth, Maria, ed. *Early Lessons*. London: George Routledge & Sons, 1856.

Edgeworth, Richard L., and Maria Edgeworth. *Practical Education*. 2nd ed. 2 vols. Boston: T. B. Wait & Sons, 1815.

Elazar, Daniel J. *Building toward Civil War: Generational Rhythms in American Politics*. New York: Madison Books, 1992.

Endler, James R. *Other Leaders, Other Heroes: West Point's Legacy to America and beyond the Field of Battle*. Westport, CT: Praeger, 1986.

Falk, Stanley L. "Major Alfred Mordecai: First Ordnance Officer to Apply Scientific Methods to Armament." *Nearprint* (November–December 1959).

Fehrenbacher, Don E., ed. *Abraham Lincoln: Speeches and Writings, 1832–1858*. New York: Library of America, 1989.

Fletcher, George P. *Loyalty: An Essay on the Morality of Relationships*. New York: Oxford University Press, 1993.

Foner, Eric. *Free Soil, Free Labor, Free Men: The Ideology of the Republican Party before the Civil War*. New York: Oxford University Press, 1970.

Franklin, Donna L. *Ensuring Inequality: The Structural Transformation of the African-American Family*. New York: Oxford University Press, 1997.

Frederickson, George M. *The Inner Civil War: Northern Intellectuals and the Crisis of the Union*. New York: Harper & Row, 1965.

Friedman, Jean E. "Antebellum Religious Identities of Northern and Southern Women." *Review & Expositor: The Journal of the Faculty of the Southern Baptist Theological Seminary* 92 (Summer 1995): 319–35.

Friedman, Jean E. *The Revolt of the Conservative Democrats: An Essay on American Political Culture and Political Development, 1837–1844*. Ann Arbor, MI: UMI Research Press, 1979.

Friedman, Jean E. *Ways of Wisdom: Moral Education in the Early National Republic*. Athens: University of Georgia Press, 2001.

Genovese, Eugene D. *Roll, Jordan, Roll: The World the Slaves Made*. New York: Vintage Books, 1976.

Gleckner, Robert F., and Gerald E. Enscoe, eds. *Romanticism: Points of View*. Englewood Cliffs, NJ: Prentice-Hall, 1970.

Goodwin, Doris K. *Team of Rivals: The Political Genius of Abraham Lincoln*. New York: Simon and Schuster, 2005.

Goodwin, Joan. "Maria Weston Chapman and the Weston Sisters." *Dictionary of Unitarian Universalist Biography*, 2001, an online resource of the Unitarian Universalist Heritage Society.

Greenwood, Janette T. *The First Fruits of Freedom: The Migration of Former Slaves and Their Search for Equality in Worcester, Massachusetts, 1862–1900*. Chapel Hill: University of North Carolina Press, 2009.

Gregory, Frances W. *Nathan Appleton: Merchant and Entrepreneur, 1779–1861*. Charlottesville: University of Virginia Press, 1875.

Gutman, Herbert G. *The Black Family in Slavery and Freedom, 1750–1925*. New York: Pantheon Books, 1976.

Hampshire, Stuart. *Justice Is Conflict*. Princeton: Princeton University Press, 2000.

Herdt, Jennifer A. *Putting on Virtue: The Legacy of the Splendid Vices*. Chicago: University of Chicago Press, 2008.

Heygate, William E., and Nathan Appleton. *The Doctrines of Original Sin and the Trinity: Discussed in a Correspondence between a Clergyman of the Episcopal Church and a Layman of Boston*. Boston: J. H. Eastburn's Press, 1859.

Heyrman, Christine L. *Southern Cross: The Beginnings of the Bible Belt*. Chapel Hill: University of North Carolina Press, 1997.

Hickey, Donald R. *The War of 1812: The Forgotten Conflict*. Urbana: University of Illinois Press, 1989.

Hillen, Andrew, ed. *The Letters of Henry Wadsworth Longfellow*. 4 vols. Cambridge: Belknap Press, 1972.

Hogue, Arthur R., ed. *Charles Sumner: An Essay by Carl Shurtz*. Westport, CT: Greenwood Press, 1972.

Holifield, E. Brooks. *The Gentlemen Theologians: American Theology in Southern Culture, 1795–1860*. Durham: Duke University Press, 1978.

Inscoe, John C., and Robert C. Kensler, eds. *Enemies of the Country: New Perspectives on Unionists in the Civil War South*. Athens: University of Georgia Press, 2001.

Johnson, Allen, ed. *Dictionary of American Biography*. New York: Charles Scribner's Sons, 1928.

Johnson, Steven. *The Truth about Patriotism*. Durham: Duke University Press, 2007.

Joyner, Charles. *Down by the Riverside: A South Carolina Slave Community*. Urbana: University of Illinois Press, 1984.

Kammen, Michael. *Mystic Chords of Memory: The Transformation of Tradition in American Culture*. New York: Knopf, 1991.

Lawson, Melinda. *Patriot Fires: Forging a New American Nationalism in the Civil War North*. Lawrence: University of Kansas Press, 2002.

Leech, Margaret. *Reveille in Washington, 1860–1865*. New York: New York Review Book, 1941.

Levi, Margaret. *Consent, Dissent and Patriotism*. Cambridge: Cambridge University Press, 1997.

Levine, Lawrence W. *Black Culture and Black Consciousness: Afro-American Folk Thought from Slavery to Freedom*. New York: Oxford University Press, 1979.

Liberman, Marcel. *Commitment, Virtue and Moral Realism*. Cambridge: Cambridge University Press, 1998.

Lincoln, William S. *History of Worcester*. Worcester: Henry J. Howland, 1862.

Lincoln, William S. *Life with the Thirty-Fourth Massachusetts Infantry in the War of Rebellion*. Worcester, MA: Press of Noyes, Snow, 1879.

Linderman, Gerald F. *Embattled Courage: The Experience of Combat in the American Civil War*. New York: Free Press, 1987.

Lockridge, Lawrence S. *The Ethics of Romanticism*. New York: Cambridge University Press, 1989.

Long, Everette B. with Barbara Long. *The Civil War Day by Day: An Almanac, 1861–1865*. New York: Doubleday, 1971.

Longfellow, Henry W. *Hyperion: A Romance*. Boston: Houghton, Mifflin, 1893.

Keegan, John. *The American Civil War*. New York: Vintage Civil War Library, 2009.

MacDonald, Edgar E., ed. *The Education of the Heart: The Correspondence of Rachel Mordecai Lazarus and Maria Edgeworth*. Chapel Hill: University of North Carolina Press, 1977.

MacIntyre, Alasdair. *Dependent Rational Animals: Why Human Beings Need the Virtues*. Chicago: Open Court Press, 1999.

Malone, Dumas. *Jefferson the President: First Term, 1801–1805*. Boston: Little, Brown, 1970.

Marcus, Jacob R., ed. *Memoirs of American Jews, 1775–1865*. 3 vols. Philadelphia: Jewish Publication Society of America, 1955–56.

May, Rollo. *Love and Will*. New York: Dell, 1968.

McAdoo, Hariette. *Black Families*. Thousand Oaks, CA: Sage Publications, 2007.

McPherson, James M. *Drawn with the Sword: Reflections on the American Civil War*. New York: Oxford University Press, 1996.

McPherson, James M. *For Cause and Comrades*. New York: Oxford University Press, 1997.

McPherson, James M. *The Negro's Civil War: How American Negroes Felt and Acted during the War for the Union*. Urbana: University of Illinois Press, 1982.

McPherson, James M. *Ordeal by Fire: The Civil War and Reconstruction*. New York: Knopf, 1982.

McPherson, James M. *Tried by War: Abraham Lincoln as Commander-in-Chief*. New York: Penguin Books, 2009.

McPherson, James M. *What They Fought For, 1861–1865*. New York: Anchor Books, 1994.

Miller, Perry. *The New England Mind: From Colony to Province*. Boston: Beacon Press, 1961.

Mitchell, Reid. *Civil War Soldiers*. New York: Viking Penguin, 1988.

Mitchell, Reid. *The Vacant Chair*. New York: Oxford University Press, 1988.

Morgan, Michael L., ed. *Classics of Moral and Political Theory*. Indianapolis: Hackett, 1992.

Morris, George S., and Susan L. Foutz. *Lynchburg in the Civil War: The City —the People—the Battle.* 2nd ed. Lynchburg, VA: H. E. Howard, 1984.

Nash, Gary B. *The Forgotten Fifth: African Americans in the Age of Revolution.* Cambridge: Harvard University Press, 2006.

Nathanson, Stephen. *Patriotism, Morality and Peace.* Lanham, MD: Rowman & Littlefield Publishers, 1993.

Neely, Mark E., Jr. *The Last Best Hope of Earth: Abraham Lincoln and the Promise of America.* Cambridge: Harvard University Press, 1995.

Nussbaum, Martha. "Patriotism and Cosmopolitanism," in Joshua Cohen, ed. *For Love of Country: Debating the Limits of Patriotism.* Boston: Beacon Press, 1996.

Oldfield, Adrian. *Citizenship and Community: Civic Republicanism and the Modern World.* New York: Routledge, 1990.

Oliver, James, and Lois E. Horton. *Black Bostonians: Family Life and Community Struggle in the Antebellum North.* New York: Holmes and Meier, 1999.

Palmer, Beverly W., ed. *Selected Letters of Charles Sumner.* 2 vols. Boston: Northeastern University Press, 1990.

Pappas, George S. *To the Point: The United States Military Academy, 1802–1902.* Westport, CT: Praeger, 1993.

Pateman, Carole. *The Problem of Political Obligation: A Critical Analysis of Liberal Theory.* New York: John Wiley & Sons, 1979.

Payne, Leonidas W., ed. *Southern Literary Readings.* New York: Rand McNally, 1913.

Pease, Jane H., and William H. Pease. *Bound with Them in Chains: A Biographical History of the Antislavery Movement.* Westport, CT: Greenwood Press, 1972.

Peckman, Morse. *Romanticism and Behavior: Collected Essays II.* Columbia: University of South Carolina Press, 1976.

Pegis, Anton, ed. *The Basic Writings of Saint Thomas Aquinas.* 2 vols. New York: Random House, 1945.

Pickett, La Salle C. *Literary Hearthstones of Dixie.* Philadelphia: J. B. Lippincott, 1912.

Piersen, William D. *Black Yankees: The Development of an African-American Subculture in Eighteenth-Century New England.* Amherst: University of Massachusetts Press, 1988.

Pleck, Elizabeth H. *Black Migration and Poverty: Boston, 1865–1900.* New York: Academic Press, 1979.

Potter, David. *Lincoln and His Party in the Secession Crisis.* New Haven: Yale University Press, 1965.

Pugh, David G. *Sons of Liberty*. Westport, CT: Greenwood Press, 1983.

Rable, George C. *The Confederate Republic: A Revolution against Politics.* Chapel Hill: University of North Carolina Press, 1994.

Raboteau, Albert J. *Slave Religion: The 'Invisible Institution' in the Antebellum South.* New York: Oxford University Press, 1978.

Rawick, George P., ed. *The American Slave: A Composite Autobiography.* Westport, CT: Greenwood Press, 1972.

Regosin, Elizabeth, and Donald R. Shaffer, eds. *Voices of Emancipation: Understanding Slavery, the Civil War and Reconstruction through the United States Pension Bureau Files.* New York: New York University Press, 2008.

Ricoeur, Paul. *History and Truth.* Translated by Charles A. Kelbley. Evanston, IL: Northwestern University Press, 1965.

Ricoeur, Paul. *The Just.* Translated by David Pellauer. Chicago: Chicago University Press, 2000.

Robinson, David. *William Ellery Channing: Selected Writings.* New York: Paulist Press, 1985.

Rosen, Michael, and Jonathan Wolff, eds. *Political Thought.* New York: Oxford University Press, 1999.

Ross, Michael, and Dale Mills, eds. *The Justice Motive in Everyday Life.* Cambridge: Cambridge University Press, 2002.

Ruan, William F. J., ed. *Collected Works of Bernard Lonergan.* Toronto: University of Toronto Press, 1996.

Samet, Elizabeth D. *Willing Obedience: Citizens, Soldiers, and the Progress of Consent in America, 1776–1898.* Stanford: Stanford University Press, 2004.

Sandel, Michael J. *Justice: What's the Right Thing to Do?* New York: Farrar, Strauss and Giroux, 2009.

Schaar, John H. *Legitimacy in the Modern State.* New Brunswick, NJ: Transaction Books, 1981.

Schave, Douglas, and Barbara Schave. *Early Adolescence and the Search for the Self: A Developmental Perspective.* New York: Praeger, 1989.

Shade, William G. *Democratizing the Old Dominion: Virginia and the Second Party System, 1824–1861.* Charlottesville: University Press of Virginia, 1996.

Smith, Kimberly K. *The Dominion of Voice: Riot, Reason, and Romance in Antebellum Politics.* Lawrence: University of Kansas Press, 1999.

Stern, Philip Van Doren., ed. *The Life and Writings of Abraham Lincoln.* New York: Modern Library, 1940.

Stout, Harry S. *Upon the Altar of the Nation: A Moral History of the Civil War.* New York: Penguin Books, 2006.

Stowe, Stephen M. *Intimacy and Power in the Old South: Ritual in the Lives of the Planters*. Baltimore: Johns Hopkins University Press, 1987.

Taylor, Charles. *Sources of the Self: The Making of the Modern Identity*. Cambridge, MA: Harvard University Press, 1989.

Thomas, Benjamin F. *Lincoln's New Salem*. Springfield, IL: Abraham Lincoln Association, 1934.

Thomas, Emory M. *The Confederate Nation: 1861–1865*. New York: Harper & Row, 1979.

Thomas, Emory M. *The Dogs of War, 1861*. New York: Oxford University Press, 2011.

Tillich, Paul. *Love, Power and Justice*. Cambridge: Cambridge University Press, 1993.

Tivnan, Edward. *The Moral Imagination: Confronting the Ethical Issues of Our Day*. New York: Simon & Schuster, 1995.

Tripp, Steven E. *Yankee Town, Southern City: Race and Class Relations in Civil War Lynchburg*. New York: New York University Press, 1997.

Turner, Justin G., and Linda L. Turner. *Mary Todd Lincoln: Her Life and Letters*. New York: Alfred A. Knopf, 1972.

Unger, Irwin, ed. *Essays on the Civil War and Reconstruction*. New York: Holt, Rinehart and Winston, 1970.

Wall, Caleb A. *Reminiscences of Worcester*. Worcester, MA: Tyler & Seagrave, 1877.

Weems, Parson M. *A History of the Life and Death, Virtue and Exploits of George Washington*. Early American Imprints, Series 1, microform, no. 39063, 1800.

Wegenknecht, Edward. *Mrs. Longfellow: Selected Letters and Journals of Fanny Appleton Longfellow, 1817–1861*. New York: Longmans Green, 1956.

Welsh, David A. *Justice and the Genesis of War*. Cambridge: Cambridge University Press, 1993.

White, Ronald C. A. *Lincoln*. New York: Random House, 1965.

Williams, Oscar, ed. *Immortal Poems of the English Language*. New York: Washington Square Press, 1960.

Wilson, Charles R., ed. *Cultural Perspectives on the American South: Religion*. Vol. 5. New York: Gordon and Breach, 1991.

Wilson, Douglas L. *Honor's Voice: The Transformation of Abraham Lincoln*. New York: Alfred A. Knopf, 1998.

Wilson, Douglas L., and Rodney O. Davis, eds. *Herndon's Informants*. Urbana: University of Illinois Press, 1998.

Wilson, James Q. *The Moral Sense*. New York: Free Press, 1997.

Wood, Gordon S. *The Creation of the American Republic, 1776–1787.* New York: W. W. Norton, 1969.

Wyatt-Brown, Bertram. *Honor and Violence in the Old South.* New York: Oxford University Press, 1986.

Wyatt-Brown, Bertram. *The Shaping of Southern Culture: Honor, Grace, and War, 1760s–1880s.* Chapel Hill: University of North Carolina Press, 2001.

Wyatt-Brown, Bertram. *Southern Honor: Ethics and Behavior in the Old South.* New York: Oxford University Press, 1982.

Zinn, Howard. *The Other Civil War: Slavery and Struggle in Civil War America.* New York: Harper Perennial, 2011.

MANUSCRIPTS

Abraham Lincoln Papers, American Memory, Library of Congress, Washington, D.C.

Appleton Family Papers, Massachusetts Historical Society, Boston.

Brown Family Papers, American Antiquarian Society, Worcester, Massachusetts.

Chase Family Papers, American Antiquarian Society, Worcester, Massachusetts.

Crawford Blagden Collection of the Papers of Wendell Phillips, Houghton Library, Harvard University, Cambridge.

George Mordecai Papers, Southern Historical Collection, University of North Carolina, Chapel Hill.

George William Bagby Papers, Virginia Historical Society, Richmond.

Jacob Mordecai Papers, Duke University, Durham.

Lincoln Family Papers, American Antiquarian Society, Worcester, Massachusetts.

Mordecai Family Papers, Southern Historical Collection, University of North Carolina, Chapel Hill.

Telfair Family Papers, Georgia Historical Society, Savannah.

Thomas Gold Appleton Correspondence, Houghton Library, Harvard University, Cambridge.

Weston Collection, Boston Public Library, Boston.

Index

About the Author

Jean E. Friedman, PhD, is Associate Professor Emerita of history at the University of Georgia, Athens. Her published works include *The Enclosed Garden: Women and Community in the Evangelical South, 1830–1900*; *Ways of Wisdom: Moral Education in the Early National Period*; and, with William G. Shade, *Our American Sisters: Women in American Life and Thought*. Friedman holds a doctorate in history from Lehigh University.

DATE DUE

			PRINTED IN U.S.A.